When Television Brought Us Together

Together

Celebrating the Shows and the Values That

Shaped America's First TV Viewing Generations

David Hofstede

WHEN TELEVISION BROUGHT US TOGETHER

ISBN – 978-1-949802-20-7

Published by Black Pawn Press

FIRST EDITION

Table of Contents

Introduction: A Window on Our Past

Is there anyone else out there who doesn't understand the world anymore?

Such a deep, anguished, Linus Van Pelt question was not in my thoughts back in May of 2012 when I started my Comfort TV blog. All I wanted to do was write about the TV shows I grew up watching, and still watch almost every day.

But when you focus your attention on one fixed period in time, it doesn't stop the rest of the world from moving forward. Every year that passed was one more year further away from the programs in the era I christened 'Comfort TV" – shows that reflected what life in America was like in the 1950s, '60s, and '70s.

We're 50 years beyond most of their debuts now. Do they still mirror how we live? Should they?

I don't mean the cosmetic stuff – the fashions and the cars and the slang. Such artifacts are fun (or groovy!) to experience again, whether with affection or slightly embarrassed bemusement. But we'll survive their passing into history.

Other changes since that time have been more profound, such as how we view each other and ourselves, and what our priorities should be. Whether traditional roles are now deemed restrictive and offensive by their very existence. What constitutes a good education, and the importance of work. Whether moral values are objective or subject to the whims of a culture. And if these lives we lead have any ultimate meaning.

Those are big questions, and most people don't look for answers in episodes of *Bewitched*, *Father Knows Best* or *The Brady Bunch*. But the answers are in there, whether the creators of these shows intended that placement or not.

A Common Thread

The shows from decades past are more than a source of happy shared memories among millions of people; they are a common thread weaved through our culture; they portrayed a time when people were more sincere and less sarcastic; more civil and less cynical; they come from an era when it felt like we were one nation (yes, under God) instead of different warring tribes. They show us families and communities that support each other. They show us cities where schools and offices and synagogues are safe.

And when we watch them again, it also brings back memories of the days before VCRs and DVRs. Back then we knew when we watched a popular prime time series like *The Carol Burnett Show* on Saturday night, we were sharing that experience with tens of millions of Americans doing the same thing at the same time.

And here's the part that will seem odd to those who grew up after that time had passed: It felt good. There was something reassuring about being part of something bigger, and feeling a tangible connection to people from one end of the country to another, even though you were doing something as inconsequential as watching a TV show.

Such connections, such common threads, are beneficial for a nation. Television was just one of many that have disappeared over the past three decades, with nothing substantial emerging to replace them. Perhaps that's one reason why we're in the state we're in now.

An Escape into a Kinder, Gentler Time

I fear we've reached the point when the characters from these shows dwell in an America we no longer recognize. And in these uncertain times there's a reassurance in returning to a place that is familiar, safe, and far removed from the instability (and sometimes outright insanity) of life in the 21st century. Such escapes can provide temporary relief, but while they're lovely places to visit you can't stay there. Fortunately, these same shows also provide valuable lessons for living in the real world.

Let's go back and share some happy memories.

Preface: Why These Shows?

Why *I Love Lucy* and not *My Little Margie*?

Why *The Love Boat* but not *Fantasy Island*?

As this book is not intended as a history of television, it will inevitably leave out many shows that will be among your favorites, so I felt an explanation was in order on the criteria of inclusion.

Quality was obviously a factor but not the only one. Many TV historians would argue that *The Defenders* was a better legal drama than *Perry Mason*. But only *Perry Mason* is profiled here. The reason (and one that applies for almost every other selection) is popularity and longevity beyond a show's first run. *Perry Mason* lasted nine seasons and aired continuously in syndication for decades thereafter. Turn on your TV now and you're almost sure to find it somewhere. That makes it far more significant than *The Defenders* when measured by cultural impact.

In some cases, a series was left out because the point being made about its content would be the same as is discussed in another chapter. *Leave it To Beaver* is a prime example of a beloved 1950s family situation comedy that provides the same viewing pleasures and sociological observations as

Father Knows Best. I chose the latter because I thought *Father Knows Best* had more to offer, including some remarkable outside-the-box episodes that can still surprise you.

Happily, with DVDs, streaming services, YouTube and retro TV channels, there is more access to television's rich history than there has ever been before. If you are a child of television who grew up with these classics, you already know that the shows celebrated here are just a sampling of all the wonderful series produced by that era. If you are discovering them for the first time, hopefully this book will be a gateway that will lead you into many more delightful experiences from a time when television brought us together.

The Adventures of Ozzie & Harriet

1952-1966 (ABC)

435 Episodes

There were higher-rated shows, there were more award-winning shows, there were more critically acclaimed shows, and there were a few shows that ran longer (though not many). But of all the series from the classic TV era only *The Adventures of Ozzie & Harriet* provides enough material for dozens – even hundreds – of TV history studies, because there are so many aspects of this endlessly fascinating series worthy of exploration.

Start with the most obvious – it is television's longest-running live action family situation comedy, and it features a real family – married couple Ozzie and Harriet Nelson and their two sons, David and Ricky.

At a time when millions of viewers have been fascinated by shows about the Kardashians and Duggars and others, here was a series that was decades ahead of its time.

Imagine the bizarre state of going to work with your whole family and acting out everyday situations like sitting around the dinner table or planning a weekend trip, on a set built to resemble the house you just left. In fact, the exterior shot of the Nelson residence in the opening credits showed their actual Los Angeles home (at 1822 Camino Palmero St.)

And when the workday is done you return home and pick up where you left off as an actual family. What must it be like to participate in a simplified version of your daily life, while simultaneously coping with any less sitcom-friendly aspects of those relationships when the cameras stopped?

The results, to me, are as captivating as they are unique. And this wasn't some short-lived sociological experiment in entertainment – *The Adventures of Ozzie & Harriet* ran for 14 years, longer if you count the radio show that preceded the television series. The show aired long enough for David and Ricky to grow up and get married, and for their wives to join the show, also playing dramatized versions of their real selves.

I still wonder who these people really were. On the show, Ozzie was a genial, laid-back patriarch who avoided household chores or any kind of labor. The fact that he had no discernible job was one of the show's running gags, though the topic was never broached. But the real Ozzie served as a producer, director and cowriter, for a series that turned out 39 new episodes in its first two seasons. He may have been the hardest-working man in 1950s television.

Harriet appeared the quintessential housewife, with her woman's club meetings and the stack of pancakes she served her family every morning for breakfast. But the real Harriet was a vaudeville performer and band singer who enjoyed hanging out at the Cotton Club. She had such a way with an acerbic punch line that you knew she was just as feisty when the cameras weren't on.

Their eldest son David was often regarded as the least interesting of the quartet, but I was always intrigued by him, because he never seemed like the type who would aspire to appearing in a TV show if that wasn't the family business. Yet in the episodes that focused on him as he progressed from high school to college, to getting married and working in a law office, he epitomized the anticipated life and career trajectory of his generation better than any other young man on television.

What was it about this one family that millions of Americans found so interesting for so long? Was that window into aspects of real people's lives a factor? Perhaps, but maybe it was simply a familial affection that compounded in viewers over time, as well as audiences seeing aspects of themselves and their own families in the Nelsons – or at least what they aspired to be.

This was a time in television when there was a lot more of that – shows about families and doctors and lawyers and police officers that depicted their subjects in a way that would engender admiration and respect from the viewing public. It wasn't done overtly to send that message; it was, rather, a natural consequence of the way a self-assured and principled nation would portray itself.

Another element that made the show special was its balance of traditional '50s and '60s stories with dashes of surrealism and a style of plot-less meandering that would be hailed as groundbreaking decades later on *Seinfeld*. From the most basic of incidents – Rick grows a beard; Ozzie decides to stay in bed all day; Harriet gets a new hairstyle – the show devised clever, labyrinthine scripts that are still laugh-out-loud funny.

You never knew where the show was going to take you. An episode about Ozzie's all-night quest for tutti-frutti ice cream features a 1920s-themed musical dream sequence. In "The Manly Arts" (1961), David and Ricky fight a gang of smugglers in a scene right out of *The Untouchables*. They did their own stunts, just as they did in a circus episode where they performed a trapeze act. In several episodes one of the Nelsons will break the fourth wall and comment directly to the viewers, sometimes in character, sometimes as themselves.

And we've come all this way without mentioning Ricky Nelson's remarkable music career, another trailblazing aspect to the series. He was the first TV star to attempt such a crossover, and remains the standard by which all similar attempts are measured. Nelson was also television's first singing teen idol, establishing the template for everyone from Davy Jones to David Cassidy to Zac Efron.

Rick formed a band in a 1956 episode, and in 1957 he performed a cover of Fats Domino's "I'm Walkin'" in the episode "Ricky the Drummer." The original was still in the top 40, but that didn't stop Ricky's version from reaching #4 on *Billboard*'s Hot 100.

Viewers watched Nelson's performances on TV and then bought his albums, and those who heard him sing on the radio would then tune into the series. That's the kind of cross-promotional win-win that makes studios, networks, agents and managers salivate. Nelson had 35 top-40 hits between 1957 and 1972, including such pop classics as "Hello Mary Lou," "Travelin' Man," "It's Late" and "Poor Little Fool." He was inducted into the Rock and Roll Hall of Fame in 1987.

Sadly, those memorable musical moments have likely contributed to the series' not faring well on DVD. Despite its quality and historic significance, music rights licensing to Ricky's catalog may be too high a price for a distributor. Ricky's son Sam Nelson teased an official DVD release, but chose to go it alone rather than work with an established company. That may not have been a wise choice at a time when the market is already in decline, particularly for television shows of this vintage.

Still, this show has been a survivor for decades already. It was never the highest rated among ABC's programming slate, yet it kept getting renewed year after year. As of this writing all of its more than 400 episodes have been uploaded to YouTube. So even if the Nelsons are no longer "America's favorite family," as lauded in the show's opening, I am confident their legacy will find a way to endure.

The Best Episodes

"The Lost Christmas Gift" (1954)

The Adventures of Ozzie & Harriet aired several delightful holiday episodes over its long run. "Does it seem to you that the boys are missing the real spirit of Christmas?" Ozzie asks his wife near the beginning of "The Lost Christmas Gift". But when Ricky's new catcher's mitt can't be found, Harriet wonders if the gift was sent to another Nelson family on the other side of town. Their visit to that home awakens the family to that missing Christmas spirit. All of the series' holiday shows, especially "Busy Christmas" and "The Girl in the Emporium" are annual traditions in my home.

"The Pajama Game" (1955)

Using "Adventures" in the title was meant to be ironic, as most episode stories were spun from the most mundane of everyday tasks. But every so often the title fit, when a seemingly harmless choice triggers a series of perilous mishaps. Here, Ozzie's decision to help Ricky with his geometry homework leads to he and his neighbor Thorny (Don DeFore) becoming stranded in the middle of downtown, in their pajamas.

"Captain Salty and the Submarine" (1956)

Ozzie happens on a children's show that's giving away a mechanical submarine for six bottle caps of Seafoam Root Beer. When he can't convince either of his sons that it would be fun and educational to order one, he does it himself. If you have a dad that enjoyed playing with your Christmas toys more than you did, this one will hit home. It gets even better when Captain Salty announces that the winner of his bicycle giveaway contest is "little Ozzie Nelson," who will appear on the show to pick up his prize.

"Ozzie's Triple Banana Surprise" (1957)

Ozzie Nelson loved ice cream, so it's not surprising that "Tutti-Frutti Ice Cream" wasn't the only classic series episode based on a frozen dessert. "Ozzie's Triple Banana Surprise" is told in flashback, as Ozzie reveals what happened to him after enjoying one of those concoctions at the neighborhood malt shop.

That night he dreams of strumming a ukulele on a tropical beach, surrounded by lovely native girls, and singing "In the Middle of an Island." A phone call from David wakes him up – he's stranded with his date at a diner because of car trouble.

Ozzie heads out to pick them up, and starts meeting the people he dreamed about. And then David isn't at the diner when he gets there. As events become more surreal Ozzie gets to the point where he's not sure what is real and what isn't anymore.

"The Duenna" (1957)

David meets Lucita, an attractive girl who speaks only Spanish. Somehow they manage to make a date, but he is confused when she calls later and he can't understand her. A half-hearted attempt to translate reveals one word familiar to Ozzie – "duenna," meaning chaperone. Apparently it's Spanish tradition for girls on dates to be accompanied by a grandmother or maiden aunt. Ozzie tags along to socialize with the chaperone, but is taken aback when the duenna turns out to be an attractive senorita with amorous intentions.

The episode plays without subtitles, except for one brief scene needed to clarify the plot. Thus, viewers are as challenged by the language barrier as David, which heightens our awareness of how difficult these situations can be. What is engaging is the good faith effort made on both sides, without any expressions of impatience or frustration.

How Times Have Changed: Photography

From 1956 to 1961, the Eastman Kodak Company sponsored *The Adventures of Ozzie & Harriet.*

This was the era in television in which a show's stars often also appeared in its commercials. Here that task usually fell to Harriet Nelson, who spoke directly to viewers at home about how much the Nelson family enjoys capturing and sharing memories of vacations and get-togethers in pictures. And when Christmas approached, Harriet would urge viewers to pick up a Kodak Brownie Starflash camera (for just $5.95!) and gift-wrap it under the tree with a tag that reads "Open Me First." That way, Dad would be ready to snap photos of the kids opening their gifts from Santa.

Photography wasn't anything new by the 1950s, but it was still something special.

Another memorable Kodak advertising campaign popularized the phrase "Kodak Moments," a sentiment to describe how the average person used photography for most of its history – as a way to capture optical memories of special events: a child's birthday party, seeing the sights on a trip to Europe, meeting a celebrity. Disneyland set up "Kodak

Picture Spots" to help amateur shutterbugs take the best pictures for their family albums.

Harriet Nelson wasn't the only TV character with an appreciation for the joys of photography.

In *The Brady Bunch* episode "Not-So-Rose-Colored Glasses," Carol is thrilled by Mike's anniversary gift – a beautiful photograph of their six children, enlarged and framed for permanent display in their bedroom (at least for one episode).

The opening credits sequence for the brilliant ABC drama series *Family* shows a series of photographs of each family member displayed on top of a piano.

And how many shows featured episodes about the end of a relationship, in which the broken-hearted look longingly at a photo from when they were still together? When the break-up is especially hostile, those photos might get folded or cut in half. That was a tactic used by Donald Hollinger's mother to erase the memory of Ann Marie on *That Girl* ("Thanksgiving Comes But Once a Year, Hopefully").

Beyond the obvious desire to save significant moments for posterity, there was a practical reason why people only took pictures of meaningful events and places – most rolls of film allowed for just 24 or 36 photo-taking opportunities, and every snap of the shutter cost money, not just in film but in developing your snapshots at Fotomat.

No such restrictions exist anymore. A cell phone can take

and store more than 50,000 photos. Freed of such attention to discretion, teens and twenty-somethings inaugurated the era of the "selfie," photos of themselves doing absolutely nothing of interest to anyone.

While there are still photojournalists, hobbyists and others devoted to chronicling our life and times through images, photography today has been relegated to feeding the raging narcissism of millennials.

After the inevitable apocalypse, as anthropologists comb through the digital records of the early 21st century, they will find millions of photos of hotel continental breakfasts, sleeping dogs, pedicured toes, car backseats, balloons, kitschy salt and pepper shakers, and other artifacts of a generation obsessed with its own self-importance. I apologize in advance for the discovery.

The Andy Griffith Show

1960-1968 (CBS)

249 Episodes

If you could step through the television screen and spend the rest of your days in any setting of a classic series, where would you choose to go?

I suspect there would be a lot of folks headed for Mayberry as seen on *The Andy Griffith Show*.

Who wouldn't want to live and work and raise a family in a close-knit community with a more relaxed pace of life? A place where neighbors knew their neighbors and actually looked out for them? A place where meals were still home-cooked, and the statues in the park were under siege by pigeons instead of angry mobs?

As John Javna wrote of this series in his book *Cult TV*: "Today the little town of Mayberry is a nostalgic dream. But when it was created, in 1960, it didn't seem so far-fetched. America was still holding on to its innocence…society was changing, but most of rural America was still untouched."

Here's a secret: There are still a few places in rural America that are like this. You probably don't know their names or their exact locales, and that's the way they prefer it. The last thing they want is to publicize their existence because that would seal their fate. Thousands of people eager to flee failing urban areas would descend on these quiet communities, and not all of them would consent to assimilate. A few would set out to transform these hamlets into the dumps they just left.

"It's so nice and peaceful here, but do so many stores have to be closed on Sundays?"

"What a lovely homespun diner. Where's the gluten-free vegan menu?"

"Why does Sweet Briar Normal School not have a Gender Studies curriculum?"

Stay off the grid as long as you can, Mayberrys of the 21st century. The rest of us will content ourselves with the one on television.

Such an idyllic setting should feature a cast of friendly and welcoming residents, and here *The Andy Griffith Show* delivers as well. Andy Griffith stars as Andy Taylor, a widower raising a young son (Ron Howard as Opie), and a sheriff in a place where crime is not a concern. The two jail cells at the sheriff's station were usually empty, unless Otis the town drunk (Hal Smith) needed to check himself in and sleep off a bender.

The character of Sheriff Andy Taylor was introduced in an episode of *The Danny Thomas Show* that aired in February of 1960. It was a way for producer Sheldon Leonard to test his appeal with viewers before investing in a new series. In "Danny Meets Andy Griffith," Andy pulls Danny over for running a stop sign, even though there's no road where the sign sits. The fine is $5, but when the sheriff sees Danny pull out a large wad of bills, he increases the fine to $100.

If that doesn't sound like Mayberry's moral compass, you're right. While Griffith could play a wily opportunist (as anyone who has seen *A Face in the Crowd* will attest), this is not a character that would carry a show for eight years. So when the series launched six months later, Andy personified compassionate law and order, and abjured the stereotype of a corrupt small-town sheriff that enjoyed throwing city slickers in jail for going 5 mph over the speed limit.

Where Andy was content with his place in the universe, his deputy (and cousin) Barney Fife (Don Knotts) craved the kind of cops and robbers action that rarely passed through Mayberry – even if he was ill equipped to cope with it. This was clearly Andy's show, but Barney was the guy that delivered the laughs. It didn't matter how often he accidentally fired his gun or locked himself into his own jail cell – it was funny every time. Of the six Emmys won by the series, five of them went to Knotts. After he left the series soldiered on, but it was never the same.

Another reason viewers found Mayberry such an appealing place is that we got to see so much of the town over the show's run, and meet so many of its residents. We knew

Andy, Barney, Opie and Aunt Bee (Francis Bavier) would be in every episode, but the series also introduced a wonderful gathering of recurring characters: gas station attendants Gomer Pyle (Jim Nabors) and Goober (George Lindsay), barber Floyd Lawson (Howard McNear), county clerk Howard Sprague (Jack Dodson), plus Helen Crump and Thelma Lou, Ernest T. Bass, Mayor Stoner, Ellie Walker, Clara Edwards, Emmet Clark, Malcolm Merriweather, the Darlings…the list goes on and on.

For those who still wish to visit the fictional home of one of television's most beloved series, the next best thing might be Mount Airy, North Carolina, Andy Griffith's birthplace and the city that served as the inspiration for Mayberry. Try to visit during Mayberry Days, which for more than 30 years has brought series fans together to reminisce about fishing holes and fresh-baked pies cooling on a windowsill.

The Best Episodes

"A Feud is a Feud" (1960)

This early first season episode highlights how the series was initially developed as a vehicle for Andy Griffith, to expand upon the persona he established in his comedy routines such as "What it Was, Was Football." Here, he explains Shakespeare's *Romeo and Juliet* to Opie:

Andy: "Goodbye, goodbye. Partin' is such sweet sorrow that I would say goodbye till it be morrow."

Opie: "What's THAT mean?"

Andy: "Well, that means I'd love to set and jaw with ya a while longer, but I got to be a-movin' on."

When Opie asks what a soliloquy is, his 'paw' responds that it's "where you kind of look away off and kinda talk to yourself," before adding, "They used to do that a whole lot back then. You do it today and somebody will take you away."

"The Pickle Story" (1961)

This episode provides a marvelous showcase for Francis Bavier as Aunt Bee, as well as a study on the drastic actions good people will undertake to protect someone they love from shame or embarrassment. Here we learn that Aunt Bee is a marvelous cook, except when it comes to her homemade pickles. Apparently they taste like kerosene, and can mess up your digestive tract for hours, if not days. So when she enters them in the County Fair, Andy knows he's got a problem.

"Barney and the Choir" (1962)

This episode is similar to "The Pickle Story" in its conspiracy of one group of residents scheming to help one talent-deficient neighbor save face. Here, it's Barney and his dreadful singing in the choir. The solution is to convince him to sing at an extremely soft volume into a "special" microphone (one that is turned off) while another singer performs his part. Sure, it's far-fetched and convoluted, but the expressions on Knotts' face as he hears "his" voice are unforgettable.

"Opie the Birdman" (1963)

If you compiled a "best of the best" list from all the memorable episodes of classic shows celebrated in this book, "Opie the Birdman" would rank at or near the top of that prestigious company. It confirms Ronny Howard's status as one of the most capable and believable child actors from any series, as it weaves a tale that begins with an act of carelessness, followed by sadness, hope, and redemption. Writer Harvey Bullock contributed scripts to a wide range of shows, from *The Flintstones* and *Hogan's Heroes* to *Alice* and *The Love Boat*. This is his masterpiece.

"The Big House" (1963)

"Here at the rock we have two basic rules...the first rule is...obey all rules."

The state police temporarily lodge two hold-up men in Mayberry's jail, allowing Barney to play hard-boiled lawman. They promptly escape – not once but three times. Poor Barney.

Annual Events

When we all shared the same handful of television networks, there were moments throughout the year when we would take a break from regularly scheduled programming for a highly anticipated special that aired just once a year. So popular were these annual broadcasts that the network that presented them was assured of a dominant ratings win, while the competition was content to concede the night, and air a rerun of something no one was likely to miss.

In our current television era of unlimited program options and niche networks, only the Super Bowl fits that description. It's amazing that any one program still commands that level of attention in a country that can't agree on anything anymore.

The Academy Awards are presented every year, though ratings have dropped precipitously over the past two decades. Films must now pass a series of quotas and litmus tests for consideration, but audience popularity is not one of them. Viewer exodus has been hastened by that trend toward honoring box-office poison, coupled with hosts and presenters who condescendingly belittle half the audience that enjoys going to the movies.

There are Christmas presentations every season, from revivals of chestnuts like *A Charlie Brown Christmas* and *Rudolph the Red-Nosed Reindeer*, to new specials hosted by current music stars. Sometimes they win their nights, sometimes they don't, but either way they play as just another option among hundreds, watched by a few but barely acknowledged. None command the attention once given to the annual specials hosted by Bob Hope or Perry Como.

If you're of a certain age, you remember when CBS's annual broadcast of the 1939 classic *The Wizard of Oz* was appointment television. Now the movie probably sits on your shelf to be enjoyed whenever you wish in 4K Ultra HD Blu-Ray, or is stored on your phone to keep the kids quiet in the car.

From my formative years I have the most vivid memories of the following two annual television events – one still exists (barely), and the other has passed into the ages.

Miss America

Quick – what is the name of the reigning Miss America? You don't know. Nobody does.

That wasn't always the case. According to Wikipedia, in the early 1960s the pageants were the highest-rated programs on American television. The day after a winner was crowned in Atlantic City, her name and photo appeared in newspapers across the country, often on the front page.

Many of them remained in the spotlight, starting with Bess Myerson, who in 1945 became the first (and still only) Jewish woman to wear the crown. She was a familiar face on TV throughout the 1950s, most notably as one of the panelists on *I've Got a Secret*.

Lee Meriwether, Miss America 1955, was part of the TV landscape for more than 50 years, and earned an Emmy nomination for her supporting role on *Barnaby Jones*. Mary Ann Mobley, Miss America 1959, appeared in memorable episodes of *Mission: Impossible* and *The Partridge Family*, and introduced the character of April Dancer on *The Man from U.N.C.L.E.*

Even Miss Americas that did not go on to a show business career became familiar faces, especially in the weeks and months following the pageant.

Today? No one really cares. Event organizers have tried updating the format, by eliminating the swimsuit competition and having contestants discuss social issues as they sashay across the stage, but they can't suppress the obvious fact that Miss America is a beauty contest. And beauty contests might as well be slave auctions in our current woke culture.

Did your family think they were watching something offensive and exploitative back then? Mine didn't. Like millions across the nation we'd gather around the TV, and pick out our favorite contestants from the opening parade of states, introduced by long-time host Bert Parks.

Usually our choices would be eliminated when the top 15 finalists were selected, so we picked new ones.

Then we watched the swimsuit competition, and the evening gown competition, and the talent competition, where there would be a few capable singers and dancers, and a few others who relied on baton twirling and questionable ventriloquism skills. Even the bad moments were kind of sweet.

The field was then cut to the final five, who would be asked to offer an opinion on some current event or cultural phenomenon. This was always the most parodied part of any pageant. One of the best takes was in the *Charlie's Angels* episode "Pretty Angels All in a Row." Kris Munroe (Cheryl Ladd), undercover in the "Miss Chrysanthemum" pageant, is asked her favorite color: "My favorite colors are red, white and blue, because they're the colors of our flag of freedom."

In the closing moments, the runners-up would be revealed, along with the amounts of the scholarships they have earned. When there were only two left, Bert Parks would solemnly intone that if, for any reason, the winner were unable to fulfill her duties as Miss America, the first runner-up would assume the title. The winner would be announced, tears would flow, and the new Miss America would receive her crown and sash and a bouquet of roses, and walk down that Atlantic City runway as Parks did his best to sing, "There she is, Miss America…"

Now what, I ask you, is so awful about that?

The title of Miss America was one that was accorded respect, and not just by lascivious males. There was a belief that winners personified the best qualities of the American woman, and it was a title aspired to by many young girls.

The title did not represent the end of a journey, but a beginning. Spend some time reviewing biographies of past contestants and you'll realize how many physicians and lawyers and broadcast journalists and high-ranking company executives received a boost in their professional aspirations from the scholarships provided by the Miss America Foundation. These were smart, capable women before they entered the contest as a means to help them realize their potential.

When Miss America winners accompanied Bob Hope to Korea and Vietnam, and when other winners visited military bases overseas with the USO, the soldiers were jubilant to see a beautiful woman that reminded them of home, or perhaps of someone special in their lives.

There is nothing wrong with this. But if enough people now think there is, I hope they just ditch the whole thing instead of changing it into something we no longer recognize.

The Jerry Lewis Labor Day Telethon

Growing up, Labor Day meant two things – the start of another dreaded school year was around the corner, and I would get to stay up later than usual to watch the Jerry Lewis MDA Telethon.

In 2011, Lewis was discharged from his duties after 45 years of service. The Muscular Dystrophy Association opted instead for a three-hour "Show of Strength" featuring pre-taped performances from a variety of entertainers.

There's no disputing that, in its last few years with Lewis as host, the telethons had become antiquated affairs. "Watching the stars come out," meant performances from Charo and Norm Crosby, the same people who were there when I was still in high school. And Jerry Lewis was turning in earlier than I used to, only to return at the end to unveil the final tote board and sing, "You'll Never Walk Alone" as the last shreds of confetti fell.

But even well past their prime, there was something comforting about these annual broadcasts, and how they conjured childhood memories of struggling against sleep after midnight, and surviving the boring local segments, which didn't have the glitz and star power of the Las Vegas national telecast.

A television show that was on all night was certainly unique, and I always vowed that one year I was going to be in for the duration. But I never made it.

Given the grim realities that necessitated its creation, some may be surprised that this was an event that millions of people actually looked forward to watching. And whatever else one can say about Jerry Lewis, it was clear this was his personal crusade. He was strongly invested in every broadcast, and genuinely grateful for the support of the firefighters and the corporate and civic groups who made an annual pilgrimage to drop off a check, and then introduce a short film about their fundraising activities that was never very interesting.

Each year we looked forward to the same regular bits; the tympani roll when the tote board added another million, as the orchestra played "What the World Needs Now is Love"; Lewis receiving a seven-figure check and exclaiming, "Oh, yeah, Oh, YEAH!" in an exaggerated Brooklyn accent, sporting the same awestruck look that Taylor Swift has when she wins another Grammy award. Other Lewis traditions – banter with Ed McMahon, some good-natured jibes at the floor director, and his comedic orchestra conductor routine.

And then there were the personal stories of the families touched by neuromuscular disease. These were tougher to watch, but once again it was apparent that Jerry cared about "his kids," and how much he enjoyed making each year's "poster child" smile and laugh, while knowing there was a chance that child wouldn't be around next year.

But telethons were not created for our hyperactive times, and as I grew up I also lost interest. I might donate via the MDA website but wouldn't manage more than an hour or two of the broadcast. Those annual *Parade* magazine covers of

Jerry and the new poster child were now accompanied by stories of disgruntled adults who bristled at the condescension they heard in the "Jerry's Kids" label, and viewed the telethon as shameless exploitation.

I can't be angry with MDA for taking the show in another direction, but what they gained in higher-profile celebrities they lost in heart and sentiment. Whatever the cause of the falling out between Lewis and the charity he served so well, there should have been a more gradual transition that allowed Jerry to step aside with dignity intact.

But with the end of the traditional Jerry Lewis MDA Telethons, "broadcast across the Love Network," another example of television that brought us together slipped away, never to return.

The Avengers

1961-1969 (BBC/ABC)

161 Episodes

May this fair dear land we love so well

In dignity and freedom dwell

Though worlds may change and go awry

While there is still one voice to cry

There'll always be an England

That's what I see when I watch *The Avengers*. I see England.

It's England awash in sophistication and civility, with respect for tradition and for the crown; a place where gentlemen know about well-bred horses and tailored suits and fine cheese and good wine, prefer vintage cars to new ones, and refuse to get flustered even in the face of killer robots and invisible assassins.

It's a nation populated by whimsical eccentrics who own shops that sell nothing but honey, or throw Christmas parties where attendees dress as characters from Charles Dickens novels.

And it is home to John Steed (Patrick Macnee) and Mrs. Emma Peel (Diana Rigg). Have there ever been two characters that better personified an idealized vision of their nation of origin?

There were *Avengers* episodes before and after this cherished partnership, but it's the 51 episodes in which they were paired that are most beloved by fans in America and the United Kingdom.

Steed could not have come from anywhere but England. His sartorial style, impeccable manners and aristocratic worldview were fashioned by a culture where such traits delineate a gentleman. Only Steed would find a dead foreign agent on his carpet, and lodge a complaint to his superiors because it's "very untidy."

Such a formidable chap required an equally eminent counterpart, and here *The Avengers* excelled first with Cathy Gale (Honor Blackman), and most notably with Emma Peel – scientist, journalist, mistress of martial arts, and an exquisite English rose who shares Steed's gift for understatement.

Their remarkable rapport, consisting of equal parts mutual respect and affection, playful banter and refined romance, remains unsurpassed by any two characters in television.

The England of *The Avengers* is not England as it is now, or even the England that existed at the time the episodes were filmed. It's an enchanting blend of reality and exaggeration, and every time I am fortunate enough to travel there I look for any signs of that place that are still around.

Finding them was always special – one could easily imagine Steed buying a bottle of champagne at Berry Bros & Rudd on St. James's Street, or spotting Mrs. Peel in the Diamond Jubilee Tea Salon at Fortnum & Mason, where afternoon tea has been served since 1707.

However, even if this England never fully existed, I think the idea of it is worth preserving and cherishing. Any attempt to explain why will require some tiptoeing, as it brings us in proximity to political topics that induce people to start shouting at each other.

Let's try it this way: for many classic TV devotees, part of the appeal of older television shows is the glimpse they provide into a specific place and time that we would love to visit.

For those of us who didn't get to travel from an early age, shows set in other countries gave us our first looks at what life was like there. When an episode would be set in England or Japan or Germany or Italy, we were given a distinct portrayal of those places.

It was different from how our own country was represented on TV; partly because we lived here and didn't need to learn about it from television, and partly because America has always been a product of people from all over the world, each contributing something unique and beneficial to our culture.

I'm sure most of us realized that all men in London didn't wear bowler hats and carry umbrellas, and all French waiters didn't wear striped shirts and berets. And of course they didn't all speak English with foreign accents. But when we saw these European locales, and they seemed so specific and exotic and appealing, it was natural to hope that, if and when we were able to travel there, they would fulfill some of those unique visions, naive as they might have been.

The Avengers was quintessentially British. Was that national culture and identity important? Or should culture be what naturally evolves over the decades and centuries?

I don't know. But it makes me happy that as long as we can watch Steed and Mrs. Peel, the England in which they lived will always be preserved.

The Best Episodes

"Death at Bargain Prices" (1966)

Pinter's Department Store is the unlikely setting for the murder of one government agent and the kidnapping of a nuclear scientist. Mrs. Peel joins the staff as a sales clerk, prompting one of those witty and cheeky dialog exchanges that fans treasure:

Steed: "I asked the chief predator where to find you and he said, 'Our Mrs. Peel is in ladies' underwear.' I rattled up the stairs three at a time."

Mrs. Peel: "Merry quips department on the fifth floor, sir."

"The House That Jack Built" (1966)

What usually makes an *Avengers* episode great is the sparkling chemistry between Steed and Mrs. Peel, so the more scenes they have together, the better. "The House That Jack Built" is the exception – it's practically a solo outing for Emma, who is lured to a vacant estate and then trapped inside. Escape routes are hidden by sophisticated electronics – the message of the piece is to be wary of machines that are smarter than men. I guess we're all in trouble now.

"A Touch of Brimstone (1966)

This is one of the series' most famous (and infamous) episodes. Debauched aristocrats revive the 18th century Hellfire Club, and recruit an undercover Emma as their new "Queen of Sin." Her costume raised concerns among network censors both in England and America, but equally memorable is Peter Wyngarde's charismatic performance as the group's dashing ringleader.

"A Funny Thing Happened on the Way to the Station" (1967)

A plot to kill the Prime Minister is assisted by a murderous (but unfailingly polite) train ticket collector. Railways figure into several *Avengers* stories, and seeing the carriages of that era and their rumbling sounds along the tracks makes this episode especially "British."

"Return of the Cybernauts" (1968)

This is a sequel to an earlier episode that introduced a group referred to as Cybernauts – near indestructible mechanical men programmed as assassins. It rates the edge over the original because of guest-star Peter Cushing. Courtly manners and sadistic cruelty never co-existed so well.

Sidebar: Foreign Relations

We buried the hatchet with our British cousins over 1776 a long time ago. But how well are people from different countries and cultures getting along in America these days? If you listen to the media, the answer would be not very well.

Much of that arises out of the national debate over immigration. Not the kind we've had for 200+ years – just about everyone agrees that legal immigration is a wonderful thing that has been intrinsic to our national growth, success and identity. But there's that other kind of immigration, which only about half the country supports.

Rather than pursue that debate, let's look instead at how vintage TV shows approached this topic.

I always like these episodes. They reveal how much bigger the world seemed in the pre-internet era. For the heartland residents of golden-age sitcoms, the chance to meet someone born outside the U.S. didn't come along every day. That perspective influenced how outsiders were portrayed, as well as how they were received by the characters viewers watched every week.

Often these shows fell back on cultural stereotypes that could be viewed as naïve now, or offensive if you're the sort that likes to be offended about everything.

But that was not how they were intended. If anything,

writers viewed these scripts as opportunities to educate viewers about the ways different populaces lived and dressed and spoke, while also offering an outsider's perspective on American life and culture. That required an emphasis on divergence, though inevitably an underlying message would emerge on how people are people, no matter where they are from.

Take "Fair Exchange," a 1958 episode of *Father Knows Best* in which the Anderson family plays host to Chanthini, an Indian exchange student played by Puerto Rico's own Rita Moreno.

"Will she have a shawl on her head and a water bucket on her shoulder?" Kathy wonders, while Bud hopes she knows the Indian rope trick. Chanthini is also not immune to jumping to conclusions: when she sees an apron-clad Jim helping with the dishes she assumes he's a servant. In her country, she says, the men don't do kitchen work. "You people have the right idea," Jim responds.

"Fair Exchange" offers a textbook example of how this story trope often plays out. "Did you know?" lessons are frequently inserted (not always gently) into the script: "What's that little red dot on your forehead?" Kathy asks Chanthini; "We get most of our tea from India," Margaret informs her family. And as we're still in the 1950s, everyone admirably tries not to offend each other. The final scene, where Bud teaches Chanthini about football, is one of those utterly charming moments that TV has long since forgotten how to create.

In "The Geisha Girl," a 1961 episode of *The Donna Reed Show*, the wife of the new doctor in town gains a reputation as a snob because she never attends social events. Donna believes such pre-judgments are unfair and discovers that the woman in question is not only Japanese, but also someone who prefers the traditional garb and subservient role of a wife common to her homeland.

Later, at a small dinner party, the other doctors' wives stare in disbelief as she serves her husband dinner and lights his pipe. The doctors find her deference admirable. "Don't let it give you any ideas," Donna cautions her husband.

Here we do see a suggestion of prejudice, though it is quickly proven false. But there is a discomfort among the ladies of Hilldale with someone who acts so submissive, and that in itself is interesting given how many women today might bristle at the traditional homemaker roles that are esteemed in TV shows of this era.

You can find the common denominator of these episodes and many others, written in Latin on US currency: E Pluribus Unum ("Out of many, one"). That motto expresses the philosophy that those who come to America from other places don't just want to live here; they want to be a part of what *Schoolhouse Rock* called "the great American melting pot." Many still do. But others now reject that sentiment as arrogant, and resist what they view as capitulation to another culture's traditions.

The final scene of "The Geisha Girl" shows what happens when Donna takes it upon herself to Americanize her new friend. After one shopping trip our visitor from Japan has joined the ranks of Hilldale's stylish Midwestern homemakers. Her husband is delighted to see her making friends and embracing her new life in a new country. Assimilation is portrayed as a triumph for the immigrant and the community. If only that were still the case.

The Bob Newhart Show

1972-1978 (CBS)

142 Episodes

Parts of this book were written during the early, unsettling stages of the Coronavirus pandemic, when thousands of people gravitated to nostalgia networks like MeTV for a respite from sad headlines. Relief was available from all of the series on these channels, but if I could only write one prescription to treat current-event anxiety, I would select *The Bob Newhart Show*.

In times when the world seems particularly disturbing, when emotions are running high and people shout over each other instead of engaging in conversation, Bob Hartley reminds us that listening is often better than talking, and bemusement may be the only sane response to insanity.

That recognition comes with patience, and practice, both of which are essential for a psychologist.

While the rest of us enjoy moments when life doesn't throw chaos in our paths, Bob's workday regularly places him in the company of people with serious issues. Some are hostile, some are confused, and some are afraid of everything from dating to upholstery. He responds to each one quietly, without judgment, and with an attempt to try and make them feel a little better about themselves and their lives.

Anger management is an attribute in short supply these days. But a lesson can be learned from watching Bob maintain his serenity as he copes with his patients, as well as other stress-inducers like Chicago winters and an eccentric (to say the least) best friend and neighbor in Howard Borden (Bill Daily).

It has been more than 45 years since Bob saw his first patient. But Bob's approach to his profession can inspire viewers toward calm, and in learning to distinguish situations where anger is justified from those where it would be better and healthier to just let stuff go. It might also ease the burden on our court dockets, since filing a lawsuit seems to be many Americans' preferred response to anything that bothers them in the slightest.

Was Bob good at his job? It would be unfair to assess his professional skills based on the realities of television. Elliot Carlin (Jack Riley) was still a patient after six seasons not because Bob couldn't cure his numerous neuroses, but because the character was simply too good to lose. That applies also to the meek Mr. Peterson (John Fiedler) and the sweet but addled Mrs. Bakerman (Florida Friebus).

Bob's sessions with this group were a consistent series highlight, as were many of the scenes set within the Windy

City high-rise where he interacted with secretary Carol Kester (Marcia Wallace) and dentist Jerry Robinson (Peter Bonerz).

After a challenging day Bob headed home to Emily (Suzanne Pleshette), which also happened to be the title of the show's theme, a contender for the title of best instrumental TV show intro music ever composed ("Home to Emily" by Lorenzo Music). Pleshette's sass was the perfect counterpoint to Newhart's button-down disposition.

As a viewer you could sense the thought put into every aspect of the series, creating distinctive roles and blending the individual aptitudes of well-cast actors into an ensemble that complemented each other's talents. This was a hallmark of the best 1970s situation comedies, which is why so many fans stayed home on Saturday nights back then (before the VCR) to enjoy a standout CBS programming lineup of *All in the Family, M*A*S*H, The Mary Tyler Moore Show, The Bob Newhart Show* and *The Carol Burnett Show.* Those were the days, indeed.

Bob Newhart would return to television four years later in *Newhart* (1982-1990). It was another success, but when it came time to wrap it up the series chose to wipe out its own history with a call back to Newhart's previous show: Bob wakes up next to Emily and describes a crazy dream about being an innkeeper in Vermont. The joyous audience reaction left no doubt of how fondly viewers remembered the show that debuted 18 years earlier. *TV Guide* ranked it as the best series finale of all time.

The Best Episodes

"Sorry, Wrong Mother" (1974)

There are many fine moments here, from Bob using a rag doll in a therapy session to his story about being jealous of his father's attention to a foster kid. But what fans remember most is the guest appearance of John Ritter as Dave, the overly friendly waiter at Uncle Yummy's Ice Cream Parlor.

"Over the River and Through the Woods" (1975)

"More goo to go!"

It's regrettable that drunk scenes have become yet another casualty of our finger-wagging age. Once they were to great comic actors what a hanging curve ball was to a .300 batter – a golden opportunity to hit one out of the park. That's what happened when Bob Newhart, Bill Daily, Jack Riley and Peter Bonerz were handed a scene in which their characters get sloshed over Thanksgiving. They hit their rhythm early and for ten minutes set-ups and punch lines are served and volleyed with perfect timing and precision. When it all comes together like this, there's nothing better.

"Bob Has to Have His Tonsils Out, So He Spends Christmas Eve in the Hospital" (1975)

The title says it all: Bob is subjected to the indignities of peekaboo hospital gowns, Howard's hospital horror stories, and an ancient nurse. There are laugh out loud moments in every scene, from the doctor's diagnosis to a raucous tree-trimming scene in Howard's apartment. The dotty nurse who takes care of Bob (veteran character actress Merie Earle) gets a laugh with every line she utters, and sometimes when she's just standing there.

"The Longest Goodbye" (1975)

This episode introduces Tom Poston in his recurring role as Bob's college roommate Cliff Murdock, aka "The Peeper." He brings out the silly side of Bob (known in college as "The Mooner" because…well, you can figure that one out). It's strange but fun to watch Bob laugh so heartily at the Peeper's practical jokes, while Emily and Carol stare in confused amazement. The "Sonny Boy" scene here is another fan favorite.

"Death Be My Destiny" (1977)

No situation comedy explored the comic possibilities of the telephone and the elevator more than *The Bob Newhart Show*. Case in point, Mr. Carlin tells Bob he always thinks other people are laughing at him; Bob says he's just imagining it, and right on cue the elevator doors open behind him, and we see a crowd of laughing passengers.

But the show's record for most elevator moments in one episode belongs to "Death Be My Destiny." This is the one where Bob steps into an empty elevator shaft.

Bob: "I was almost touched by Father Death"

Emily: "That's Father Time, Bob. It's Old Man Death"

Bob: "No, it's Old Man River"

Emily: "Are you sure?"

Bob: "Whoever he was, I felt icy fingers up and down my spine"

Emily: "That's Old Black Magic"

Bob vows to never get on an elevator again, but as he counsels a patient on how to conquer fear, he finally takes his own advice. However, the elevator at his office building still has a few more surprises in store.

How Times Have Changed: Psychiatry

Bob Hartley was a psychologist, not a psychiatrist, though that distinction was irrelevant to those tuning in on Saturday nights in the 1970s.

As this exchange from *The Dick Van Dyke Show* illustrates, perhaps no other profession has been more lampooned by yesterday's television.

Rob Petrie: "What do you think, Phil?"

Psychiatrist: "What do you think?"

Rob: "Well, I... I thought I'd come over here and find out what you think."

Psychiatrist: "What I think doesn't matter. It's what you think."

Rob: "Well, what I think you think?"

Psychiatrist: "No, what you think you think."

Rob: "I don't know what to think."

"The Brave and the Backache" (1964)

Was this merely an example of irony in humor, to make therapists as addled as their patients? Perhaps – but I would suggest that more people were dubious about the entire discipline of psychiatry in the 1950s-1970s, and these shows reflected a belief that all this head-shrinking stuff was a bunch of double talk and hooey. Today, when half the world is in therapy for something, television has responded accordingly with more sympathetic portrayals (*The Sopranos, Huff, Private Practice*).

As with so many other elements of classic TV, there was predictability to encounters with psychiatry. Once a story headed in that direction, savvy viewers figured they could look forward to scenes built around at least one of these two experiments.

The Inkblot Test

Is this still part of the therapist's arsenal, or has it been undermined by decades of sitcoms in which everyone who looks at inkblots sees something pornographic? *F Troop*'s Corporal Agarn saw "a beautiful Indian girl in a short skirt bending over a campfire," to which Roaring Chicken responds, "I like your inkblot better than mine."

On *The Golden Girls*, Dorothy interpreted an inkblot as "John Forsythe lying naked in a pool of honey." And after a psychiatrist questions why Maxwell Smart interprets every blot as a couple hugging or kissing, Max responds, "You're the one with the dirty pictures."

That Girl built an entire episode around inkblots. In "There's Nothing to Be Afraid of But Freud Himself," Donald interviews a psychiatrist who has developed a more accurate way to use inkblots to identify personality traits. Ann thinks one of them looks like a spider, and discovers that means she is stubborn, argumentative and impulsive. When Don hesitates to question that verdict it almost ends their relationship.

The Word Association Test

"I'll say a word, and you say the first word that pops into your head."

The most famous TV example of this is a *Saturday Night Live* sketch with Chevy Chase and Richard Pryor that can't be quoted here. But it also dates as far back as *Gilligan's Island* and *The Donna Reed Show*, when Mary uses it on her friends and is dismayed to find that the word most associated with her is "wholesome."

Once again, the comic potential in such scenes is abundant, as when Cousin Itt takes the test on *The Addams Family*:

Mortimer Phelps: [to Itt] "Now I'll say a word and you say whatever pops into your mind. Uh... bird."

Gomez: "Vulture."

Morticia: "Molting."

Gomez: "Mating."

Morticia: "Nesting."

Gomez: "Billing."

Morticia: "Cooing."

Gomez: "Lips."

Morticia: "Red."

Gomez: "Kiss me!"

Mortimer Phelps: "Please! Now, I will not tolerate any more interruptions."

Gomez: "Really, old man, you don't understand true love when you see it."

In season three of *Bewitched*, Endora conjures up Sigmund Freud to settle a fight between Samantha and Darrin in "I'd Rather Twitch Than Fight," while Larry and Louise Tate offer the services of their psychiatrist for the same reason. When the two doctors meet, their disagreement about the root of the argument almost results in a fistfight. Think of it – two learned men trusted with helping a couple to avoid conflict threaten to beat each other up. Once again, psychiatry does not fare well.

Dr. Alfred Bellows on *I Dream of Jeannie* was a psychiatrist, though you'd also occasionally see him conducting physical exams. The show's best recurring gag would have Bellows enter a room just after Jeannie caused some chaos, leaving poor Tony to try and explain why it's snowing over his house, or why there were circus animals in his living room.

In season four's "Dr. Bellows Goes Sane," Bellows compiles three years of such bizarre incidents into a dossier presented to General Peterson. Upon reading it, he decides it is Bellows who is ready for a padded cell. The doctor is fired, and replaced by another psychiatrist (wonderfully played by the equally batty Joe Flynn).

And while it wasn't commonly referred to in the series, Dr.

Zachary Smith on *Lost in Space* was an intergalactic doctor of environmental psychology. Again, not exactly a role model for the profession.

Was there any TV shrink you'd trust with your mental health? I'd nominate Dr. Sidney Freedman, who made occasional visits to the 4077 on M*A*S*H. As played by Allan Arbus, his most famous quote was "Ladies and gentlemen, take my advice...pull down your pants and slide on the ice."

That is advice worth 100 bucks an hour.

The Brady Bunch

1969-1974 (ABC)

117 Episodes

The Brady Bunch aired from 1969 to 1974, but it never really went away. Through decades of syndication, where the series would routinely dominate its time slot and attract new generations of fans; through reunions and revivals, tributes and parodies, *The Brady Bunch* has become not only a pop culture touchstone for the baby boomers who grew up with its characters, but with their children and grandchildren as well.

I wouldn't call it my favorite show, but it's the one I most closely associate with the warm, nostalgic feelings engendered by the television classics of the past.

For a series that never ranked among the top 25 shows in any of its five seasons, the enduring popularity of *The Brady Bunch* defies all logic, and far surpassed the expectations of anyone involved with its creation.

In addition to its syndication success, no other series – including *Star Trek* – has inspired as many successors over more than 45 years.

The Brady Kids (Animated series)

The Brady Bunch Hour (Musical-variety series)

The Brady Girls Get Married (Made-for-TV movie)

The Brady Brides (Situation comedy)

A Very Brady Christmas (Made-for-TV movie)

The Bradys (Drama series)

Brady Home Movies (TV special)

The Real Live Brady Bunch (Staged performances of original *Brady Bunch* episodes)

The Brady Bunch and *A Very Brady Sequel* (Theatrical films)

The Brady Bunch In the White House (Made-for-TV movie)

Growing Up Brady (Made-for-TV movie)

My Fair Brady (Reality TV series)

The Brady Bunch Exposed (Australian TV documentary)

It's a Sunshine Day: The Best of the Brady Bunch (CD)

A Very Brady Renovation (Home renovation series)

There have been books as well, from series star Barry Williams' *Growing Up Brady* (which inspired a TV movie adaptation) to *Love to Love You Bradys*, co-written by series star Susan Olsen, to *Brady, Brady, Brady: The Complete Story of the Brady Bunch* by series creator Sherwood Schwartz.

Rarely has a year gone by since 1969 without some new acknowledgement of the series, whether it's an original cast reunion, the debut of new collectible merchandise, or yet another film/television/stage adaptation of America's happiest family.

If you're over the age of 40, you know the details of the

Bradys' lives more intimately than those of your own family. You probably can't name three Billie Eilish songs, but you still know all the words to "It's a Sunshine Day." You can't resist smiling when you order pork chops and applesauce in a restaurant. You still break appointments by saying "Something suddenly came up."

Yet as much as I love the series, I still find it difficult to pinpoint any one reason for why it has been so embraced.

For me, as an only child, I've always found myself drawn to shows about large families. Watching them was a way to vicariously experience what it may have been like to have a childhood surrounded by loving, but sometimes frustrating siblings, while actually growing up without ever having to wait in line for a bathroom or a telephone.

The series also exists in an ideal time loop that served it well in perpetual syndication. Just as Greg (Barry Williams) graduates high school in the final episode, and his life is about to become less certain as he heads to college and into the working world, the reruns revert back to the beginning, with the marriage of Mike (Robert Reed) and Carol (Florence Henderson), and we get to watch the kids grow up again, safe and happy.

But perhaps the main reason why the show resonated so well with viewers, beyond the likability of its appealing cast, was just how "normal" it was. While the bunch came together in a unique way – widower with three boys marries widow with three girls – the singular challenges of a blended family were mentioned only a few times in the first season, and then forgotten.

Occasionally we had reminders that this was a sitcom; Marcia (Maureen McCormick) went to a school dance with Davy Jones, and an eccentric archaeologist abducted the Brady boys when the family went to Hawaii. But most of the slice-of-life stories were middle class America personified: siblings fight and then make up; a middle child is jealous of her older sister; teenage peer pressure leads to a bad decision; school plays, ballet lessons, pony league baseball, neighborhood bullies, slumber parties, tonsillitis, and breaking mom's favorite vase by playing ball in the house.

The show could have been set anywhere in American suburbia, and that's how it was presented. We assume it was California because of an episode set at the beach, occasional glimpses of a palm tree, and the fact that no one ever came home from work or school knocking slush off their galoshes, even in the Christmas episode.

But in the 1970s, whether you grew up in Newport Beach or Nebraska, Florida or Fort Worth, New England or New Mexico, the Bradys were us, if you were blessed to grow up in a loving household. If they were not who you were, they were probably who you wanted to be.

The Best Episodes

"The Dropout" (1970)

Los Angeles Dodger great Don Drysdale compliments Greg's slider, and from that moment nothing else matters but baseball – not even completing school assignments: as Greg explains to his concerned parents, "I'm going to be a baseball player – they don't have to know anything!"

His life-plan proves short-lived after the cocky, would-be Cy Young winner gets clobbered in a Little League game, and then decides he never wants to play baseball again. That leads to the best father-son scene in a series that was never as sentimental as *Father Know Best*. But it would be hard to find a better cautionary tale about hubris than this 30-minute show.

"The Liberation of Marcia Brady" (1971)

Long before the Boy Scouts opened their membership to girls, Marcia Brady attempts to join Greg's Frontier Scouts group. Greg wants to show her how silly she looks, so he tries to join Marcia's club, the Sunflower Girls – but he's too old, so Peter (Christopher Knight) is coerced into the job. That sets up the episode's most memorable scene, in which Sunflower Girl Peter tries to sell cookies door-to-door.

The Liberation of Marcia Brady" aired just six months after Mary Richards first walked into the WJM newsroom. It provides some still-funny moments and a look at how the early stages of feminism and the women's movement were being discussed in the average American household.

"The Personality Kid" (1971)

With the exception of "Two Petes in a Pod," almost every Peter episode is a series highlight. These are also some of the funniest shows in the run, whether Peter is secretly recording his siblings' conversations ("The Private Ear") or being consumed by guilt after breaking mom's favorite vase ("Confessions, Confessions").

Still, "The Personality Kid" is an episode everyone remembers, and with good reason. The story has Peter coming home from a party distraught because someone told him he has no personality. His parents expect it to blow over, but when it doesn't we find Mike doesn't have much tolerance for self-pity: "Stop moping around! If you don't like your personality, improve it! Change it!" Thus we get a famous sequence as Peter takes various personalities for a test drive, one being that of Humphrey Bogart.

It's hard to explain why the "pork chops and applesauce" scene still makes me laugh, even though I've probably watched it 50 times. It isn't just Christopher Knight's awful Bogie impression, in which "swell" becomes "schwell"; it's the reactions from Carol and Alice (Ann B. Davis) that progress from befuddled to bemused, and how it becomes contagious as both adopt the same facial tics and pronunciations.

"Today I Am a Freshman" (1972)

Marcia's uneasy transition into high school sent a reassuring message to young girls that no one is immune from insecurity, even someone as smart and beautiful and poised as Marcia Brady.

To boost her social life at her new school, Marcia joins every club available, leading to a series of amusing scenes as she tries her hand at archery, scuba diving, karate and yoga. While this is happening, the episode's B-plot has Peter building a working volcano, which he tests as Marcia is considered for membership in Westdale High's most exclusive club, The Boosters.

For a television writer, bringing the A-plot and B-plot of an episode into a perfect simultaneous payoff is the ultimate accomplishment. "Today I Am a Freshman" accomplishes this goal about as well as it could be achieved.

"Amateur Night" (1973)

This was the most celebrated and the most successful of the show's occasional musical episodes. The kids purchase a silver platter for their parents' anniversary, but Jan (Eve Plumb) miscalculates the cost of the engraving, leaving them $56.23 short. In desperation, they attempt to raise the money by performing on a TV talent contest.

The performance of "It's a Sunshine Day" in this episode is as famous a moment as the series produced. The song has become an indelible moment from 1970s pop culture. In the years since it has been featured in episodes of *Family Guy* and *Castle*, in commercials for the Playstation video game console and the Amazon subsidiary Audible, and it provided the title for a 1993 CD collection of Brady songs.

Sidebar: More Brady Moments

Of all the various spinoffs and tributes the series inspired, these two may be the most remarkable.

The Real Live Brady Bunch

Sisters Jill and Faith Soloway grew up on Chicago's Near South Side, where endless *Brady* reruns provided a safe haven from the drama of their parents' unhappy marriage. Their devotion continued through high school, college, and a post-graduate gravitation to the city's local theater community.

When Faith became a musical director at Second City, she wrote a parody song based on Jefferson Airplane's "White Rabbit" that incorporated a Brady reference in the lyric "Go ask Alice." Around the same time, the Soloways discussed their *Brady* love with Jill's friend Becky Thyre, who astonished the siblings with a perfect imitation of Marcia, complete with hair flip.

From these meager inspirations, the sisters conceived *The Real Live Brady Bunch*, in which *Brady Bunch* scripts were performed verbatim by actors both too old – and in some cases too chunky – for their roles.

The show opened in June of 1990 at the 110-seat Annoyance Theatre, a rundown loft on Broadway Ave. that specialized in subversive comedy/improv pieces. It played once a week on Tuesday nights, described by one local paper as the darkest of dark-night slots.

"We thought five people would show up," said Jill of the show's debut. But within a month, lines began forming for tickets by 11AM, and hundreds of people were turned away every night. A second show was added, but the sell-outs continued. Astonished, Jill and Faith would go up to the roof of the theater to marvel at the length of the lines. The show would later play successfully in New York and Los Angeles, where in 1992 Davy Jones reprised his role in the episode he originally appeared in 20 years earlier.

"We did it just to have fun and, all of a sudden, reporters were asking our views on the 70s and family dynamics and why the show was so popular," Jill reflected. "And I think we were just these two Jewish girls wanting to be in a big Gentile family that had family meetings and potato sack races."

A Very Brady Renovation

The Brady Bunch home, as shown on the series, is located just off Ventura Blvd. in Studio City, California. Though no episodes were actually filmed there, the house became famous over the years and attracted a steady flow of fans. When it was put up for sale in 2018, it was purchased by the HGTV network, which set out to turn the structure into the actual Brady residence. Among the many challenges – an interior layout that in no way resembled the sets used for the series, and the fact that this one-story house would now need a second floor.

The network recruited many of its top designers and renovators for the project, as well as the original Brady kids.

The entire undertaking was a completely impractical thing to do, requiring thousands of hours and millions of dollars. But seeing the results, it feels like time and money well spent. The four episodes of *A Very Brady Renovation* were a sugar rush of the sweetest kind of nostalgia. The reactions of the cast and other visitors at seeing a "real" Brady house illustrated the pull we all feel from the shows we loved growing up. Now, when are they going to let us visit?

The Code of Practices for Television Broadcasters

Even if you have ever heard of The Code of Practices for Television Broadcasters, you've seen its seal appear after the closing credits of TV shows that originally aired between 1952 and the late 1970s.

Of the many factors that separate shows from the classic TV era from the current television landscape, the Code of Practices may be the most consequential – and the most divisive.

In four single-spaced, two-column pages, this document provided a set of guidelines specifying what is acceptable content for a television series, and what is not.

According to its Preamble, "It is the responsibility of television to bear constantly in mind that the audience is primarily a home audience, and consequently television's relationship to the viewers is that between guest and host."

This is the first sign that these guidelines have long since passed into a bygone age. Would you welcome the inhabitants of the *Big Brother* house as guests in your home?

The Code continues: "Television, and all who participate in it, are jointly accountable to the American public for respect for the special needs of children, for community responsibility, for the advancement of education and culture...for decency and decorum in production, and for propriety in advertising."

Antiquated? Perhaps. Words like 'decorum' and 'propriety' are no longer prevalent among television executives and producers, unless they are used as examples of what doesn't draw ratings.

The Preamble is followed by a list of subjects that must be approached with prudence. More quotes from the text:

"Profanity, obscenity, smut and vulgarity are forbidden."

"Attacks on religion and religious faiths are not allowed."

"In reference to physical or mental afflictions and deformities, special precautions must be taken to avoid ridiculing sufferers from similar ailments and offending them or members of their families."

"The presentation of cruelty, greed and selfishness as worthy motivations is to be avoided."

"Criminality shall be presented as undesirable and unsympathetic. The condoning of crime and the treatment of the

commission of crime in a frivolous, cynical or callous manner is unacceptable."

"The use of animals, both in the production of television programs and as a part of television program content, shall, at all times, be in conformity with the accepted standards of humane treatment."

"Racial or nationality types shall not be shown on television in such a manner as to ridicule the race or nationality."

"News reporting should be factual, fair and without bias."

I'll pause for a moment until you stop laughing at that last one.

What is being communicated is not primarily about censorship; unlike the Comics Code Authority, which in 1971 famously rejected an issue of *Spider-Man* because it depicted drug use, the Code of Practice allowed a wide range of topics to be included in television dramas or comedies, including drugs. However, it required that behavior that is considered wrong, illegal or destructive be presented as such.

As the document later states in a section on children, "Crime, violence and sex are a part of the world they will be called upon to meet, and a certain amount of proper presentation of such is helpful in orienting the child to his social surroundings. However, violence and illicit sex shall not be presented in an attractive manner, nor to an extent such as will lead a child to believe they play a greater part in life than they do."

Television has not only moved beyond that dictum to a staggering extent, a case could be made that much of the medium's programming is now an endorsement of behaviors once condemned.

Did these restrictions limit creativity? Or did the Code establish protections that helped television to maintain a suitable standard in programming content that would be preferred by the majority of its viewers?

A 1965 article in *TV Guide* revealed that there were indeed writers that felt hamstrung by the restrictions of network standards and practices. Among those quoted for the piece were Gene Roddenberry (*Star Trek*), Bruce Geller (*Mission: Impossible*) and Sterling Silliphant (*The Naked City*). These were not industry benchwarmers seeking excuses for why their scripts were rejected. Yet somehow they still managed to create exceptional television within a business that had to serve both art (better shows meant bigger ratings) commerce (advertisers would not buy commercials on a show that was offensive to viewers), and an adherence to commonly held values.

One last brief point about content: A series like *The Defenders* exposes the fraudulent claim that stories about the dark side of humanity require graphic visual detail for sufficient impact. There are some very unsavory topics in these episodes, but they are handled effectively and without exploitation, in a way that satisfied 1960s broadcast standards. Today, good luck finding any network capable of such discernment.

Sadly, it was inevitable that television would eventually grow beyond any concerns over being a well-behaved guest in a viewer's home. The cable TV industry was not limited by whatever broadcast restrictions remained at the time of its introduction, and those running the networks felt forced to keep up with edgier content.

But I am grateful that television, in its first three decades, strived for something beyond entertainment. Many of the series created during this era remain among the finest ever produced. And if you have children you can let them watch any of these shows without worrying about inappropriate content.

A Default Setting of Kindness

"What separates classic TV as a whole from current TV?"

Some differences are obvious, from the assertion of more traditional values to the family-friendly content. But I have always felt it runs deeper than that.

There is something primal in the DNA of these shows that is no longer found in much of today's television. Exactly what it is, however, can be difficult to put into words.

But I think I've finally figured it out. No single description will fit hundreds of series from the 1950s through the 1970s. But as a general summation of philosophy I think this one is pretty close.

Classic TV shows, and more specifically the characters in them, originate from a default setting of kindness.

The outlook that emanates from these shows, particularly the situation comedies, is a positive one that is embodied in the demeanor of their characters, who start each new day feeling satisfaction with their lives, their families and their careers.

This being television, complications are regularly introduced into these contented environments, and its denizens are not immune to sadness, frustration or disappointment. But these too are managed in a civilized manner, and by the next episode they have reverted back to their default setting, eager to face the possibilities of another day.

Work was not an ordeal. Most breadwinners approached a trip to the office not with dread but with appreciation for their jobs. Joe Friday (*Dragnet*) loved being a cop. Rob Petrie (*The Dick Van Dyke Show*) reveled in the camaraderie and shared creativity he enjoyed while writing for *The Alan Brady Show*. Pete Dixon (*Room 222*) cared about the educations and the futures of his high school students. Pediatrician Alex Stone (*The Donna Reed Show*) gamely smiled through the screams and tears of his patients. Jim Anderson (*Father Knows Best*) sold insurance, an occupation associated only with tedium – and carried out his tasks with integrity and professionalism.

Homes were happy places where functional families lived. Children were blessings, not burdens. Doorbells and phone calls were answered with a smile. Communities were closer and neighbors knew each other. Church on Sunday was the rule and not the exception.

I could cite countless shows and episodes that would support these positions, but this isn't about specific moments; it's about the overall impression expressed throughout this entire era. Audiences enjoyed spending time each week with these characters because they were admirable people. They still do.

Of course there are exceptions: Sgt. Bilko, as brilliantly played by Phil Silvers – inveterate gambler, con man and sycophant; Herbert T. Gillis (*The Many Loves of Dobie Gillis*), perennially frustrated by working long hours, rude customers and a deadbeat son; bus driver Ralph Kramden (*The Honeymooners*) had a short fuse that was exacerbated by the repeated failure of his get-rich-quick schemes.

But exceptions only reinforce the argument that most TV Land denizens in this era were basically contented people. Now, look at any list of recent popular or critically acclaimed series. What's the most common default setting for the characters?

I see a lot of people that are self-centered. I see characters that believe the world owed them a better life than the one they have, who wake up every day into a deck that is stacked against them. I see people that resort to snark because they are uncomfortable with sincerity.

Is that more realistic? Perhaps. But that wasn't the question and that, for me, is not the top priority of a television show.

I try to have a default setting of kindness. Sometimes it doesn't last until breakfast, but it's important to have aspirations. When I need a refresher course in how it's done, I always know where to look.

The Dick Van Dyke Show

1961-1966 (CBS)

158 Episodes

Perfection is the elusive, likely unobtainable goal that many of us strive toward through our work in a fundamentally imperfect world. 99.9% of us will never get there.

I think *The Dick Van Dyke Show* got there.

I love every series celebrated in this book, but I can also identify where and when they occasionally slipped: the introduction of a new but unnecessary character (Cousin Oliver on *The Brady Bunch*; Emily on *Family Affair*); a final season that lacked the quality and freshness of previous seasons (*Bewitched, Get Smart*); the strongly felt absence of beloved characters (*The Mary Tyler Moore Show, Mission: Impossible*).

Such drawbacks are all too common and even understandable given the challenges of sustaining viewer interest in a long-running series. That *The Dick Van Dyke Show* managed to sidestep them as nimbly as Rob Petrie (occasionally) sidestepped that ottoman in the series' opening credits, is a remarkable achievement.

How did the stars align so to create such a perfect show? It began with Carl Reiner, who conceived the series as a starring vehicle for him, before realizing he was the one weak link in an otherwise good idea. So he kept the concept of a show about a television comedy writer, and retreated to his typewriter to churn out wonderful scripts for 55 of its episodes, including 11 of the first 12 shows.

Taking over for Reiner as series lead Rob Petrie was Dick Van Dyke, largely unknown at the time outside of Broadway, where he had costarred in the hit musical *Bye Bye Birdie*.

The choice was inspired. Van Dyke was debonair and charismatic, projected a natural intelligence that made him believable as a talented writer, and was also as adept at physical and slapstick comedy as anyone since Charlie Chaplin and Buster Keaton.

Other roles were also ideally cast. Mary Tyler Moore was the last to be hired and the least experienced participant, but seemingly overnight she emerged as a gifted comedic actress in episodes such as "My Blonde-Haired Brunette," "The Curious Thing About Women," "The Life and Love of Joe Coogan" and "Pink Pills and Purple Parents" among many others. Viewers could also feel the palpable mutual affection she shared with her TV husband.

Showbiz veterans Rose Marie and Morey Amsterdam played Sally Rogers and Buddy Sorrell, Rob's cowriters of *The Alan Brady Show*, and Carl Reiner found a role better suited to his genius as the short-tempered dictatorial star of that show.

Bald, bespectacled Richard Deacon played Mel Cooley, the show's producer (and Alan's brother-in-law), a perfect target for Buddy's hilarious rapid-fire insults.

Larry Matthews played the Petries' son Richie. He didn't add much, but he wasn't an unwelcome distraction either.

The Dick Van Dyke Show excelled both as a family sitcom and a workplace sitcom. Perhaps because of my own choice of career my favorite moments were those set in Rob's office. It's not surprising that Carl Reiner saw the comic possibilities in a writer's room for a variety series, having worked for Sid Caesar in writer's rooms that at various times included Mel Brooks, Woody Allen, Neil Simon, Larry Gelbart, Mel Tolkin and Selma Diamond.

Not only were these scenes funny and entertaining, there was an authenticity to them. Who better than real veteran TV writers to relate the frustrations of long days waiting for comic inspiration, and then developing a tiny seed of an idea into a bit that made an audience laugh? The series also received outstanding script contributions from Bill Persky and Sam Denoff (who later created *That Girl*), Garry Marshall (who later created *Happy Days*), and Dale McRaven (who later created *Perfect Strangers*).

On the Petrie home front, Rob and Laura gave us a glimpse into a romanticized suburban lifestyle to which many of us still aspire. Who wouldn't love to attend one of their parties at 148 Bonnie Meadow Rd., where witty conversation is exchanged, and guests and hosts perform polished song-and-dance numbers in the living room?

I was five years old the first time I saw this show, in the kitchen of a duplex in Skokie, Illinois. I would eat dinner and watch the series in syndication on Chicago's WGN-TV, channel 9. It made me laugh, and it made my mom laugh.

After a few years of constant exposure I lost touch with the Petries for a while, only to rediscover them in the 1980s when my home was wired for cable and I discovered Nick at Nite. Once again, *The Dick Van Dyke Show* was a nightly tradition, and it had lost none of its appeal. And when the series was released on Blu-Ray, I had a welcome pretext to watch every show again in order, now with a stunning clarity that I could never have imagined more than 40 years earlier. Buddy's putdowns of Mel Cooley still made me laugh, even though I've heard them a thousand times before.

That's the enduring legacy of a great television show. And it's one that Rob Petrie, for all his other talents, never fully embraced.

The great irony in *The Dick Van Dyke Show* is how Rob assessed his own vocation. By all accounts he was one of the best television writers in the business, yet he believed he would only be validated as a "real" writer if he wrote a novel.

In the episode "A Farewell to Writing" Rob becomes envious when an old friend has his book published. "I'm not a writer," he concludes. "You are a writer, and a good one,"

Laura tells him, to which he responds, "Then why I am I sitting here reading someone else's book instead of my own?"

There's a similar conversation in "I'm no Henry Walden," as Rob and Laura prepare to attend a cocktail party for a world-renowned poet. "I don't know who invited me and I don't know why," he tells Laura, because the other guests are all "serious writers."

"What am I?" He asks. "All I write is jokes. Nothing I write has any real permanence about it. Alan says it on the television once, and pfffft! It's gone forever."

That episode aired in 1963, before anyone could conceive of videocassettes or DVDs, or shows that would live in perpetuity on nostalgia cable networks. So while Rob may have needed a published book to validate his life's work, it's his work for television that would emerge as more prominent and more influential. His talent, like all of the real TV writers working in this era, would unify our culture, entertain generations of viewers, and continue to show us a way of life worthy of emulating.

Very few novels have ever done that.

The Best Episodes

"Where Did I Come From?" (1962)

There were several series episodes featuring flashbacks to earlier moments in Rob and Laura's life. This is the best of them, as the couple reminisces about the days before the birth of their son. Rob takes the role of nervous expectant father to hilarious lengths.

"The Curious Thing About Women" (1962)

Watching this episode first in syndication as a kid, and many times thereafter, my future career aspirations were inspired by the office scene where Rob, Sally and Buddy develop an unremarkable event (Laura opening Rob's mail before he gets a chance to read it) into a classic comedy sketch. I can't think of another scripted moment on TV where the abundant joy of creativity that writers occasionally experience was more perfectly expressed. The scenes with Mary Tyler Moore and the inflatable raft were pretty funny too.

"I Am My Brother's Keeper/The Sleeping Brother" (1962)

These episodes introduced Dick Van Dyke's brother Jerry, playing Rob Petrie's brother, Stacy. The bizarre plot has Stacy trying to break into show business but only being able to perform while he's asleep (due to a rare, advanced form of sleepwalking). Despite that contrivance the shows are smart and funny, particularly during the cast performances at those Petrie house parties that made the suburbs looks so cool and sophisticated.

"Coast-to-Coast Big Mouth" (1965)

The first episode of the show's fifth and final season contains the most memorable of Carl Reiner's always-welcome appearances as Alan Brady. The story has Laura going on a game show and getting tricked into revealing that Brady is bald. Rob's horrified reaction is hilarious, but the highlight finds Laura trying to save her husband's job. Her confrontation with Alan, as he sits glowering at his desk behind a display of now-useless hairpieces, remains one of the series' best moments.

"Obnoxious, Offensive, Egomaniac Etc." (1966)

The writing staff takes out their frustrations with their boss by writing childish insults in their copy of a script – which is accidentally sent to Alan Brady's office. Can they retrieve it before he reads it?

The Donna Reed Show

1958-1966 (ABC)

275 Episodes

"That Damn Donna Reed" is the title of a 2001 episode of *The Gilmore Girls*. It opens with Lorelei Gilmore (Lauren Graham) and her daughter Rory (Alexis Bledel) watching an episode of *The Donna Reed Show*. Rory's boyfriend Dean drops by with pizza and asks, "Who's Donna Reed?"

She was "the quintessential '50s mom with the perfect '50s family," Lorelei responds.

"Is it a show?" he asks.

"It's a lifestyle," says Lorelei.

"It's a religion," says Rory.

After such facetious praise they proceed to mock the show mercilessly (but because *Gilmore Girls* is brilliantly written, also very cleverly). They scoff at Donna's contented domesticity, the scenes of parents and children doing chores together, and the simple pleasures of everyday life.

"I don't know," says Dean. "It all seems kind of nice to me."

Yes, Dean, it was. In fact *The Donna Reed Show* is as nice as TV gets. There seemed to be an extra measure of warmth and grace and kindness that emanated from each episode, unmatched even by such equally wholesome programs as *Father Knows Best* and *Leave it to Beaver*.

That gentle, openhearted quality can be attributed largely to the lady whose name appears in the show's title. Donna Reed was a known and loved presence for audiences dating back to when George Bailey wanted to give her the moon in *It's a Wonderful Life*. If television thrived on performers who would be greeted as welcome guests in America's homes, no one could be more welcome than this enchanting, classy lady, a Hollywood star when that still meant something, and yet as relatable and approachable as your next-door neighbor.

There's a reason Donna played a character named Donna, just as Mary Tyler Moore played a Mary and Roseanne Barr played a Roseanne: with each of their respective shows the hope was that audiences would see the characters as an extension of the women portraying them. It worked every time – just ask those Gilmores, who never referred to her as Donna Stone of Hilldale. That's Donna Reed on TV, smiling as she bakes another cake and always looking like she just got back from the beauty salon.

With top billing, an Academy Award and a distinguished film career already behind her, Reed might have been expected to carry the show – and perhaps she could have managed it. Thankfully, that wasn't necessary. The casting of Carl Betz as her husband was perhaps the most important key to the series' success. Television is littered with star vehicles that failed because the star overshadowed everyone else in the room. *The Bob Newhart Show* got it right. Shows like *The Jimmy Stewart Show* and *The Smith Family* with Henry Fonda did not – and didn't last.

Dr. Alex Stone, a patient pediatrician with a quick wit and easygoing parenting style, was a man that audiences would believe could attract someone as wonderful as Donna. Both knew how lucky they were to find such ideal partners.

Shelley Fabares's Mary, as effortlessly luminous as her TV mom, had impeccable manners, but could also be vain and manipulative. Remember that girl in high school who knew how attractive she was, and used it to her advantage? That was Mary Stone. Sometimes, as in "Mary's Double Date" she got caught playing two interested boys off each other, and paid the price. "You played a dangerous game, and you lost," Donna admonished (would her mom ever do that? Never!)

But just when you think you've got Mary pegged, along comes an episode like "Decisions, Decisions, Decisions," when she's out with a pompous jerk who takes her to a fancy restaurant and can't pay the check. She shows such commendable poise and maturity that you fall in love with her all over again.

And Jeff Stone (Paul Petersen)? Simply one of the most credible and authentic sitcom kids ever. I'm in my 50s and there are still times I wish I had his self-assurance.

Donna Stone was a homemaker, a role now deemed burdensome and exploitative, and not just by the Gilmore girls. But here is another situation where TV shows of the past do not get enough credit for self-awareness from the current arbiters of what is culturally desired. *The Donna Reed Show* confronted that stereotype head on in a 1960 episode appropriately titled "Just a Housewife." Donna put the detractors in their place, while reaffirming the value, dignity and fulfillment of the life she chose to lead.

Another Gilmore jibe at the series was that "nothing happens" in every episode – meaning there were no crises that threatened the stability of the family or the security of their daily life.

You won't always find challenging content in most of these vintage series, but that is not a creative flaw. Rather, their consistency and predictability is an important part of their enduring appeal. I for one would never want to watch an episode of *The Donna Reed Show* in which Donna gets cancer, or Jeff is critically injured in an auto accident. That was not why these shows were made.

Today's TV critics praise shows that avoid stories that are too "fan-friendly." But I cannot imagine a writer or producer from any popular show in the 1950s saying, "I've got an idea for a story that will really devastate the audience. It will make a lot of them angry and they may stop watching, but I still think it's the right thing to do."

That was not an option. And with very few exceptions I don't think it should be.

If you asked Tony Owen, (Donna Reed's husband and the show's producer), or Ozzie Nelson or Sherwood Schwartz, they'd tell you that escapism was what they hoped to offer. The philosophy was that viewers had their own problems. When they settled in for a night of TV, the last thing they wanted was to watch characters going through the same stressful realities that they had to endure.

Shocking an audience is easy. Telling stories week after week, season after season, without resorting to such tactics, and still keeping your fans coming back for more – that's an achievement.

Let's end this piece where it began, with *The Gilmore Girls*. Peeved by Dean's admiration for the domesticity of *The Donna Reed Show*, Rory tries to teach him a lesson by inviting him over for a home-cooked dinner. She greets him at the door in a '50s style dress, apron, pearls and heels, and serves each course with a smile. She also confesses to doing some research into the series, and discovering that Donna was an un-credited producer and director on her show, which made her one of the first woman television executives.

Even worse – Rory confesses that her turn as a happy homemaker was fun, except for one slip - she neglected to serve rolls with the steak and mashed potatoes: "Donna Reed would have never forgotten the rolls."

So true, Rory. So true.

The Best Episodes

"Three-Part Mother" (1958)

The series' pilot serves as the perfect introduction to the Stone family. Still new in town, Donna is pressured to attend a lecture by her husband, on the same evening that Jeff has a basketball game and Mary must introduce her mother to the members of her girl's club. How can she conquer this dilemma? She's Donna Reed – nothing is beyond her.

"The Ideal Wife" (1959)

"Everybody can't be as sweet as Donna."
"I'm so lucky to have a mother as sweet as you."

Donna finally hears the word 'sweet' once too often and decides it's time to become a more demanding wife and a strict disciplinarian with the children.

Does it last? Absolutely not – but it's fun to watch her try.

"Sleep No More My Lady" (1959)

The preternaturally beautiful Donna Reed could never be Lucille Ball, and her series rarely put her in the type of bizarre situations that Lucy Ricardo caused every week. But that doesn't mean she couldn't thrive in physical comedy or farce. In "Sleep No More My Lady" Donna inadvertently overdoses on tranquilizers before her husband is to deliver a speech at a medical convention. That scene, and the hotel room hijinks that follow, offered Reed a rare chance to be something other than the poised and perfect homemaker.

"Donna's Prima Donna" (1962)

Shelley Fabares will be the first to tell you she's not really a singer. But with the right song, the right arrangement, and backing vocals by the likes of Darlene Love, "Johnny Angel" (performed in this episode) became her first and only #1 hit. She recorded several albums after the song's unexpected success, but never got close to a hit again.

"My Dad" (1962)

Medical emergencies impose upon several father-son activities, and also force Alex to miss a school performance where Jeff planned to sing a song honoring his father. Paul Petersen's singing career was not as successful as his TV sister's but his performance of the song "My Dad" reached #6 on the Billboard chart, and 50 years later it can still reduce a grown man to tears.

How Times Have Changed: Healthcare

In its third season, *The Donna Reed Show* aired an episode entitled "Never Marry a Doctor." Near the beginning, Dr. Alex Stone receives a call at his office about a child that is sick. The call went directly to the doctor, not to a receptionist who puts the nervous parent on hold for several minutes, before offering them the option of going to the emergency room, or making an appointment for a week from Thursday.

Dr. Stone then collects his medical bag and heads off to the patient's home. When he arrives, he does not hand the child's mother a multiple-page questionnaire that wants to know every medication everyone in the family has ever taken, and whether her third cousin has ever had malaria. He does not request to see a picture ID, an insurance card, or a referral from another physician.

Instead, Dr. Stone does something that will now likely confuse any viewers under the age of 30: he examines and treats the patient – in other words, health care.

After the exam, the boy's father tells Dr. Stone that he's been out of work for a while and can't pay the bill. "Don't worry about that," Alex tells him. "Medical service is something you have to have when you need it, not when you can afford it. I can wait."

Is it any wonder why so many people prefer television from this era?

When this episode first aired in 1960, these scenes would not have struck viewers as unrealistic. Similar moments were commonplace in the dramas and comedies of the 1950s through the 1970s.

When we compare the way things were in the classic TV era to how they are now, we find that most pursuits are more efficient and more convenient than they used to be. On *The Dick Van Dyke Show*, Alan Brady's writing staff didn't have computers so they still wrote their scripts on a typewriter, with multiple carbons so there would be more than one copy. Phone calls are now made with a voice command or one touch of a saved number, instead of dialing a rotary phone. Debit cards offer an easier way to pay for a purchase than writing a check. Photographs can be viewed a second after they are taken.

But with health care we seem to have gone the other way. I grant you there are better treatment options for a variety of conditions today than when Ben Casey and Marcus Welby were handing out prescriptions, but those breakthroughs came from research laboratories and universities. At the grassroots level where doctors see patients, it seems like we've regressed…and lost something precious in doing so.

Another memorable program comes to mind: "Samantha's Da Vinci Dilemma" from the fourth season of *Bewitched*. The story had Aunt Clara trying to conjure up a house painter to help Sam, and instead zapping up Leonardo Da Vinci. In the episode's best scene, Leonardo wanders into a museum and hears a guide praising a modern sculpture that looks like a block of stone with a crack in it – because that's all it is. He is shocked to discover what has become of the trade he once practiced.

If Aunt Clara were to zap Alex Stone into a 21st century physician's office, I wonder if he wouldn't feel the same way.

Sidebar: Ask Your Doctor About...

It is hard for me to adequately express my hatred for a type of television commercial that once did not exist at all – the prescription drug ad.

This is a level of resentment that far surpasses the annoyance we have all felt with certain commercials: used car ads where every line is screamed instead of spoken; commercials that change the lyrics to popular songs to sell cat food; the subtle advancement of social justice agendas where the practical person of color has to explain something simple to the doltish white guy in the office.

Prescription drug ads irritate me at a more primal level. I find their very existence odious.

I'm a proud capitalist and have never felt I had the right to tell anyone how honestly-made income should be spent, whether that's a CEO salary some might consider exorbitant, or paying $10,000 for a limited-edition wristwatch that provides the same time of day as Mickey Mouse.

But the sheer pervasiveness of this one type of product ad makes one question unavoidable: Why are drug companies spending this much money ($60 billion a year by some estimates) to promote the benefits of products that no one can actually go out and buy?

I doubt physicians are being persuaded by commercials

featuring an elfin redhead dressed like a human digestive tract, or a woman walking around town trailed by her anthropomorphic bladder. But I'm sure over the past decade they've become fed up with calls from patients, wondering why they are not getting the same stuff that helped that nice woman on TV go bowling with her family.

No wonder the American Medical Association has called for a ban on prescription drug ads. Can't come too soon.

I also wonder what return on investment companies receive for all this advertising, particularly since some of these drugs are meant to treat conditions that are extremely rare.

Cars and candy bars and household cleaners are promoted via a medium that reaches into everyone's home, because almost everyone buys them. But when I see Danny Glover pretend to break into spontaneous tears and laughter to illustrate the symptoms of Pseudobulbar Affect (PBA), I wonder why a national advertising campaign is deemed appropriate for a product that 99.3% of Americans will never want nor need.

And stop with that "PBA" stuff too. Suddenly every illness has to have a cute nickname. Atrial fibrillation is now "A-Fib" (any relation to J-Lo?). Will epilepsy soon become "Shakey Shake"?

I abhor the length of these spots. There is no such thing as a 30-second pharmaceutical commercial. The extra time is needed to accommodate the comical litany of side effects lawyers demand be verbally enumerated. This is always immediately preceded by the reluctant admission: "(drug name) is not for everyone." These bits have been parodied plenty already, but that recognition should not distract us from the utter insanity of some of these stipulations.

Take Jublia, which you may do if you have toenail fungus. The condition is unsightly, but you can live a perfectly contented life with it if you wear socks. Jublia frees you from this burden, but if you're pregnant and you rub it on your toe, it could harm your unborn fetus. If it could inject something into your system powerful enough to do that, what else could it do?

Oh, and it's also flammable. Apply it to your foot by candlelight and you might burn down your house.

But the champion in the side effect sweepstakes is still Chantix, a drug that allegedly helps you quit smoking. Taking it, we are warned, could create "suicidal thoughts or actions." Is there any other way to interpret "suicidal actions" than killing yourself? At what point does the cure become more dangerous than the condition?

I have one more selfish reason for diving toward the mute button every time one of these ads appears; I don't like to be reminded of sick and dying people while I'm trying to watch Gilligan get off the island.

Does that make me selfish and heartless? Fine. I've been in

hospitals and had conversations with doctors about medication for relatives in serious straits. It's not fun. It isn't supposed to be fun. So when COPD is portrayed with a cartoon wolf in a green sweater, or when an ad for a heart disease drug shows someone wistfully singing, "The sun will come out...tomorrow" from *Annie*, in a way that suggests he's not entirely sure he'll be around to see it, it's beyond tasteless.

If you have a conscience you don't try to "sell" medication for people coping with late-stage cancer the same way you peddle remedies for a stuffy nose or a sore back. You have those conversations in private, with medical professionals and patients and their families.

Unfortunately, the very idea of privacy barely exists anymore, as those of the millennial ilk broadcast every virtue and sin they commit to social media. As always, television does not shape culture, it merely reflects it. I wish there was something I could take to change that reflection. Maybe I'll ask my doctor.

Dragnet

1967-1970 (NBC)

98 Episodes

Here is where I may lose some of you.

My fellow classic TV fans have reached near-unanimous consensus that the 1967-1970 version of *Dragnet* pales in comparison to its earlier TV run (1951-59). But it's the latter version that I came to treasure, primarily through the years it played on Nick at Nite, back when that cable channel was worth watching.

Eventually I did check out the original version, which was darker and grittier though not (to me) necessarily better.

Back then, Jack Webb's iconic portrayal of Los Angeles Police Detective Sergeant Joe Friday had a lean and hungry look. He hated bad guys and made it his personal mission to bring them to justice. But by the late 1960s, Friday had the hangdog expression of a veteran cop who had seen it all. Not world-weary, perhaps – he still reported to work eager to make his city safer. But years of seeing the worst of humanity up close have taken their toll.

There was something noble in that persistent sense of duty, in the face of whatever new danger and heartbreak the day may bring. That's why I prefer the 1960s series.

Dragnet was never a show about the cool renegade cops who "play by their own rules." It was not an action-packed series with tire-screeching car chases and guns blazing. This is a meticulous, dialogue-driven procedural about two middle-aged L.A. police officers (played by actors who will never grace a poster on a teenage girl's wall) who show up for work every day and do their best to serve the city that pays their salary.

From 1967 to 1970, viewers tuned in to watch Friday and Officer Frank Gannon (Harry Morgan) solve what were typically routine cases, while wearing the same drab suits in almost every episode. They ran down leads that didn't pan out. They sat at their desks filling out reports. They made awkward small talk until the boss called them into his office.

Why was this so compelling? I think it starts with the authenticity and attention to detail that Jack Webb insisted on in his depiction of cops at work. *Dragnet* humanized the men who wear the badge, and made them admirable not because of super-heroic deeds, but through their decency, compassion and dedication. As one merchant tells Friday in "The Big Shooting", "Whatever we pay you people, it's not enough."

It was also a series that was unequivocal in its recognition that there should be consequences for breaking a law, whether classified as a misdemeanor, a felony or a capital offense. Once that was not an unfamiliar concept, but it may play differently for generations raised in an era when law enforcement is viewed with mistrust or open hostility. One can only imagine what Joe Friday would think of sanctuary cities.

What else made it memorable? It began with a theme song (composed by Walter Schumann) that opened with four notes as familiar to TV fans back then as the first four notes of Beethoven's Fifth Symphony. It added catchphrases to the language: "This is the city," "The story you are about to see is true. The names have been changed to protect the innocent," "Just the facts."

Dragnet also sounded like nothing else on television. The unique staccato rhythm of the dialogue was often parodied in its day – some readers might remember a famous skit on *The Tonight Show* featuring Webb and Johnny Carson, and some missing copper clappers. Perhaps that's another reason the '60s show gets a bad rap.

Don't expect that derision from police officers, however. Real cops felt tremendous respect for Jack Webb, and the honor he brought to their profession. The Los Angeles Police Department actually retired Friday's badge number – 714 – to acknowledge his contribution to the law enforcement community. During the show's original run the LAPD frequently received calls asking to speak to Sgt. Friday. The response was always the same: "Sorry, it's Joe's day off."

The Best Episodes

"The Big Interrogation" (1967)

A rookie cop (played by future *Adam-12* star Kent McCord) is wrongfully accused of robbing a liquor store. Friday and Gannon are assigned to interrogate the officer, who is understandably angry that the city he signed up to protect now thinks he's a crook. When he announces his plan to leave the force, Friday launches into a nearly four-minute speech on what it means to be a police officer. It should be required viewing at every police academy graduation.

"The Christmas Story" (1967)

Friday and Gannon try to track down a missing statue of the baby Jesus, stolen from a church's Nativity scene. The statue is only worth a few dollars, but as the priest explains, it's the only Jesus his parishioners know. On Christmas Eve they return to the mission to break the bad news about their investigation, when their eyes are drawn to the church entrance, where a little boy transports the missing statue in a red wagon. He had prayed for the wagon, and promised Jesus the first ride. "Paquito's family, they're poor," explains the priest in the last scene. Friday looks around at the symbols within the church and responds, "Are they, Father?"

"The Big Departure" (1968)

If you liked Friday's speech in "The Big Interrogation," you'll also appreciate how he and Gannon educate some teenagers who decide to establish their own country, by stealing everything they need to get it started. Every time a movement like "Occupy Wall Street" springs up, somebody posts this speech to YouTube as a response to their grievances. And it still works.

"The Big High" (1967)

What made the 1960s *Dragnet* seem corny and out-of-step to some viewers was the hard line it took against illegal drugs, including marijuana. Several episodes were devoted to that subject, none more memorable than "The Big High."

A concerned father reports that his daughter and her husband are using marijuana. Friday and Gannon drive out to their spacious, tastefully-decorated Sherman Oaks home and meet a smart, personable couple. The woman's husband says that one day marijuana is going to be like liquor, "packaged and taxed and sold right off the shelf." "I doubt it," Gannon responds – and now we know he was wrong about that. But these were conversations happening in homes across the country. The foreshadowing of the final scene is hardly subtle, but that doesn't blunt its impact.

"Management Services: DL-411" (1969)

The assassination of Dr. Martin Luther King had a profound impact on the nation. And though Los Angeles was more than 1,700 miles away from Memphis where it took place, the city was on alert for how that event would impact their community. What follows is an almost documentary-like introduction to the LAPD's Emergency Control Center. "It's like one big finger on the city's pulse," Friday explains. Though history tells us L.A. was quiet in the aftermath of the assassination, this episode depicts how a big-city police force copes with a potential crisis.

The Dukes of Hazzard

1979-1985 (CBS)

147 Episodes

I wrote a book about *The Dukes of Hazzard* back in 1998, but that's not why the show is included here. It is here because the series epitomizes one of the themes of this book – how our culture has changed.

I was born and raised in the Chicago area and moved to Las Vegas in 1982. I have spent little time in our Southern states, outside of passing through the region during a road trip from Chicago to Orlando. What I knew of the South from a distance likely fell into stereotypes both positive and negative: stock car races, country music, Cracker Barrels, SEC football and downhome, unpretentious "Hey, y'all" charm. Also, a few pockets where they're still not quite ready to admit defeat in the War Between the States.

Like all such assessments it's part true and part not, but *The Dukes of Hazzard* ran with those representations, and didn't back down from one that is now considered toxic – the Confederate flag (painted on the roof of the General Lee) as a symbol of Southern pride. It gave few people pause during the show's original run, but the controversy re-emerged with greater intensity in 2015, following a racially motivated church shooting in South Carolina, and again in 2020 after a Minneapolis police officer was charged with murdering a man named George Floyd.

At one point the furor reached such a pitch that the series was pulled from syndication, and DVD season sets were removed from store shelves. This, while Civil War statues were destroyed on college campuses and in city parks.

Series star (and later U.S. Congressman) Ben Jones (Cooter) defended his show. "I think all of Hazzard Nation understands that the Confederate battle flag is the symbol that represents the indomitable spirit of independence which keeps us 'makin' our way the only way we know how,'" he wrote. "That flag on top of the General Lee made a statement that the values of the rural South were the values of courage and family and good times."

John Schneider, who played Bo Duke, echoed that sentiment. "If the flag was a symbol of racism, then Bo and Luke and Daisy and Uncle Jesse were a pack of wild racists, and that could not be further from the truth."

Heritage or hate? That is the question, and the best answer is one that will satisfy almost no one. "Different people at different times have used the Confederate flag as a symbol of both – and of other things," according to the American Civil War Museum. "Trying to reduce the flag to a single meaning distorts the flag's history and ignores the very real influence that history has had on perceptions and meanings."

Perhaps the easiest course would be to determine that hate trumps heritage, and eradicate the Confederate flag, or relegate it to museums, for the greater good. But the moment that happens other symbols will come under attack, including those that have no association with anything as unsavory as racism. We saw this in 2020 when the removal of Confederate statues was a precursor to the removal or destruction of statues honoring Ulysses S. Grant, Theodore Roosevelt, Abraham Lincoln, Francis Scott Key, and George Washington, as well as a few prominent abolitionists. The more bowdlerization is emboldened, the faster it spreads.

Real solutions to what remains of racial disparity will take time, and serious thought, and intelligently appropriated investment. It will require asking difficult questions and facing hard truths. It's much easier for self-appointed bigotry warriors to ban symbols and send *The Dukes of Hazzard* (along with *Gone with the Wind*) back to the vault for a few months, so everyone knows how much they care.

Has that worked yet?

Flag or no, Southern pride is apparent in every *Dukes of Hazzard* episode, and not just on the roof of the General Lee. It was embraced wholeheartedly by those who lived in their own Hazzard Counties – rural towns throughout the South where residents formed a special connection with the series. It became so popular that it cut into attendance at the near-sacred Friday night high school football games. Fan gatherings still happen every year, where *Dukes* faithful drive their homemade General Lees, meet the show's stars, and talk about favorite episodes over beer and barbecue.

Surprisingly, *The Dukes of Hazzard* was also a top-ten hit that pulled solid ratings in New York, Boston, and Chicago. Apparently you don't have to reside below the Mason-Dixon Line to enjoy watching a car fly over a train, or to admire the most stunning pair of legs since Betty Grable's (belonging to Catherine Bach as Daisy Duke).

It wasn't the best show – even its stars admit to that. The scripts could be mind-numbingly repetitive: Some suspicious out-of-town slickers would hit town planning some nefarious act, usually with the cooperation of corrupt County Commissioner "Boss" Hogg (Sorrell Booke). Their crimes would be pinned on "them Duke boys," Bo (Schneider) and Luke (Tom Wopat), who would spend the rest of the episode trying to clear their names, and outrun Sheriff Rosco P. Coltrane (James Best).

But even if you weren't sure if you were watching a new episode or a rerun, the series had a different rhythm than any other show at the time. Stories were introduced and narrated in the friendly down-home cadence of a balladeer – country music legend Waylon Jennings. The lawbreakers were the heroes and the local law was the villains. And everybody still kind of liked each other even when they were at odds.

The characters were engaging, and the setting was welcoming. If you get those two elements right, viewers will find you.

I'm still amused by the confusion *The Dukes of Hazzard* engenders in certain people from certain places. Asking them why the show was popular would be like asking them to solve any of the toughest unsolved conjectures in mathematics - and they'd still have a better chance with the equations.

It ties in to the belief that there are two Americas, not necessarily defined by geography or race or education or income. Sometimes I think there are more like five or six Americas, but only one of them is still thinking clearly.

It's the one that understands why an 18-year-old high school valedictorian would choose to enlist in the army instead of accepting a scholarship to Stanford.

It's the one that abhors actual racism, and is equally disgusted by manufactured racism, which is just as cruel and intolerant.

It's the one that sees the flaw in "you have your truth, I have my truth" thinking, because inevitably your truth and my truth will come into conflict, and those situations are resolved not by whose truth is authentic, but by who has the most muscle behind their viewpoint.

And yes, it's the one that likes *The Dukes of Hazzard*.

The Best Episodes

"High Octane" (1979)

The first five episodes of the series were filmed in and around Covington, Georgia. When the ratings proved impressive enough to indicate the show might last, Warner Bros. opted to shoot the rest in California. There was a more authentic "Southern" feel to these early shows, and "High Octane" was one of the stand-outs, offering a fairly accurate portrayal of the ongoing battles between moonshiners and the Treasury Agents assigned to catch them.

"The Ghost of General Lee" (1979)

Two crooks steal the General Lee and drive it into a lake. Rosco arrives in time to watch the car sink, and assumes Bo and Luke are dead. They return in time to witness their own memorial service, and decide to stay deceased long enough to foil Boss Hogg's latest insurance scam. This was John Schneider's favorite episode and it's a good choice. "The Ghost of General Lee" offers the usual thrills and comic bits, along with some moments of genuine emotion – plus, Daisy painting the Confederate flag on the roof of a decoy General and exclaiming, "I just love that flag!" Uh-oh.

"Granny Annie" (1979)

Veteran character actor James Best will always be best known for his unforgettable comic portrayal of the sputtering Sheriff Rosco, but TV fans will also remember him from a wide range of roles on great series, from *Honey West* and *The Twilight Zone* to *The Andy Griffith Show*. "Granny Annie" is listed here for one scene in which Rosco, captured by this week's thugs, is fearful that they're going to kill Boss Hogg. He calls Bo and Luke and begs for their help to save him. In less than two minutes he delivers an impassioned plea for mercy that seems both out of place on such a fun-loving show, yet also embodies everything the series was about.

"Find Loretta Lynn" (1980)

This episode marks the first guest appearance by a country music star, something that became a regular occurrence with the debut of Boss Hogg's celebrity speed trap. Several episodes would close with a country singer, having been pulled over, agreeing to perform at the Boar's Nest instead of paying a fine. Over six seasons the show featured performances from The Oak Ridge Boys, Tammy Wynette, Mickey Gilley, Dottie West, Roy Orbison and more.

"Carnival of Thrills" (1980)

Three words: Bo vs. Luke. The only time the two cousins ever fell out was after Bo fell for Diane (Robin Mattson) owner of a traveling carnival. She convinces Bo to take the place of her injured stuntman and attempt the dangerous "Leap of Life" over 32 cars. Luke thinks it's too dangerous and lets Sheriff Rosco impound the General Lee so Bo can't go through with it. That prompts a well-shot knock down, drag-out brawl, and Bo moving out of the Duke farm. A better-than-usual script and a thrilling climactic stunt are among the highlights of the series' third-season opener.

Family Affair

1966-1971 (CBS)

138 Episodes

Rich people on television are rarely portrayed as admirable. Usually millionaires will either be corrupt and immoral (J.R. Ewing), a Scrooge McDuck caricature (Thurston Howell III), or shallow and materialistic (Blair Warner).

That's not surprising if you think about it. Most viewers can only dream of the opulence enjoyed by these characters, so why not focus more on their foibles than their virtues?

Family Affair is an exceptional sitcom, not just in the sense of being well written and performed, but also in how it varied in both content and style from other situation comedies of its era. This was particularly true in Brian Keith's portrayal of Bill Davis.

Bill, who owned a civil engineering business that builds bridges and skyscrapers around the world, had a white-collar lifestyle but a blue-collar work ethic. He lived in a stylish Manhattan apartment, employed a British gentleman's gentleman servant, and enjoyed an active social life. The last thing this contented bachelor wanted was custody of two six year-old twins and their teenage sister. But they were his brother's kids and he took them in, because it was the right thing to do.

Imagine having an idyllic life instantly upended by responsibilities you never expected or wanted. Bill could have said no – other Davis relatives had done so before him, and from what we're told of the family they all had a lot less to lose. But Bill said yes, with no clue what that would entail.

The circumstances of their arrival on Uncle Bill's doorstep were not forgotten after the pilot. The twins' insecurity and separation anxiety inspired several first season shows. Contrast this with any other series from that era that featured a widowed parent – *The Brady Bunch, My Three Sons, The Partridge Family* – in which none of the children ever displayed a moment of anxiety over such a traumatic experience.

That doesn't mean *Family Affair* is a depressing show, but it's an honest show. And there's a remarkable grace and compassion that permeates how sensitive moments are handled, and an emotional authenticity that is extraordinary for escapist entertainment.

As previously stated, Brian Keith is wonderful here, and Sebastian Cabot as Mr. French was a perfect foil for three rambunctious kids. Anissa Jones (Buffy) is almost spookily effective as an actress, meriting comparison to Jodie Foster at that age. It takes Johnnie Whitaker (Jody) a couple of seasons to catch up but he gets there eventually. And Kathy Garver's

Cissy was a first crush to many boys and one of TV's most well-behaved teenagers – which made her moments of rebellion all the more interesting.

All of that was likely not enough to redeem the 1% on TV, but it was a good try.

The Best Episodes

"Fat, Fat, the Water Rat" (1967)

So many people who grow up poor never realize how little they had, because they were part of a loving and supportive family. Likewise, it never resonates with Buffy and Jody that their circumstances with Uncle Bill are what most people would consider rich – they're just relieved to finally have a permanent place to stay. There's a lot to unpack in this wonderful episode, and it starts from the premise that how we view our lives is different from how others see us.

When Buffy's dance class is canceled she wanders outside and meets a group of kids that Mr. French derides as "street urchins," but for the next hour she has the time of her life playing simple games and getting her clothes dirty. She'd love to play with them again but she heard their leader say he didn't like "fancy kids," and deep down she knew she was one of them.

After she recounts her adventures to Uncle Bill, they both dress down and head back to that neighborhood so Buffy can hang out with her new friends. One of the boy's fathers asks if Bill is down on his luck and offers to give some of his daughter's old dresses to Buffy. So you can imagine the reaction of these kind, humble people when Mr. French, dressed to the nines, arrives to tell Bill he needs to return a call from Washington DC.

As fences get mended, we see how perceptions can be altered – on both sides – a message too often lost in this era of identity politics.

"The Toy Box" (1967)

Uncle Bill does his best Rob Petrie impression and trips over Jody's skateboard. That mishap inspires a new Davis home rule: any toys not put away properly will be locked up and donated to charity.

You probably see where this is going. One inadvertent jostle as Buffy runs off to wash for dinner lands her beloved doll Mrs. Beasley on the floor, and when Mr. French sees the doll lying there he is devastated at the thought of what happens next (Sebastian Cabot is amazing in this very brief scene). Thankfully, Uncle Bill believes the experiment has served its purpose, and not only commutes Mrs. Beasley's sentence, but also liberates all the other confiscated toys. Whew!

"Flower Power" (1969)

Prim and proper Cissy is lured into the East Village pad of some freewheeling hippies who spout deep thoughts like "We can just be...here we just are." Will Uncle Bill's eldest turn on, tune in and drop out? Veronica Cartwright plays Jo-Ann, one of the flower children whom Cissy finds fascinating, until little Buffy opens her eyes to the pitfalls of a life with no responsibilities.

"The Good Neighbors" (1970)

Buffy wonders why the residents in their apartment building don't all know each other and socialize like neighbors did back in her home state of Indiana. She sets out to change that, by inviting everyone in the building to a get-acquainted party in the lobby.

On a typical sitcom, the residents would all be so charmed that they would cast aside their big city cynicism and realize how much they've been missing by their withdrawn ways. But here, Buffy waits by the elevator to greet all her New York neighbors with punch and cookies, and...

"Feat of Clay" (1970)

Bill receives a valuable pre-Columbian statue from a girlfriend and colleague. Buffy and Jody take it to school for show-and-tell, and break it on the way home. To cover up the accident they create a replica out of modeling clay, and everyone accepts it as the real thing – including art experts when it is displayed in a museum. This is a nice bookend episode with "A Matter For Experts," from the show's first season. Both stories explore how the people who make the most fuss about knowing what they're talking about…may actually be more clueless than the rest of us.

Sidebar: A Salute to Mrs. Beasley

Mrs. Beasley was the best friend to Buffy Davis on *Family Affair* from the first episode of the series until its final episode, five years later. By then, most young girls had started to outgrow their dolls, as illustrated in the most heart-shattering manner possible by Jessie the cowgirl in *Toy Story 2* (thanks, Sarah McLachlan!).

But it never seemed odd for Buffy to still care about her constant companion, though one might wonder how Anissa Jones felt about playing some of those scenes when she was 13 years old.

This is one of those situations where I wonder whether series creator Don Fedderson had a purpose in selecting the type of doll that was right for Buffy, or if it just seems like a wonderfully perceptive choice in retrospect.

Most little girls prefer baby dolls, so they can play the mother; or they may be drawn to the wish-fulfillment appeal of Barbie, with her Malibu dream house and square-jawed boyfriend and endless closet full of perfect outfits.

Mrs. Beasley, with her old-fashioned blue polka-dot dress and spectacles, looked like a kindly grandmother. That seems strange at first, but it makes perfect sense that a little girl who lost her parents would be more comforted by the presence of a mature image than by an infant. Here was an older person who cared about her, who was never going to leave her behind.

The doll's most memorable appearance came in the first season episode "Mrs. Beasley, Where Are You?" in which Mr. French accidentally knocks her off the terrace ledge of Uncle Bill's deluxe apartment in the sky. Buffy's crippling separation anxiety - a recurring theme throughout season one, is brought back to the fore as Buffy tries to cope with another loss: "People you love always go away. I know."

Family Affair. Not for the faint of heart.

How Times Have Changed: School

The sound of a lone bugle is heard through the second-story window of a high school classroom.

Immediately the students seated at their desks rise in unison, without being prompted, turn toward an American flag, and along with their teacher recite the Pledge of Allegiance.

That scene takes place near the beginning of "The Exile," a 1964 episode of *Mr. Novak*. It has nothing to do with the rest of the episode. It's just something that happened at the fictional Jefferson High School, as it happened in thousands of actual schools across America at that time.

A good school is not defined by reciting the Pledge, but there is a reason that such rituals endured for decades. It was meant, for a moment, to unify teachers and students with diverse backgrounds, beliefs, and interests into a common conviction: we're fortunate to be here, and to enjoy the benefits this country provides us.

You may not always see the Pledge recited in other school-based series from this era, but it would be a reasonable assumption that it was part of the school day. No one would watch that scene from *Mr. Novak* and find it anomalous.

The tradition is still in place here and there, but now sags under the weight of relentless court challenges, and a U.S. history curriculum that would cause any student body to question what America has done to deserve their fidelity. In a 2018 editorial Nathan J. Robinson, editor of *Current Affairs* magazine, summed up the feelings of many in our current times: "This dumb, creepy ritual should never have been imposed on kids."

Next to homes and offices, schools were among the most frequent settings for scenes and stories in every family situation comedy, from *Leave it to Beaver* to *The Brady Bunch*, *The Donna Reed Show* to *Family Affair*. Those portrayals were largely accurate in their details – the sizes of the classrooms, the subjects that comprised the school day, the lunchrooms and the playgrounds, the sports teams and the after-school clubs and activities, and the paralyzing fear that accompanied a trip to the principal's office.

From age five to age 18, young people spent a sizable chunk of their lives in these institutions, and parents did not have to think twice about trusting that arrangement. Lessons would be learned, teachers would be qualified, discipline issues would be controlled, and nothing would happen that clashed with the values of the community in which they all reside. In short, amidst work pressures and paying-the-mortgage pressures and keeping the car running and the refrigerator full, it was one less thing to worry about.

Sure, in inner cities and lower-income areas the challenges were greater. But even without the resources taken for granted in the suburbs, dedicated teachers and administrators went above and beyond to compensate for economic shortcomings and made the most of what they had, as depicted in shows like *Room 222* and *The White Shadow*.

When we watched an English teacher like Elizabeth Sherwood (Carol Mayo Jenkins) on *Fame*, we knew there were real English teachers introducing young minds to the genius of William Shakespeare and Charles Dickens, Harper Lee and Emily Dickinson.

On *Room 222* Pete Dixon (Lloyd Haynes) taught American history to a diverse class of students, some who may have felt marginalized by some prevailing attitudes from 200 years ago. He encouraged open discussion and conflicting opinions. In the episode "The Lincoln Story," the discussion touched on the Civil War and slavery, and when facts and legends don't coincide. But the objective was always education, not indoctrination.

I will always consider myself very fortunate to have gone to the public schools I attended, where parent-teacher night was packed like a matinee of *Hamilton*. It's a reminder of how the success of a school is determined not just by teachers, but also by the families of the students that go there.

There have always been private schools and religious schools, as well as families who opted for home schooling.

But for decades the overwhelming majority of American parents were confident that our elementary, junior high and high schools accepted the important responsibility of educating America's children, and did a great job with it.

That began to change over the past 20 years as a result of a number of factors, including Common Core, the greater reliance on standardized testing, and the emergence of special interest groups with objections to certain lessons, certain courses, and certain extracurricular activities.

As social activism began to supersede the three "R"s, boards of education forgot the wisdom of Margaret Mead, who advised that children should be taught how to think, not what to think. According to the Pulitzer Center's 2020 annual report, more than 3,500 classrooms incorporate materials from The 1619 Project, an attempt to reframe American history around slavery. It doesn't matter that its teachings have been unequivocally discredited on even the most basic facts by a consensus of historians – the objective is not to study the past, but to reshape the future.

For the first time, we must face the realization that the schools we've always trusted really have no obligation to excel, because they cannot be replaced regardless of their performance. Charter schools and religious schools can provide competition but face strong pushback from teacher's unions and other organizations that are personally and financially invested in maintaining a virtual monopoly.

As this is written we may be approaching a tipping point on schools. Perhaps there will still be a Pledge of Allegiance in 20 years – but who knows what young minds will be pledging allegiance to.

Father Knows Best

1954-1960 (CBS/NBC)

203 Episodes

There's something remarkable about *Father Knows Best.* You can watch any dozen episodes and be entertained by the wholesome charms with which this 1950s sitcom is identified. And then you'll discover a story that is so compelling in its content that you could write a college thesis about it.

To some extent this is true of many shows from an era we now group into a collective memory of innocent nostalgia. To some these family situation comedies are nothing more than sanitized portrayals of a traditional family that may provide a few simple pleasures, but are no longer relevant to the way we live today. Some actually find them offensive – a reactionary fantasy of a Middle America that never really existed, where Dad brings home the bacon, Mom is happily chained to her stove, and together they raise unfailingly polite kids.

Those who hold such opinions have either never watched shows like *Father Knows Best,* or they just weren't paying attention when they did. There was far too much talent involved to create something so bland, both in front of the camera (Robert Young, a sturdy, calming presence as patriarch Jim Anderson), and behind the camera (gifted writers Roswell Rogers and Paul West, who penned more than 160 of its episodes).

If certain formulas tended to repeat themselves – first dates, first jobs, eccentric neighbors and relatives – keep in mind that these are moments and rites of passage that many families experience in the non-scripted world as well.

Still that doesn't mean *Father Knows Best* turned a blind eye to societal change, and what was happening in the world outside its secure bubble of suburban contentment.

In the 1955 episode "Woman in the House" the Andersons meet Jill Carlson, the younger and free-spirited wife of one of Jim's oldest friends. She smokes, she talks a little too loud for the heartland, and at one point she asks Margaret if she's ever read Kafka.

Margaret, played with quiet dignity by Jane Wyatt, can barely hide her discomfort, which only deepens after Jill becomes their houseguest for a few days. At one point she breaks down, ashamed by how provincial her life seems to this strange outsider, and by her own intolerance. This being *Father Knows Best*, both Margaret and Jill are changed for the better through the experience, but it's the culture clash that makes "Woman in the House" so fascinating.

Even more surprising is "The Bus to Nowhere" (1956), in which Betty Anderson (Elinor Donahue) experiences full-tilt existential angst that shakes her to her core. Her family dismisses her anguish as "just a mood" and "rubbish," but Betty is disconsolate – "I don't know anything anymore," she confesses. In the climax she's at the bus station ready to go wherever her savings will take her. I won't spoil the ending and how she finds her way back, but "The Bus to Nowhere" is worthy of study and debate in college classes devoted to philosophy and theology. It's one of the most profound and extraordinary episodes in 1950s television.

But whether the plot revolves around our most deep-seated anxieties or something has simple as planning a high school picnic, every episode of *Father Knows Best* has something to say about the human condition – what makes us noble, what makes us flawed, and what sometimes makes us inexplicable, even to our fellow humans.

The Best Episodes

"Bud the Philanthropist" (1957)

Bud's Sunday school teacher requests donations to buy a radio for a young newspaper boy, who suffered a broken leg in a hit-and-run car accident. Bud (Billy Gray) has $10 (the equivalent of $100 now) that he reluctantly donates, though he had been saving for a pair of track shoes. And then his class bestows the credit for his anonymous generosity onto another student.

"Bud the Philanthropist" is a perfect little morality play, of the kind that was commonplace in prime time in a bygone age. And when you see how often boorish behavior in our culture is applauded instead of condemned, it's easy to see why such stories have fallen out of favor.

"The Art of Romance" (1957)

Bud and Judy like each other but are too shy to admit it. While Jim offers Bud advice on how to make the first move, so he can keep the upper hand in the relationship, Betty coaches Judy on the strategies of getting a boy to do what you want him to do. "Men think they're so clever and I can't understand why – they haven't outsmarted us yet." Betty says.

While Jim and Betty engage in a move and counter-move showdown, with Bud and Judy as the chess pieces, both become so competitive they forget that Bud and Judy actually want to get together. We think dating and romance have been radically transformed in this "woke" culture, but "The Art of Romance" reminds us that human nature is not so easily reshaped by social scientists.

"Father's Biography" (1958)

It's a classic family sitcom dilemma that has played out on other series as well: Jim has an important opportunity to advance his career and community status, but the event he must attend to do so is on the same night that his young daughter Kathy (Lauren Chapin) will read the essay she wrote about her father at a school assembly. What will he do?

What separates this episode from other such stories is a powerful dream sequence in which Jim appears before St. Peter, wondering if he'll be granted entry into heaven. Jim defends his decision on that fateful night, asserting that being a great man is not as important to him as being an ordinary man who is loved by his family.

"A Friend in Need" (1958)

In the middle of the night, a lost dog named Duchess shows up on the Anderson doorstep. Within days she becomes a beloved member of the family, despite the likelihood that the dog's real owner may turn up. Yes, it's shameless sentiment, but the story is beautifully told.

"Mister Beal Meets His Match" (1958)

Betty, writing a story for college, casts her family in a new version of the *Faust* tale. Mysterious stranger Harry Beal sells Bud a set of books that seem to grant wishes, but you don't get something for nothing (or at least, that was a lesson still taught in the 1950s). Jim discovers to his horror that the gifts in the books were received at the forfeiture of their souls. A panicked Jim offers Beal his own soul in exchange for theirs. The harrowing parts of the tale are played straighter than you might expect.

Sidebar: Twenty-Four Hours in Tyrantland

"Twenty-Four Hours in Tyrantland" ranks among the most memorable television episodes ever created. One reason: It never actually aired on television.

In 1959, the U.S. Department of the Treasury approached the producers of *Father Knows Best* about filming a special episode of the series that would promote the sale of United States savings bonds. Their request was granted, with the AFL-CIO union covering production costs, and the actors donating their time and talents.

The finished episode was distributed to schools, churches and civic groups, to encourage viewers to buy bonds as a sound investment, as well as a way to protect the nation from foreign enemies.

When I first watched it, based on the little I had heard, I expected some shallow piece of propaganda, with dire warnings of the Communist threat expressed in fevered tones reminiscent of *Reefer Madness*. I should have known better.

The episode was written by Roswell Rogers, the series' most talented and prolific scripter. He wasn't capable of hackwork, and he got the story's message across without pushing any of the Anderson family to act differently from their established characters.

The story opens with Jim trying to recruit his family into

Springfield's savings bond campaign. Margaret is ready to help, but the kids are predictably less than enthused. Bud was already TV's prototypical teenage slacker, Betty's highest priorities were usually boys and a new formal for every dance, and little Kathy was always self-centered.

Jim is understandably disappointed in their lackluster response. "Do you kids realize what would happen if everyone in America was as little concerned with our way of life as you are? Why, freedom would go zinging right out the door! It could happen much easier than you think. And if it did, if this freedom was suddenly taken away from you...you couldn't take it. I don't think you could handle it for 24 hours." Bud responds, "How much you wanna bet?"

And that gives Jim an idea. If the kids endure 24 hours under tyrannical rule, they'll each win $18.75 to spend any way they want. If they lose, they'll have to spend that money on a savings bond. The kids jump at what appears to be a cinch bet – they have no idea the lengths to which Dad is about to go to prove his point.

"This is the most important lesson they've ever had," Jim tells his wife. "If our young people don't think enough of our way of life to try to preserve it, I shudder to think what's going to happen to America."

Are you shuddering yet, Jim?

Maybe "Twenty-Four Hours in Tyrantland" would seem corny to millennials. But that's probably how they'd react to any *Father Knows Best* episode. The world has changed so much since then. This was a show written at a time when no one would have anticipated there would be interest in this series 70 years later. It was directed solely at a Cold War audience that had watched the Soviet Union invade Hungary, and heard Nikita Khrushchev openly and repeatedly threaten the West with nuclear annihilation.

What could someone living in a quiet Midwestern town do to prevent such a catastrophe? Buying a bond wasn't going to reduce Soviet aggression. But perhaps it was a way to feel a little less powerless.

Are Family Sitcoms Idealized?

Perhaps the most frequent observation about family situation comedies in the classic TV era, especially among those who dislike them, is that they are unrealistic because they present an idealized view of family life. In fact, this viewpoint is now so ubiquitous that even folks who enjoy these shows largely accept it.

But I don't. Never have, and never will.

Before anyone objects, let's take a closer look at the term 'idealized.'

The Oxford Dictionary defines something idealized as "regarded or represented as perfect or better than in reality."

That's actually two definitions, as "perfect" is hardly the same as "better than in reality."

To me "perfect" connotes an absence of conflict; a life free from worry over health issues or money issues or relationship troubles. But these topics were frequently explored in sitcoms from this era. Granted, problems were almost always resolved with no real harm done, but there are dozens of examples of episodes where a dream job didn't come through, or the boy a young girl had a crush on didn't ask her to the dance, or a chance at public acclaim turned instead into a moment of embarrassment. These were struggles that would have been familiar to viewers.

With "perfect" off the table, those seeking to make this case must now try and prove "better than reality." That should be pretty easy, right?

This is where you'll hear people say things like "*Father Knows Best* was idealized because Robert Young was a kind, understanding dad, but my dad was a drunk with a bad temper," or "the kids on *The Brady Bunch* always had money to buy new clothes and go out on dates, but in my family we had to struggle just to pay the bills and put food on the table."

Well…okay. But we have to acknowledge that no television show could ever encapsulate a recognizable reality for everyone in such a large and diverse nation. So it's unfair to expect *Leave it To Beaver* or *The Donna Reed Show* or *The Cosby Show* to epitomize everyone's personal experience.

But if these shows managed to approximate the real lives of some families in America, then that "better than reality" indictment is nullified. And I believe they do.

We all realize there were families in 1955 that did not get along as well as the Andersons on *Father Knows Best*. But for many of them, the series provided not an unrealistic portrayal to be derided, but a paradigm to which they could aspire.

If you disagree, then you would need to offer examples of situations or behaviors from episodes of these shows that would not be achievable by a real family in the era the episode aired. If anyone tries, I'll look forward to those responses.

Shows like *Roseanne* have exacerbated this assessment. "Now that's a *real* family!" you hear critics rave, and perhaps those caustic (but still loving) relationships are indeed more familiar to a higher percentage of the viewing audience. My parents never spoke to each other the way the Conners do, so for me that show was a reality I didn't recognize.

What saddens me most about this topic is how readily we dismiss happy, loving, well-adjusted traditional families as an impossible fantasy. What does that say about us: that a series about a middle-class couple and their kids can be put into the same category as a show about a man with a talking horse?

The more this perception persists, the more grateful I am for these shows, and for the DVDs and cable networks that continue to air them every day. In a culture that continually celebrates the lowest common denominator, they represent what is possible when we treat those closest to us with patience, tolerance and compassion.

If you see your childhood in these shows, as I often do, then you have been blessed. If you didn't, then aspire to them as a reality worth pursuing, and a road map for how to get there. It's not as hard as you might think.

The Fugitive

1963-1967 (ABC)

120 Episodes

Taking my TV viewing preferences as a whole, there didn't seem to be much hope that I would enjoy *The Fugitive*.

It's a somber show that is not fast-paced or action-packed, there is almost no humor, and the protagonist, Dr. Richard Kimble, suffers through the most tortured existence of any character ever created for television.

For someone who values the older shows as a means to occasionally escape the harsher realities of life, a show as relentlessly downbeat as *The Fugitive* is an unlikely destination.

And yet...I would cite it as one of the television's ten best shows, and I am entranced by it every time.

The series is justly revered among TV fans, but it's still not as celebrated as it should be, because it was not syndicated as often as the sitcoms and lighter dramatic fare of the 1960s. Like *The Defenders*, it is one of television's crown jewels, but its achievements may one day be lost to the ages.

The premise of *The Fugitive* is covered in an opening credits sequence narrated by William Conrad: Indiana doctor

Richard Kimble (David Janssen) is convicted of murdering his wife and sentenced to death. He claims he saw a one-armed man fleeing the scene. No one believes him. He escapes when the train taking him to prison derails. The police lieutenant escorting him to the death house, Philip Gerard (Barry Morse) becomes obsessed with his recapture.

From such broad stroke set-ups TV shows both great and terrible have been made. But *The Fugitive* was *Les Misérables* for television, as compelling in its medium as Victor Hugo's literary masterwork.

The pilot, "Fear in a Desert City," provides a perfect illustration of the series' strengths. Kimble is working as a bartender in Tucson, just one more in a litany of menial jobs. Throughout the show's four seasons he is most often found in rural areas, a skilled physician taking day labor work and trying to blend in among poorly educated people. Though he keeps his head down and doesn't talk much they sense he's not like the rest of them. Some react with kindness, some with curiosity, some with hostility.

David Janssen, who inexplicably never won the Emmy for his portrayal of Kimble, inhabits this role on a cellular level. You believe his every skittish reaction to a squad car parked across a street; the lonely desperation of a man trying to prove his innocence by tracking down the real killer of his wife in a world that predates Google by 30 years; a "victim of blind justice" cast adrift in a relentlessly dark and hostile world bereft of any permanent home, prospects or friends.

But he's still a doctor, which was a brilliant decision on the part of series creator Roy Huggins. As much as Kimble needs to distance himself from his former life to stay alive, he is also compelled by his vocation and his conscience to help if someone needs medical attention. As soon as he does, he knows people will wonder how a migrant worker picking strawberries in Salinas knows how to perform a tracheotomy, and his days there will be numbered. Yet Kimble repeatedly compromises his own safety to help the kind of person that society ignores.

Lt. Gerard was Javert to Kimble's Valjean, and a formidable adversary throughout the run. Gerard only appears in about one-third of the episodes in every season – another wise and all-too-rare example of restraint in service of the drama. If Kimble kept narrowly escaping Gerard 25 times a season, the series becomes a Road Runner cartoon. This way, when Gerard does get close, it ratchets up the tension to unbearable levels.

Once you grasp the premise, you know that in a typical episode Dr. Kimble is not going to be captured, or killed, or exonerated, because that would be the end of the show. Yet the series teases each of those outcomes repeatedly, and does it so well you can't help but wonder how Kimble is going to get out of another no-win situation, or how the end of his nightmare will elude him once more.

For a series so groundbreaking in its format, its lack of permanent setting or supporting cast, and its inversion of traditional hero and villain roles, there was one cliché to which *The Fugitive* was not immune. That would be Kimble's capability to make every woman he approaches fall in love with him. The show had to be aware of how this trope became abused. But perhaps, given the tribulations he endures for four seasons, it seemed only fair to allow him a few hours of pleasure with guest stars like Lois Nettleton, Suzanne Pleshette, Hope Lange and Susan Oliver.

For its first three seasons, *The Fugitive* aired in black and white, and that seemed fitting for a somber series with a grim protagonist running for his life through a hostile world. Many of its best episodes like "Search in a Windy City" and "Brass Ring" had a film noir quality fostered by the light and shadow of black and white cinematography. When the series switched to color for its fourth and final season, Dr. Kimble's life didn't get any better, yet it still appeared a little less dark and dangerous.

That would be my only criticism if it were not for the finale, which at the time of its broadcast became the most-watched episode of network television in history, garnering an astonishing 73 share. This may be the quintessential example of when television brought us together – even Super Bowls don't generate that degree of national attention now.

Yes, "The Judgment" delivers a satisfying end, but it's not

perfect. I always thought the final moment between Kimble and Gerard should have been more substantive. And it would have been wonderful to round up some previous characters Kimble met in his travels, in brief clips in which they read a newspaper account of his exoneration and smile.

Still, since most shows back then did not receive the luxury of a definitive final installment, we are fortunate that Kimble's saga ended at all. There was concern over how it would impact the series' syndication appeal, and perhaps that proved to be valid. But viewers were so invested in the series that they deserved closure.

If you missed *The Fugitive*, put it on your to-do list now. Something this good should never be forgotten.

The Best Episodes

"Fear in a Desert City" (1963)

Not every series arrives fully formed, but *The Fugitive* debuted with an episode that instantly brings viewers into the harsh realities of Richard Kimble's life on the run. It's hard to imagine anyone tuning in back then and not getting hooked.

"Nightmare at Northoak" (1963)

Working as a school bus driver in a small New England town, Kimble rescues his young passengers when a fire breaks out on the bus. He is hailed as a hero, but doesn't want any publicity for his actions, knowing that his photo in the newspaper will put Lt. Gerard back on his trail. This episode features the first confrontation between Kimble and Gerard since the doctor's escape from custody. The scenes between Janssen and Morse are always a series highlight.

"The Girl from Little Egypt" (1963)

What really happened the night Helen Kimble was murdered? This episode fills in the details, presented in flashback while Dr. Kimble lies unconscious in a hospital, after being hit by a car. It confirms his innocence, while lamenting the sad reality that sometimes our imperfect justice system punishes the guilty and condemns the innocent. How ironic that "The Girl From Little Egypt" is set in San Francisco, where more than 40 years later a man shot and killed a woman in broad daylight on the city's Pier 14, and was found not guilty by a jury.

"Angels Travel on Lonely Roads" (1964)

Richard Kimble hitches a ride with Sister Veronica, a nun who is traveling to Sacramento to renounce her vows. What makes this two-part episode work is a wonderful performance by Eileen Heckart as Veronica, and the conversation she shares on the road with Kimble about the existence of miracles, and science vs. faith. The show was so well received that it was the only *Fugitive* episode to inspire a sequel, "The Breaking of the Habit."

"The Iron Maiden" (1964)

Kimble is working construction on a missile silo in the Nevada desert. The site is visited by a U.S. Congresswoman, who is injured at the bottom of the shaft. While Kimble tries to help her, a press photographer snaps a photo that makes the national news. Gerard sees it and immediately heads for the site. Before he arrives an accident strands several workers, including Kimble, 200 feet below the surface. By the time the equipment is fixed, his identity has been exposed. There's only one way out of the shaft, and when he surfaces Gerard will be there waiting for him. How will he escape this time?

How Times Have Changed: Television Seasons

September used to be a month television fans anticipated with the same excitement as any of the festive holidays that followed. This was when new programs debuted and old friends returned with new episodes. It was fun and exciting and for kids it helped take some of the sting away from the end of summer and the start of school.

It hasn't been like that for a long time. New shows now debut on Netflix and Hulu and a dozen other places every week, and if we don't watch them now we can get around to it next month or next year.

Maybe that's why so many shows go undetected by most viewers. In fact, hundreds of television series have debuted and disappeared over the past 20 years, with the majority of the country unaware of their existence.

Take a show like *The Marvelous Mrs. Maisel*, winner of Emmys, Golden Globes and Screen Actors Guild awards. It averaged 1.9 million viewers per episode. That is 0.57% of the U.S. population.

For most of its history that's not how television worked. While there have always been movies, plays and books that went virtually unnoticed, television was different because all of it emanated from a single source, located in almost every home in America. Within that source there were just three national networks and a few local stations, so programming options were limited. We were all watching the same stuff.

During the classic TV era television could be good or bad, but it was never invisible. It was prominent. It was important. It was the primary source of entertainment and information for three generations of people throughout the western world.

And it had a season that started in September. One way we knew it was almost here was when the *TV Guide* Fall Preview Issue arrived in our mailbox (with a particularly resonant thud, as it was usually twice the size of the average issue).

Reading the descriptions of the new shows and seeing the cast photos, we'd all decide which ones we were definitely going to check out. When an intriguing new series dropped into a time slot opposite one of our returning favorites – oh, the agony. I wonder in 1973 how many were lured away from *Gunsmoke* on Monday night to watch a new sitcom starring Diana Rigg. On Friday should we stick with *The Odd Couple*, or watch Sally Field in *The Girl with Something Extra*?

Television networks also eagerly endorsed their new programming slates beginning in late summer, with extravagant musical promotions featuring all of their top stars. There was a sense of company pride in these spots, which also engendered a familial relationship between network and viewer. Look, we thought, at all these rich and famous people, taking time out of their busy schedule to invite us to watch their shows.

If you're old enough you may still remember some of these campaigns: "You and Me and ABC," "NBC: Just Watch Us Now" and CBS's "Looking Good." I always enjoyed the ABC promos the most, from "Still the One" to "Come on Along with ABC." They were the top dog network at the time such promos were in vogue, and were happy to invest the time and money to keep it that way. The days of presentations like this are gone forever.

And so, sadly, is the television season.

What constitutes a "season" for a show today? For some streaming series it's eight or 12 episodes. Most network series manage to reach 22 shows, but they usually don't debut until October, and then disappear again in a few weeks after airing a "fall finale." Contrast that with some typical first seasons from an earlier era:

Leave it to Beaver:	39 episodes
The Donna Reed Show:	37 episodes
Gunsmoke:	39 episodes
Naked City:	39 episodes
Bewitched:	36 episodes
The Twilight Zone:	36 episodes
The Adventures of Ozzie & Harriet:	39 episodes

Today's television actors, writers, directors and creative teams earn many times what their golden age counterparts did, for doing a lot less work.

The end of television seasons is just one reason why even quality shows are now missed by 99% of the country. And given the sheer volume of them, and the rapidity with which they come and go, we are at a point I never thought I'd see: a new television series has been reduced to the impact of a YouTube video. It holds your interest for a few seconds, and then it disappears from the memory.

Get Smart

1965-1970 (NBC/CBS)

138 Episodes

Does a situation comedy have to be funny to be successful?

For me, the answer is no. There are many older shows I watch in which laugh-out-loud moments are rare. I still enjoy them because of their familiar characters, their worldviews and their values, and because they have been a part of my life for as long as I can remember. Watching them is like visiting old friends.

But funny is good too – and *Get Smart* is as funny as TV gets.

Humor is subjective, so many of you may have another choice for the series that produced the most hilarious moments. How blessed we were through that era when television gave us so many contenders for the title – *The Honeymooners, Your Show of Shows, The Phil Silvers Show, I Love Lucy, Green Acres, Rowan and Martin's Laugh-In, The Carol Burnett Show, Taxi, Cheers.*

Perhaps *Get Smart* clicks with me because it was a show tailored to the sense of humor of 12 year-old boys – and no matter how old I get, that's apparently where my maturity level ceased. I assume that's something I have in common with the show's creators, Mel Brooks and Buck Henry.

Get Smart gave us brilliant moments of physical comedy - Max did more damage to himself than KAOS could ever inflict. It gave us catch phrases to volley back and forth among friends at school: "Missed it by that much," "Sorry about that, Chief," "Would you believe..." It gave us a hero who was still cool even as he stumbled through every mission, and an attractive and capable partner in Agent 99 (Barbara Feldon) that was crazy about him even when he did dumb things.

And it gave us comedy that lampooned the cultures and traditions associated with different ethnic groups. It was not the show's most frequent go-to source for laughs, but with recurring characters like Detective Harry Hoo and The Claw (don't say it!), this seemed like the most logical place to address another way in which older series are being marginalized by those who find their content offensive.

You know what apparently isn't offensive? *Game of Thrones*, a series that won an Emmy for Best Drama. That's a show that has featured, among other things, multiple rapes and graphic beheadings, a woman paraded naked through the streets and pelted with garbage, a child strapped to a stake and set on fire, and a brother and sister spending a special kind of quality time with each other that siblings don't usually share.

Isn't it wonderful living in such enlightened times? But I digress.

I don't pretend to have all of the answers on this. What I do know is that for centuries, the dissimilarities between groups of people could be exaggerated and mined for humor. Television is rife with examples, from Bill Dana's character of Jose Jimenez in the 1950s to portrayals of Native Americans on shows like *F Troop* in the 1960s, to the 1970s and Nancy Walker's interfering, guilt-inducing stereotypical Jewish mother Ida Morgenstern on *The Mary Tyler Moore Show* and *Rhoda*.

Most consumers of popular culture understand that humor exists outside of polite society, and may be offensive by its very nature. Still, the overwhelming majority of viewers maintained a practical sense of what may be funny, and what crossed a line into cruel and offensive.

The difference is context. And context matters.

Think of it this way: There have been films and television shows that have depicted the violent murder of a teenage girl, in a scene that is harrowing to watch and disturbing to think about. Viewers know that all the promise in that young life will now be unfulfilled, that the girl's parents are about to be informed of a life-altering tragedy, and that a family and community will never be the same.

And then there are movies like those in the *Friday the 13th* series, in which teenage girls are brutally murdered on screen, and the audience reaction is…laughter? Sometimes applause? Genre fans rank these scenes by the creativity of the kill and how well the special effects make the murder look real. They are not meant to be taken seriously.

If horror films are allowed that distinction, comedy deserves the same privilege.

As we enter this strange new era when an Eskimo Pie triggers outrage, it remains to be seen how drastically the rules for what is considered funny will be rewritten. But how comedy evolves in the future should not cancel shows that were created in an earlier time.

Must they be reconsidered at all? There's no getting past that now, and the impulse behind reassessment has sadly culminated in an unsettling trend toward censorship. That strikes me as a terribly misguided solution, especially as it can never be applied in a way that will satisfy every potentially aggrieved party. Some groups will inevitably get favored nation protection, while others will wonder why any slights directed toward their group are ignored.

Last year, the MeTV network began scouring through its program library to seek out and expunge any word, image, costume or expression that might generate an outraged tweet. One of the casualties of this crusade was a tiny plaque showing a confederate flag in Richie's room on *Happy Days*, which is now blurred out. But the large Nazi swastikas in *Hogan's Heroes* remain intact.

The only solution, for these shows and for *Get Smart*, is to let the material play as it was originally created. Broadcasters can run a disclaimer or a parental guidance warning before the show if deemed necessary, but stop trying to reshape art from the past to fit a present standard.

Thankfully, *Get Smart* had many other comedic weapons as well – the multiple locks on Max's door, Hymie the robot (Dick Gauthier), and the Cone of Silence (see sidebar).

And it had Don Adams, in one of those magical matches of an actor with a role perfectly suited to his appearance, and that optimized every arrow in his comic arsenal. He won the Emmy as Best Actor in a Comedy Series three years in a row for his work as Agent 86, and it's amazing that TV Land has not yet dedicated a statue in his honor somewhere in Washington, D.C.

That setting, and how it tapped into derision over the capabilities of our leaders in the nation's capital, also brought viewers together from across the political spectrum. At a time when the Vietnam War dominated headlines, Republicans wondered why U.S. forces were not winning, while Democrats wondered how we ever got involved over there in the first place. *Get Smart* offered a welcome chance to laugh at the folks in charge of the country – and to hope there wasn't too much truth in its satire.

The Best Episodes

"Mr. Big" (1965)

Everything that made *Get Smart* one of the funniest series from any decade was already in place in its first episode, written by Mel Brooks and Buck Henry. You got your shoe phone, your Cone of Silence, and a villain sure to incite offense in humorless defenders of political correctness.

"Washington 4, Redskins 3" (1965)

A rogue band of Indians called the Red Feathers demand the return of their stolen land, or they'll unleash a powerful new weapon. Max infiltrates the tribe and winds up engaged to the chief's daughter. Agent 86 in buckskins is funny by itself, but "Washington 4, Redskins 3" also unveils one of the most unforgettable sight gags in the history of television. The first time I saw it, I thought I'd never stop laughing. And as with "Mr. Big," much of the content from the title on down will now be scrutinized in a way that was not intended.

"The Amazing Harry Hoo" (1966)

Is this a straight send-up of Charlie Chan movies, or is it mocking the preposterous casting of white actors as Asian characters? Either way, the result is yet another culturally insensitive but classic episode.

"A Man Called Smart, Part 1" (1967)

You'll want to watch all three parts of this story, which was originally intended for theatrical release. But it's the first segment that features a masterpiece of slapstick comedy starring Don Adams, a stretcher and a revolving door. Adams, whose distinct voice and catchphrases were a big part of the show's success, never utters a word throughout the sequence, and still earns huge laughs. There is also an innovative opening chase scene that portends Adams' association with the cartoon series *Inspector Gadget*.

"Maxwell Smart, Private Eye" (1967)

Budget cuts force CONTROL personnel into taking part-time jobs. Max becomes a private detective in this *Maltese Falcon* parody. Don Adams' Humphrey Bogart impression is spot on, and every moment in his rundown office is comedy gold, from the wastebasket tosses to the non-existent fire escape exit, to comedian Buddy Hackett as a nearsighted assassin.

Sidebar: Your Tax Dollars at Work: The Cone of Silence

Introduced in the first episode of *Get Smart*, the Cone of Silence would rouse some of the biggest laughs on what many would argue is still the funniest television series ever created.

Was this merely an inspired visual gag, or a subtle comment on government incompetence? Imagine how many millions of dollars were poured into research and development on something that never did its job. Not the first time, and certainly not the last. Fill in your favorite boondoggle here.

Its presence in the series' pilot suggests that this was a moment that would help sell the show: Maxwell Smart, dedicated and eager but also clumsy and dense, awaits assignment from the head of the secret government espionage agency CONTROL. The Chief (Edward Platt), Max's boss, hints at how vital this upcoming mission will be. Not willing to take any chances, Max demands his orders be given only within the security of the Cone of Silence. The Chief, exasperated as if he already knows Uncle Sam got stuck with a clunker, calls for it anyway.

The scene works so well that it could have been reprised with only minor variations in future episodes and still earned a laugh. But that would have been too easy for a show with this much genius in its origins. The Cone of Silence would make ten more appearances over the show's five seasons, and the question was never whether it would function as designed, but how it would fail once again.

In "KAOS in CONTROL" (1965) the Cone still impairs communication between Max and The Chief, but those outside can hear every word they say.

It appears once again in "My Nephew the Spy" (1965) after Max insists that regulations call for all security measures to be taken in such vital circumstances. The Cone is lowered, and the Chief asks Agent 86 what he discovered about KAOS headquarters. Max responds, "Nothing."

"Hubert's Unfinished Symphony" (1966) features the debut of the portable Cone of Silence, which looks even more ridiculous than its predecessor. How unfortunate for the Chief, who spends most of the episode with his head stuck inside.

When Max and 99 are on assignment in England in "That Old Gang of Mine" (1967), the London CONTROL office provides its own variation, the Umbrella of Silence. Surprisingly it's up to the task, but other complications ensue.

In "A Tale of Two Tails" (1968) we learn that the Cone was invented by Professor Cohn. "The Cone of Silence was invented by a Professor Cohn?" Max asks, as he looks up at it; "That's funny...it doesn't look it." One more example of a joke that worked 40 years ago and would now generate demands for sensitivity training.

With the Cone on the fritz again, Max and the Chief opt for the CONTROL secret word file. Once you see how that works you'll wonder if it was created by the same guy who wrote the federal tax code.

And though it's not canon I should mention that a high-tech version of the Cone appears in the 2008 *Get Smart* film with Steve Carrell. It still didn't work.

How Times Have Changed: Telephones

Among its many accolades, *Get Smart* was also the first series to feature a character with a mobile phone – even if it was embedded in his shoe.

The cell phone as we know it was decades away when Max was talking to the Chief on his wing tip. But once the device achieved mass-market penetration it marked yet another permanent divergence from the world as it existed in the classic TV era. It was the end of the line for stories that relied on characters not being able to communicate important information to each other, because they did not have access to a telephone.

Example: On *The Dick Van Dyke Show*, the flashback episode "The Attempted Marriage" (1962) depicted Rob and Laura's almost wedding. Rob, still in the army, was en route to the church when his jeep broke down. He arrives hours late, long after the guests had left believing Laura had been jilted. That show could not be presented now – Rob's cell phone would have dispatched a cab to pick him up, and he then could have called Laura to let her know he'd be a little late.

In the 1960s pay phones were the only option for someone

in Rob's predicament. They were usually housed in telephone booths, which are also now about as commonplace as the TARDIS-like police boxes on the streets of England. "But where will Superman change?" is a joke that only people my age would still make. That association dates back to the 1940s *Superman* radio series, but Clark Kent's phone booth transformation was surprisingly never shown on television's *The Adventures of Superman*. However, we do see a phone booth in the opening credits of *Get Smart*, where it serves as the entrance to CONTROL headquarters.

Perhaps TV's most famous pay phone was the one Mike Brady installed in the family room of his home in the *Brady Bunch* episode "Sorry, Right Number" (1969). Tired of paying sky-high phone bills, he hopes this drastic step will teach his kids to be more discerning in how much time they spend chatting with their friends. Today they would all have their own phones, hopefully on a volume discount plan.

Using a telephone back then was a very different experience. Incoming calls were signaled by a pleasant bell-like ring instead of a harsh electronic tone; numbers were dialed on a rotary device – any call to a phone number with a lot of nines and zeros required extra time and effort to place (and yes, we were annoyed when we saw them); phone numbers were found in the telephone book.

When was the last time anyone on television spoke to a telephone operator? That too was once a common occurrence, though operators were often portrayed as hindrances to communication rather than helpful public servants. Lily Tomlin personified the profession as the snarky Ernestine on *Rowan & Martin's Laugh-In*. But if they were not among the people in our neighborhood, we wouldn't have the lovely song "Operator" by Jim Croce, or the Partridge Family's "Echo Valley 2-6809".

I wonder if anyone else is nostalgic for the pre-cell phone era. I have an iPhone, but I'm not crazy about using it. People now look at those of us with landlines like we still churn our own butter. So be it. But that landline will never get hacked and send my bank account information to someone in China.

Another benefit to landlines is that they are tethered to your home or office, which limits the number of people exposed to your conversation. Why do people with cell phones in restaurants and parks and other public venues insist on chatting at a volume that requires everyone in their immediate vicinity to participate?

And when you get an unwanted call from a telemarketer or scam artist, pressing a button to terminate the call on cell will never feel as satisfying as slamming down a receiver with authority.

Oh, and cell phones could give you cancer too, according to some studies, so win-win. The end of public civility, and a deadly illness – neither of which will ever be traced to a phone with a cord attached to it.

Society was actually able to function quite efficiently before the development of the 5G network, though that news may be shocking to anyone under the age of 20. Sure, it was different. Back then it seemed like a big deal to place or receive a long distance call, which is why for most families they became a treasured part of holiday celebrations. Television commercials for the phone company would dramatize such special moments with phrases like, "Reach out and touch someone," and "The next best thing to being there." An overseas call? That was almost supernatural.

I'm glad cell phones were not around during the era of television celebrated by this book. Think of your favorite family sitcom from the 1950s or '60s, and about the scenes spent sharing the details of everyone's day around the dinner table. Then think of that same scene, with mom, dad and the kids all staring at their own phones, texting friends and checking emails.

Gilligan's Island

1964-1967 (ABC)

98 episodes

You cannot do a book with this premise without giving *Gilligan's Island* its due. If you find that hard to believe, you're not alone.

For the first generations of kids to grow up with television, this show was inescapable. In nearly every city across America, it played for years in reruns, usually during the afternoon just in time for after-school viewing. Through that familiarity and repetition, it entered our national bloodstream, to the point that most of us can still sing the theme song even if we haven't watched an episode in 20 years.

I get how that happens. You invite characters into your home every day as you would friends, and enjoy spending time with them. You remember days when you were home sick from school, and a *Gilligan's Island* episode came on that made you forget about your flu for a while.

It's a credit to Sherwood Schwartz that two of the shows he created, this one and *The Brady Bunch*, are as cherished by baby boomers as any television series in history. Both are more loved by fans than admired by critics, and who really cares what they thought anyway? Both gave us characters that penetrated the popular culture to a depth and extent far beyond their simplistic pedigree.

It's a series that existed outside current events, which has also helped it to age gracefully. Nothing that happens in almost every episode would give away that *Gilligan's Island* is more than 40 years old. You can put your kids down in front of it now and they'll still be taken with the silly but good-natured escapades.

So I'm in the minority here because I never really "got" this show. I mean, there's not much to get, really – seven stranded castaways, sing-along theme, "Ginger or Mary Ann" debate (the correct answer is Mary Ann) – but why do so many of my fellow TV enthusiasts find such pleasure in repeat viewings of this silly sitcom?

A couple of years ago I decided to give it another chance. I borrowed all three seasons on DVD and watched every episode in order. And it still did nothing for me.

What did resonate was a theory I recall reading about how Gilligan (Bob Denver) sabotages every rescue attempt because he likes the island and prefers it to the outside world. He doesn't do it on purpose, because he realizes that means disappointing his friends, but when it comes time to send that message or fire that flare or accomplish whatever responsibility with which he has inexplicably been trusted, he screws it up. He just can't help himself.

If true, this is less an indictment of Gilligan as it is of his fellow castaways. Despite repeated blunders they still, invariably, assign him some critical task that can make or break their salvation.

I don't need realism from my escapist TV, and that ship has already sailed when you're watching a show in which three characters wear the same outfit for three years, while four others sport new clothes from a seemingly inexhaustible supply that was packed for a three-hour tour. But at some point, the other islanders would have boosted their odds of rescue by banishing Gilligan to the nearest cannibal-populated island.

For anyone who needs proof that American cared about the plight of Gilligan, the Skipper (Alan Hale, Jr.), Mr. and Mrs. Howell (Jim Backus and Natalie Schaefer), Ginger (Tina Louise), the Professor (Russell Johnson) and Many Ann (Dawn Wells), I give you the 1978 TV movie *Rescue from Gilligan's Island*, which reunited the original cast except for Tina Louise.

The timing was perfect; ten years of build-up was just right, and the cast still looked enough like their characters so their reunion would be nostalgic and uplifting, rather than desperate and sad.

The movie earned an amazing 52 share of the audience, so it was undoubtedly a success in every way except creatively. If anything, *Rescue* was even dumber and more juvenile than an average episode of the series. One sequence with Gilligan paddling around in the water with a shark seems to go on for hours. Worse, its popularity paved the way for *The Harlem Globetrotters on Gilligan's Island* (1981), an even greater atrocity that featured the unforgettable image of Lovie Howell (still played by 81 year-old Natalie Schaefer) face-guarding Sweet Lou Dunbar in the post.

Don't take my lack of affection too seriously. There is probably a show or two in this book that you never cared for either. That's all right – we're still friends.

The Best Episodes

"Don't Bug the Mosquitoes" (1965)

The famous pop band The Mosquitoes (Bingo, Bango, Bongo and Irving) land on the uncharted isle for some relaxation. The episode's highlight is a performance of "You Need Us" by The Honey Bees – Lovey, Ginger and Mary Ann. It's dreadful, but at least it's dreadful in an interesting way.

"The Producer" (1966)

This episode is better known as the Hamlet show. The castaways create a musical version of Shakespeare's tragedy set to various classical themes.

"All About Eva" (1966)

Bob Denver and Jim Backus also played multiple roles during the show's three seasons, but Tina Louise's dowdy performance as Eva Grubb was the series' most memorable departure from the usual monotony of foiled island escapes. The episode "All About Eva" also earns bonus points for blending two familiar chestnuts into one story – the dual role and the "plain Jane becomes a knockout" transformation.

Happy Days / Laverne & Shirley

Happy Days
1974-1984 (ABC)

255 Episodes

Laverne & Shirley
1976-1983 (ABC)

178 Episodes

Nostalgia is not limited to one generation.

While we now have fond memories of America from decades past, there were those in the 1970s who remembered the 1950s as a happier and more innocent time. That may have been one of the inspirations that prompted Garry Marshall to create *Happy Days*, but the show as it was conceived was not the show it ultimately became.

In its first season viewers met the Cunningham family of Milwaukee – dad ran a hardware store, mom was a housewife, Richie went to high school, Joanie to junior high. A third sibling named Chuck was introduced and subsequently forgotten even by his closest relatives.

The stories lived fully in the time the show was set: there were episodes about beatniks and broken down Studebakers, the Cold War and backyard bomb shelters, biker gangs, corrupt TV quiz shows, and teenagers trying to sneak into burlesque clubs.

And then a supporting character, that appeared regularly in the show's first season but was unbilled in the opening credits, became the most popular television character in America: Arthur Fonzarelli. Fonzie. The Fonz. He was played by Yale Drama School graduate Henry Winkler, who was almost 30 but suddenly found himself appearing on the cover of *Tiger Beat* magazine alongside Shaun Cassidy and the Bay City Rollers.

By the show's second season Winkler was listed second in the credits behind the top-billed Howard. By the third season, Fonzie was the focal point of nearly every episode.

The calendar on the wall at Howard Cunningham's hardware store still displayed a 1950s date – but did it really matter anymore? Not when a poster of The Fonz sold in numbers surpassed only by an iconic image of Farrah Fawcett in a red swimsuit.

While the series lost much of its nostalgic ode to the Eisenhower years, *Happy Days* deserves our appreciation for leveraging the adulation young fans felt toward The Fonz to do some good in the world, instead of just cashing in with more lunch box and trading card sales. Episodes were built around Fonzie having to wear glasses, taking out a library card, overcoming a fear of singing in public, reading Shakespeare, becoming a policeman (temporarily), and going back to high school to get his diploma. If the Fonz said something was cool, it was cool – and in the late 1970s that had more impact than any public service announcement costing tens of thousands of taxpayer dollars to produce.

It became a different show then, perhaps not better but still entertaining. The remaining cast members all accepted Winkler's ascent with grace, trading fewer lines for the security of continuing paychecks. Howard (Tom Bosley) and Marion (Marion Ross) remained models of Midwestern middle class domesticity; Richie, like John-Boy Walton, developed an interest in journalism, back when it was still practiced correctly; Potsie (Anson Williams) and Ralph (Don Most) filled out Richie's circle of friends; Joanie (Erin Moran) grew up on TV, as sitcom kids are wont to do, into an attractive and assertive young woman.

But that second golden age did not last either. In the show's fifth season it unwittingly created the pop culture reference "jump the shark,' to identify the moment in a television show's run when it begins to lose what made it special. It was a funny way to remember the ludicrous scene of Fonzie, garbed in t-shirt, leather jacket and water skis, jumping over a net-walled area of water containing a man-eating shark. Others ascribe to the black t-shirt theory, contending that the show really lost its mojo when Fonzie switched from white to black t-shirts. By its final years the cast had turned over almost completely, and the series would be unrecognizable to someone who stopped watching in its first season.

It happens. Eleven seasons is a long time. However, Fonzie's leather jacket still resides in the Smithsonian, a testament to that character's impact on the popular culture when television was still a true mass medium.

Happy Days begat several spinoffs, but *Laverne & Shirley* deserves special mention as it succeeded to the point where it drew higher ratings than its predecessor. After a one-shot appearance as good-time gals on *Happy Days*, the characters were softened into best friends and roommates who worked at a brewery by day and dreamed of catching the eye of a rich doctor by night. Lenny (Michael McKean) and Squiggy (David L. Lander) filled the wacky neighbor roles, Phil Foster bellowed as Laverne's bombastic dad, and Eddie Mekka played dance teacher Carmine Ragusa, Shirley's back-up plan if she couldn't strike it rich in marriage. Or, as she put it: "I can date other men, and Carmine can date ugly women."

The vintage setting eventually became an afterthought here as well. But in the physical comedy antics of Laverne DeFazio (Penny Marshall) and Shirley Feeney (Cindy Williams) older viewers could recall similar moments from Lucy Ricardo and Ethel Mertz back when they first fell in love with television. That gave the series a nostalgic vibe apart from its setting.

There was also an opposites-attract element in their relationship reminiscent of *The Odd Couple*, a series that also featured Penny Marshall. Where Laverne was pragmatic about the future, Shirley remained optimistic they could make all our dreams come true (to quote the show's theme song). Laverne was open to relationships (in the parlance of the series, she would "vo-dee-oh-doh-doh"). Shirley would save herself for marriage. It was a friendship tested but never cleft.

As with *Happy Days*, the magic didn't last to the final episode: a relocation from Milwaukee to Los Angeles proved disastrous, and Cindy Williams' departure left Laverne on her own in the show's final season. But for a while this was the #1 show in America, and once that was a mountain only a classic could climb.

The Best Episodes

Happy Days

"Give the Band a Hand" (1974)

Richie and Potsie lose the money their band just earned in a crooked poker game. Howard returns with his son to the scene of the crime to set things right. This first season episode exemplifies *Happy Days* before Fonzie: a single-cam series with a subtle laugh track, instead of a show filmed before an amped-up live audience; stories with quieter moments and dialogue that didn't lean so heavily on punch lines and catch phrases. It was still a good show, but one that likely would not have lasted as long as what it became.

"Richie Fights Back" (1975)

It's not hard to see why Henry Winkler's Fonzie stole the show. Here, as he defends Richie against a pair of bullies, he conveys power and self-assurance with every movement and facial expression. Still, Richie is tired of getting bailed out of trouble by his best friend, and takes martial arts lessons so he can take care of himself. Many funny moments in this one, as well as a showcase for Pat Morita as malt shop owner "Arnold."

"They Call It Potsie Love" (1975)

Amidst Fonzie-mania here was a sweet episode in which Joanie develops a surprising crush on Potsie after he serenades here with "Put Your Head On My Shoulder." The story gave both characters a chance to break out of their narrow confines and play something more substantive.

"Fonzie Loves Pinky, Pts. 1-3" (1976)

This three-part story had an epic feel to it back in the day, as Fonzie was matched with a female that was his equal in cool. Backstage tensions kept Roz Kelly from reprising her role as

Pinky Tuscadero, but this story arc, featuring the villainous Malachi brothers and a no holds-barred demolition derby, brought an already popular series to further heights of pop culture prominence.

"They Shoot Fonzies, Don't They?" (1976)

This is the dance marathon episode, where Fonzie partners with Joanie even though he's exhausted from pushing his broken-down bike 12 miles. At the climax, the Fonz performs a Russian folk dance called the Kazatsky with an athletic, show stopping virtuosity that is completely unexpected from the character or from Henry Winkler.

Laverne & Shirley

"Angels of Mercy" (1976)

Laverne and Shirley become hospital volunteers. The scene everyone remembers is Laverne's attempt to change the sheets on a bed still occupied by a large, unconscious man.

"Laverne and Shirley Meet Fabian" (1977)

Occasionally the show remembered it was set in the 1950s, as in this episode in which Laverne and Shirley pose as hotel maids to meet Shirley's singing idol, Fabian (who plays himself). Of course, they end up on the ledge outside his top-floor suite.

"Guinea Pigs" (1977)

The girls are invited to a fancy cocktail party but can't afford the $20 admission. To earn the money they volunteer at the Institute for Behavioral Sciences – Shirley is only allowed to eat dirt as part of a nutrition study, while Laverne is deprived of sleep. They make it to the bash, and that's when the after-effects of their experiments kick in. What follows is more than five minutes of non-stop laughs.

"The Diner"

A fan favorite – Laverne and Shirley work in a diner. It's not easy to explain why Laverne droning "Betty please" into a microphone is so entertaining. That may be one of the great mysteries of our age. But yes, it's really funny.

"Dinner for Four" (1978)

The scene with the "Murphy bed" is straight out of *I Love Lucy*, and another standout physical comedy set piece. But "Dinner for Four" also has some poignant undertones, as the excitement over dates with two handsome and accomplished men turns to mortification when they discover the real reason for the invitation.

Hello From Hooterville!

The Beverly Hillbillies
1962-1971 (CBS)

274 Episodes

Green Acres
1965-1971 (CBS)

170 Episodes

Petticoat Junction
1963-1970 (CBS)

222 Episodes

When looking back at the popular 1960s series created by Paul Henning, and why audiences loved them, the formula for success was simple: city vs. country.

In *The Beverly Hillbillies* we watched the Clampetts cling to the trappings and traditions of their rural lifestyle despite living in the luxury environs of Beverly Hills.

Petticoat Junction featured a train called the Cannonball that served the citizens of Hooterville. That train was under constant threat of shutdown by big city railroad executive Homer Bedloe (Charles Lane).

On *Green Acres*, New York attorney Oliver Douglas (Eddie Albert) chooses farm living in Hooterville over the opulence of Manhattan (and the objections of his wife), but soon discovers that everything he does is the exact opposite of what is acceptable among his neighbors.

Three different shows, all top-20 hits for CBS in the 1960s, each with a different premise and different tone. But for Henning they all flowed from happy memories of small town life and growing up on a farm in Missouri.

He first channeled those childhood memories into the story of a poor mountaineer who strikes oil, and moves his family to Beverly Hills.

Buddy Ebsen, then considering retirement, was convinced to come back to work in *The Beverly Hillbillies* as family patriarch Jed Clampett. It was a triumph of casting that was echoed in the discoveries of Max Baer, Jr. and Donna Douglas as Jethro and Elly May, and the selection of veteran stage actress Irene Ryan as the irascible Granny.

Debuting in September of 1962, *The Beverly Hillbillies* was the #1 show in America after just three weeks on the air. It stayed at or near the top of the ratings for its first two seasons, and remained in the top 20 through most of its nine-year run. "Not since *I Love Lucy* hit the airwaves 14 years ago has a single show so laid the industry on its ear," wrote *Los Angeles Times* TV critic Cecil Smith in 1965.

While the series became one of television's highest-rated and most successful situation comedies, it was also among its most frequently maligned by those who think TV should have loftier aspirations. "If television is America's vast wasteland," one observed, "the 'Hillbillies' must be Death Valley." "The series aimed low and hit its target," wrote UPI's

Rick DuBrow. "We're liable to be Beverly Hillbillied to death," added talk show host David Susskind, "Please write your Congressman."

What these guardians of decorum failed to observe was that, while the Clampetts may have been unsophisticated, the series itself was anything but. *The Beverly Hillbillies* mixed its broad fish-out-of-water hijinks with shrewd observations about a cynical and dysfunctional world that baffled the simple, honest Clampetts. If these critics didn't see themselves and their own biases in the goings-on, they just weren't looking.

After the *Hillbillies'* meteoric rise to the top of the Nielsen ratings, CBS President James Aubrey asked Paul Henning to create another series, no pilot necessary. Henning recalled stories his wife Ruth told him about her grandparents, who owned a little hotel beside a railroad track in rural Missouri. That became the basis for *Petticoat Junction*.

Bea Benaderet, a national treasure from television's golden age, starred as Kate Bradley, proprietor of the Shady Rest Hotel, alongside Edgar Buchanan as Uncle Joe, whose inveterate laziness was interrupted only by get-rich-quick schemes that never worked.

Henning's daughter Linda played the youngest of the three Bradley girls, and was the only sibling to stay for the entirety of the series. Unlike *The Beverly Hillbillies*, *Petticoat Junction* endured several casting upheavals, as well as the passing of Bea Benaderet in 1968. The series was at its best in its first two seasons, with Kate running the hotel, Charlie (Smiley Burnette) and Floyd (Rufe Davis) running the train, and Kate's three daughters as the characters were originally envisioned, before they became more interchangeable with each recast: boy-crazy flirt Billie Jo (Jeannine Riley), introverted intellectual Bobbie Jo (Pat Woodell) and tomboy Betty Jo.

But despite its production challenges and difficulties, *Petticoat Junction* never lost its bucolic charms or the chance to provide a half-hour of escapist TV to viewers during the turbulent 1960s. As its theme song urged, "Forget about your cares, it is time to relax."

After his second success Henning once again received carte blanche to create another series, and this time he relied on fellow writer Jay Sommers for a concept. Sommers had a bound volume of radio scripts from the 1950s called *Granby's Green Acres*, about a banker who worked in the city and longed to be a farmer.

Though Henning never wrote an episode of *Green Acres,* as executive producer he made one huge contribution to series' success by casting Eva Gabor as Oliver's wife, Lisa. Gabor was an inspired choice as the glamorous, somewhat ditzy socialite.

It was Matt Groening, creator of *The Simpsons,* who described *Green Acres* as the story of Oliver Douglas in hell.

Indeed, while the city vs. country conflicts fueled many storylines, this series carried them into the realm of the surreal. It may have shared the same Hooterville setting as *Petticoat Junction*, but *Green Acres* has more in common with Lewis Carroll and Monty Python.

The series also featured some of the best character actors of the era in memorable supporting roles: Pat Buttram and his yodeling voice as shady salesman Mr. Haney, Frank Cady, also a regular on *Petticoat Junction*, as level-headed Sam Drucker, owner of the local general store, and Alvy Moore as bewildered county agent Hank Kimball, the ideal personification of government bureaucracy.

The Paul Henning era of television ended in 1971, when CBS decided it was time to abandon the rural-themed series that helped make the network #1 for that television season. All three of his shows moved immediately into syndication, and are still picking up new fans 50 years later.

Henning, who died in 2005 at the age of 93, left behind a rich legacy of classic characters, family friendly laughter and a celebration of rural life and country values. He was never a household name, but it would be hard to find a household in America that had never met Jed Clampett, Uncle Joe Carson or a precocious pig named Arnold.

The Best Episodes

The Beverly Hillbillies

"The Giant Jackrabbit" (1963)

This is probably the most famous episode of *The Beverly Hillbillies*. The 'A' plot has Granny in full Wile E. Coyote mode, trying to trap a kangaroo she mistakes for a jackrabbit. The 'B' plot has the Clampetts trying to order food from a caterer – in the annals of funny one-sided phone conversations their attempt merits comparison with the best of the master, Bob Newhart. When this episode was first broadcast, it became the highest-rated half-hour show in television history.

"Jed Buys the Freeway" (1963)

Jesse White plays a con man that "sells" several Los Angeles landmarks to Jed, including the Hollywood Bowl, Griffith Park and the Hollywood Freeway. White built a busy career playing variations on hucksters, until he gained a more sympathetic reputation as the lonely Maytag repairman.

"Flatt, Clampett and Scruggs" (1965)

Granny is homesick for the hills, so Jed arranges for a couple of old friends to visit – Lester Flatt and Earl Scruggs, known outside of Hooterville as the legendary bluegrass duo that perform the series' theme song. These delightful visits became annual events for a few years, and offered the added delights of casting gorgeous Joi Lansing as Earl's wife, Gladys.

"The Gloria Swanson Story" (1966)

It's a running gag through all of Paul Henning's shows that the movie theaters in Hooterville and nearby Pixley are not up to date on new film releases. As a result, during a time when Hollywood's biggest stars included Michael Caine and Steve McQueen, the Clampetts still idolized Douglas Fairbanks and Mary Pickford. So what better series to feature a guest spot from silent screen legend Gloria Swanson?

"The Indians are Coming" (1967)

Co-written by series creator Paul Henning, "The Indians are Coming" opens with the Clampetts learning about a minor border issue between their oil land and the adjoining Crowfeet Indian reservation. To the Indians, it's a simple matter easily settled, but to Granny this can only mean one thing – the Crowfeet are on the warpath: "Except for John Wayne, nobody knows injuns like me!" Yes, it will likely rile the over-sensitive, but it's another hilarious episode that features a perfect grace note cameo from – you guessed it – John Wayne himself.

Petticoat Junction

"The Little Train Robbery" (1963)

Two would-be crooks try to hold up the Hooterville Cannonball, but nobody takes them seriously. So instead the would-be robbers and would-be victims head back to the Shady Rest together for a home-cooked chicken dinner. If only that approach worked in some of our more crime-ridden cities.

"Bedloe Strikes Again" (1963)

Homer Bedloe brings two top executives to Hooterville, hoping they will scrap the Cannonball as an embarrassment to the C&FW Railroad line. Before they arrive, the locals transform the train's coach into a luxury travel experience complete with meal service, barber, manicurist, and a musical floorshow.

"Bobbie Jo and the Beatnik" (1964)

Bobbie Jo is romanced by a hippie poet from New York City, played by guest-star Dennis Hopper. He's the type of angry young man that rarely visits Hooterville, and the culture clash inspires several hilarious moments, as when Uncle Joe asks him what type of poetry he writes: "My poetry is a cry of anguish in the tortured night!" From that, Uncle Joe concludes he must write jingles for indigestion commercials.

"The Ladybugs" (1964)

Even Hooterville was not remote enough to avoid Beatlemania. The three Bradley sisters fall for the Fab Four, though Kate's reaction is typical of many older folks of the day.

Uncle Joe: "It's the new sound!"
Kate: "You mean, instead of music?"

Joined by Sheila James (Zelda on *The Many Loves of Dobie Gillis*), they don mop top wigs and form their own band. It was a gimmick designed to sell records, which didn't work, but the quartet actually made an appearance in character on a 1964 broadcast of *The Ed Sullivan Show*.

"Betty Jo's Dog" (1964)

The series opened its second season introducing a new character – a stray dog adopted by Betty Jo. The dog, unnamed on the series but called "Higgins" by his trainer, often astonished viewers with the remarkable and complex tasks he was trained to do. Whether running and jumping on cue, picking up objects and carrying them to a specific place, turning off lights or picking up phones, Higgins became known as "the one-take dog," because he always got the scene right the first time.

After *Petticoat Junction* ended its run in 1970, the dog was cast as the star of a hugely successful family film that (according to IMDB) was made for $500,000 and grossed more than $39 million. From then on Higgins had a new name – Benji.

Green Acres

"Don't Call Us, We'll Call You" (1965)

The first season of *Green Acres* features one long story arc as Oliver and Lisa Douglas leave New York for Hooterville, so Oliver can pursue his farm livin' dreams. Every episode brings more bizarre frustration; here, having just mastered the generator in the previous episode ("You can't have a 2 with a 6"), he now finally gets his phone installed – at the top of a telephone pole outside his bedroom window.

"I Didn't Raise My Pig to Be a Soldier" (1966)

The army drafts Arnold Ziffel. Oliver tries to intervene, but cannot convince the draft board or the FBI that they're trying to induct a pig into the US Army.

"The Beverly Hillbillies" (1967)

A truly weird episode of television. The citizens of Hooterville launch a community theater production of *The*

Beverly Hillbillies, featuring Oliver as Jethro and Lisa as Granny! The result is every bit as crazy as it sounds.

"Das Lumpen" (1967)

The series aired multiple flashback episodes explaining how Oliver and Lisa met and fell in love during World War II. However, being *Green Acres*, every flashback told a different version of the same story. This one is my favorite, especially in the moments featuring Lisa playing cello with the Budapest Chamber Trio.

"The Case of the Hooterville Refund Fraud" (1970)

Green Acres just kept getting nuttier with each passing season, and yes, that's a compliment. I could try to summarize the plot of "The Case of the Hooterville Refund Fraud" but it won't do the episode justice: the town folk receive an unexpected (and undeserved) windfall and Mr. Haney convinces them to invest in monkey racing, in which little monkeys race around a track chasing after a wooden banana. Some things are better experienced than described.

It's Magic: Bewitched/I Dream of Jeannie

Bewitched	I Dream of Jeannie
1964-1972 (ABC)	*1965-1970 (NBC)*
254 Episodes	*139 Episodes*

The 1960s inaugurated a trend of popular situation comedies (and a misfire or two) with supernatural or fantasy elements. *My Favorite Martian* introduced audiences to a telepathic alien; *Mr. Ed* featured a talking horse; *My Mother the Car* reincarnated Jerry Van Dyke's mother into a 1928 Porter automobile. *The Munsters* and *The Addams Family* debuted in the same week in 1964.

Two of the most enduring examples of the genre were *Bewitched* and *I Dream of Jeannie*, shows that remain inextricably linked in the syndicated memories of those who love TV classics. They were frequently paired in reruns on UHF channels when that was the lone haven for television's past, and then for years as "The Magic Hour" on Nick at Nite.

The association is obvious: both shows feature a beautiful blonde woman with the power to bestow almost any wish. I don't even want to contemplate where today's television would take that concept.

The premise of *Bewitched* is a thinly veiled treatise on intolerance. The series thrived during an era in which a situation comedy built around a mixed-race couple could never crack a network's prime-time schedule. But when the mixture is that of a pretty witch named Samantha (Elizabeth Montgomery) and a down-to-earth advertising man (Dick York, and later Dick Sargent as Darrin), the fantasy element diffused the tension of cultural clashes and the wrath of disdainful in-laws, so memorably represented by Agnes Moorehead as Endora, who imbued the word "mortal" with all the scorn of a racial epithet.

It's possible to enjoy this frothy, sophisticated series for decades and never get the connection. Those looking only for a half-hour of nose-twitching escapism could easily be diverted by its delightful range of recurring characters – dotty Aunt Clara (Marion Lorne), practical joker Uncle Arthur (Paul Lynde), Sam's grandiose Shakespeare-quoting father Maurice (Maurice Evans) and kooky cousin Serena (also played by Elizabeth Montgomery), Darrin's sycophantic boss Larry Tate (David White), bombastic Dr. Bombay (Bernard Fox), and nosy neighbor Gladys Kravitz (Alice Pearce, later Sandra Gould).

Such a sterling stable of always-welcome performers provided an embarrassment of riches for the show's writers, who mixed and matched them for eight mostly marvelous seasons. And when they were otherwise occupied, Endora's endless array of creative tortures upon her hapless son-in-law produced moments of comic embarrassment that somehow, with Sam's help, always resulted in yet another satisfied client at McMann & Tate.

But the show's take on prejudice was acknowledged early on. "*Bewitched* is not about cleaning up the house with a magic wave, zapping up the toast, or flying around the living room. It's about a very difficult relationship, and people see that," Elizabeth Montgomery once said. "They know there's something going on besides the magic. When the show is viewed carefully, its other elements may be observed."

As much as Darrin rails against Sam's use of witchcraft, he ultimately accepts that her powers are part of who she is, and he should not try to change her. And though Sam's parents believe their daughter has married beneath her standing, their prejudice is no match for Darrin's love.

I Dream of Jeannie did not share the thoughtful aspirations of its unofficial sister series. The comedy was broader, the jokes more obvious, the stories less nuanced.

But in Barbara Eden and her pink harem attire, the series introduced a character that will forever be part of every classic TV retrospective. Gwen Wakeling, an Academy Award winning costumer (for 1950's *Samson & Delilah*) designed that celebrated outfit, importing satin shoes from Italy and braided cording trim from France. If you look closely you'll see Eden is also wearing a teardrop diamond on a herringbone chain, a gift from her husband Michael Ansara.

But here's a challenge, for the next time you happen by a *Jeannie* rerun or pop in an episode on DVD: avert your glance from Barbara's bare tummy and focus on Larry Hagman as her hapless master, Tony Nelson.

Why? Hagman is teaching a master class in physical comedy. On some level we see it, as the only genuine laughs in *I Dream of Jeannie* are the immediate after-effects of a disastrous Jeannie blink, as Tony contends with sudden bizarre costume changes and disappearing furniture. But we may not appreciate the remarkable timing and commitment he brings to these moments, complicated by the additional challenges created by the show's pre-CGI special effects.

Think about it – when Tony is sitting on a chair, and Jeannie makes that chair disappear, Hagman must first sit in the chair, then sit immobile as filming stops while the chair is removed, then squat in the same position until the cameras roll again, and only then react to what appears to be a split-second vanishing in the finished episode. That's a lot more difficult than just falling down.

Major Nelson's Air Force uniform also added to the impact of these moments. As the Three Stooges taught us, it's always funnier to watch a man of dignity take a pie in the face.

I could cite episodes to illustrate Hagman's gifts, but as this is *I Dream of Jeannie* it really isn't necessary. The series repeatedly recycled about a half-dozen plots over the course of five seasons, all of which included one or two moments of slapstick. When they befall poor Tony, it's the one time he deserves the accolade of Master.

Hagman hated the scripts and was fed up with the series long before it ran its course. But to his credit he, like the similarly disgruntled Kate Jackson on *Charlie's Angels*, always delivered when the director called action. His complaints were valid, but producers were more concerned about whether Jeannie's navel was ever exposed on camera. Generations raised on *Shameless*, *Girls* and *True Blood* would be astonished to learn that Barbara Eden's belly button was once considered too risqué for network television.

Besides sharing a similar premise, both series also generated incredulity among viewers that wondered why the mortals loved by Jeannie and Samantha were reluctant to exploit the amazing capabilities at their disposal.

Why would Darrin Stevens continue to trudge to his office at McMann & Tate day after day, week after week, year after year, to create advertising campaigns just to help a blustery CEO sell more dog food? Why not instead allow Samantha to twitch up an estate on Long Island or Martha's Vineyard, and spend the day playing golf, enjoying a gourmet dinner every night, and fully take advantage of opportunities the rest of us could only dream about?

The answer is that Darrin, and *Jeannie's* Major Anthony Nelson, saw value in work, and appreciated the lifestyle they had because it was one they earned. As Thomas Paine observed, "What we obtain too cheap, we esteem too lightly." The lesson that nothing worth having comes easy used to be taught in our schools and reinforced in our homes. But like so much else it has fallen by the wayside in times when politicians gain support by how much they're willing to give away free to entitled constituents.

For real-world examples of this tenet, one need only look at all of the lottery winners who were handed the kind of financial windfall you and I would need a genie to conjure, only to find their lives became worse instead of better. Magic or no magic, always be careful what you wish for, because you just might get it.

The Best Episodes

Bewitched

"A is for Aardvark" (1964)

The question of why Darrin resists the lure of better living through witchcraft has never been more eloquently expressed than in this first season episode. Story: Darrin sprains his ankle, leaving him bedridden. Samantha grows weary of waiting on him and hexes their home to respond to his requests. After just three days with his new power, Darrin is ready to quit his job and travel the world in luxury. How will

Sam bring him back to his senses?

"A Vision of Sugar Plums" (1964)

Before he became Will Robinson on *Lost in Space*, Billy Mumy guest stars here as an orphan who doesn't believe in Santa Claus. Samantha realizes there is only one way to break through his cynicism – fly him to the North Pole to meet the real Santa. This is my favorite Christmas episode of any series.

"The Joker is a Card" (1965)

"Yaga-Zoo-Zee, Yaga-Zoo-Zee, Yaga-Zoo-Zee-Zim!"

Paul Lynde debuts as Uncle Arthur, and it's an appearance for the ages. Every moment he's in this generates the heartiest laughs this series ever produced, especially when he offers to teach Darrin a spell to put Endora in her place.

"Divided He Falls" (1966)

Endora is enraged when Darrin tells Sam he has to cancel their Florida vacation because of his job. She splits Darrin into two people, so his fun loving self can go to Florida while his work self stays home. Samantha reluctantly goes along, but quickly discovers that a husband who is all play or all work can be equally insufferable.

"My Friend Ben"/"Samantha for the Defense" (1966)

A standard *Bewitched* set-up – Aunt Clara tries to summon an electrician but zaps up Benjamin Franklin instead – is elevated into the series' best two-part outing on the strength of its shrewd scripts and guest star Fredd Wayne. Wayne takes a gimmick and gives it real depth – he captures Franklin's wit and principles as well as the scientific curiosity and wonder you'd expect to see in an open-minded man suddenly transported 200 years into the future.

The highlight is the courtroom trial in "Samantha for the Defense," in which Franklin must convince a judge that he is who he says he is, against all logic. It's like an Independence Day version of *Miracle on 34th Street*.

I Dream of Jeannie

"The Lady in the Bottle" (1965)

The series' first season was slightly more ambitious than those that followed, a quality that was apparent here in its debut episode. After his space capsule misfires and he lands on a desert island, Major Nelson is delighted to encounter a genie that can rescue him – and then exasperated when she refuses to leave. By the end of the pilot Jeannie has put Tony in the suspicious crosshairs of psychiatrist Alfred Bellows (Hayden Rorke), and ended his impending marriage to the daughter of his commanding officer.

"My Master, The Rich Tycoon" (1966)

When he wasn't playing Uncle Arthur, Paul Lynde guest-starred on just about every 1960s series, always transforming each character into a variation on his own persona. His infectious laugh and sardonic smirk could make straight lines funny and punch lines funnier. He appeared on *I Dream of Jeannie* three times in three different roles. This one is my favorite: Upon arrival at Major Nelson's home he mocks the décor, prompting an affronted Jeannie to blink up all sorts of priceless art treasures, including a Ming vase and a Renoir painting. The way Lynde reads the line "A real Renoir? In Cocoa Beach?" could not be surpassed. After taking the tour of Tony's suddenly sumptuous home, he reveals himself as an IRS agent ready to send the astronaut to jail for unlisted income.

"Jeannie Breaks the Bank" (1966)

Like Paul Lynde, John McGiver was always a welcome presence in a guest spot on a familiar series. His specialty was stuffy authority figures, such as the banker who turns down Tony's loan request in this episode. Jeannie adds a few zeros to her master's bank account, and suddenly the bank can't do enough for one of its most valued customers. Some of the best moments in this series begin with Jeannie blinking up some craziness, and then disappearing just as Dr. Bellows walks in, leaving Tony to explain the inexplicable. In this episode, Tony tries to find a logical reason for the sailboat in his living room ("It was too big for the bedroom?")

"My Master the Thief" (1966)

At a museum exhibit Jeannie spots a pair of slippers that belonged to her – 2000 years ago. She blinks them out of their display case, causing an international incident. When Tony can't convince her to return them, he attempts to break into the museum to put them back. Here we get another fine example of Dr. Bellows attempting to expose the insanity he's witnessed around Major Nelson, and falling short once again.

"Jeannie, My Guru" (1968)

The series devoted several episodes to celebrating and sending up the counterculture, perhaps most famously in "The Mod Party" (1967). But I like this show better. Tony gets tricked into covering up the romance between General Schaeffer's hippie daughter (Hilary Thompson) and her longhaired boyfriend. In the process his home becomes a haven for every hippie in Cocoa Beach, including the Lewis and Clarke Expedition, a real band that featured Michael Martin Murphy ("Wildfire")

Sidebar: TV's Most Famous Bottle

Jeannie's bottle is one of television's most instantly recognizable props. And like many TV stars, it had some cosmetic work done between seasons.

As any *Jeannie* fan knows, the original bottle was smoked glass with leafy gold filigree. It appeared only during the show's first season, which was broadcast in black and white. It wasn't until 2006, when a colorized version of season one was released on DVD, that viewers finally got a non-monochromatic glimpse at that first bottle.

The series' switch to color coincided (not coincidentally) with the introduction of the classic metallic purple version. It's a beautiful piece with a pearlescent sheen and highlights in turquoise, orange, brass and pink. If you'd like to get as close a look as the series provides, check out the season three episode "Genie, Genie, Who's Got the Genie?" (Part II).

There was also a third bottle belonging to Jeannie's sultry sister, featuring a green variation on the familiar purple design.

While talented artists at Screen Gems created the finished versions of these bottles, the actual bottle used for these makeovers could be found as close as the local liquor store. It was a 1965 Beam's Choice bourbon whiskey decanter from Jim Beam, 11 inches tall, just over 14 inches with the stopper in place.

Whose idea was it to use this particular bottle on the show? According to Steve Cox's book *Dreaming of Jeannie*, no one is really sure. Director Gene Nelson may have the best claim, but its discovery has also been attributed to series creator Sidney Sheldon and a still-anonymous employee in the studio's art department.

Less than ten bottles were made during the show's five-year run. One of them is still owned by Barbara Eden. Others pop up at memorabilia auctions every so often, but there is almost no way to guarantee their authenticity. That hasn't stopped them from selling for more than $15,000.

If that is out of your price range, you can pick up a glass reproduction online for around $300 made by Mario AC Della Casa (the only person licensed by Sony) at jeanniebottles.com. No Jeannie fan's home is complete without one.

Looking Back vs. Looking Forward

What is it about people who prefer watching older shows to current television? Why are we like that?

The title of this chapter offers the most basic theory – some prefer looking back to looking forward. But is it really that simple?

I know I don't look at everything this way. It's nice that light bulbs last longer now, and I'm glad that research that once required driving to the library can now be conducted at a computer in my jammies.

However, while many aspects of our lives have improved with the passage of time, I think just as many have regressed. And that's where "things were better in my day" thinking starts, and why it can be comforting to look back at those times. The television shows of an earlier era provide a window into that bygone world.

For instance, if you think schools were better run and taught a more appropriate curriculum when Beaver Cleaver or Opie Taylor or Peter Brady were going to class, that belief will be reinforced by the classroom scenes from their respective shows. Familiar subjects are taught, history lessons will not assume that everything that happened in America since Jamestown was wrong, and teaching will be portrayed as a noble profession.

If you are sure that people were more civil to each other back when you were a kid, you'll find that reflected in how characters behave in classic television. If you have fond memories of a time when there was nothing controversial about public restrooms or police officers or "Merry Christmas," you are almost certainly someone that feels more at home in the shows of the past.

Part of this appeal comes from the fact that we lived through these eras ourselves, and they didn't seem so bad to us, then or now. I get that not everyone feels this way. There are many who experienced those times less happily than I did. And there are those of later generations who believe the shows of this time portray an era that was less sophisticated, less enlightened, and less inclusive.

Does that mean those of us who prefer *Nanny and the Professor* to *Masters of Sex* are less sophisticated? I don't think so. But it might mean that we define sophistication differently.

Does it mean we don't care about inclusion? It actually might, to be honest. It's not that we're against it – we just don't always view entertainment through that prism. I'll watch a dozen straight episodes of a 1950s sitcom and not even be aware that I've never seen a person of color. And if I did see one it wouldn't register as a person of color – it would be a character contributing to the story being told – no more, no less.

And then I'll watch *Room 222* with its racially diverse cast, and be equally captivated – not because of the diversity, but because it's an intelligent and wonderful show.

I've yet to meet a classic TV fan in favor of discrimination or anyone being mistreated. But we also see through the artificiality of forced diversity – that means how, beginning around the late 1970s, every toy commercial would have three white kids and one black kid. Even as children it was hard not to pick up on the pattern, and to think it was rather silly.

Now, maybe there were African-American kids watching at the time who needed to see that, and who am I to tell them they are wrong? But I wonder if the same objective could have been achieved in a less flagrant way. Why not two and two, or three African-American kids and one white kid? What about the Latino and Asian and disabled kids? Once you start down that path, you wind up where we are now, with every commercial looking like a 1980s Benetton ad.

How about this – figure out how many kids you need for the commercial, and then cast the ones that read the lines best – no matter what race or gender they are.

Such merit-based criteria would not satisfy the forward-looking TV fan, who is obsessed with the agendas that dictate how television shows are now put together. Just a few years ago CBS was loudly chastised for scheduling too many shows about white men on its fall roster. Rather than defend the programming slate that they invested several months and several million dollars developing, the network quickly assumed self-flagellation mode, desperately apologizing and vowing to do better.

Were the shows good or not? No mention of that.

The forward-looking viewer is happy that today's shows are engineered not to offend anyone with the exception of a few acceptable targets – Christians, dopey white guys, Southerners who have to be racist because, really, why else would they live down there?

Ironically, the shows of the past shared that goal of not offending viewers. But they managed to get there without focus groups and sensitivity training. Amazing, isn't it?

Have I answered the question? I don't know. I'm dancing around the obvious conclusion that devotees of older shows are also fonder of the times in which they were made. And those who find old shows to be dated and trite also believe just about everything is better today than it used to be.

That's probably still too simple. I'm sure there are thousands of people with a more progressive outlook who can laugh at *I Love Lucy* or appreciate the simpler charms of *Bewitched*. The difference is that they see them as nice places to visit, while other fans take a look at where the culture is headed, and wish we could go back and live in their bygone worlds. Even with a nosy neighbor like Mrs. Kravitz.

The Love Boat

1977-1987 (ABC)

250 Episodes

Classic TV viewing is rarely influenced by current events. However, at those moments when the world situation seems more depressing than usual, many of us find ourselves drifting toward less challenging shows.

When a temporary escape from dire headlines is warranted, the carefree appeal of a frivolous series like *The Love Boat* is particularly welcome. What sounds better to you right now – another story about pandemics and congressional infighting, or an open smile on a friendly shore?

Granted, if you see a Breaking News bulletin about a mass shooting and immediately pop in a *Love Boat* episode to avoid the painful details, that's not healthy. It's a variation of the 'safe spaces' that have taken root on college campuses, and deserve all the derision they have received.

I watch a lot of news each day, and when there's a major story I'll often stay with it for hours. As a former journalist I am interested not just in what is being reported but how the facts are (or are not) being communicated.

But when you dwell too long in that headspace, it alters your perspective. It becomes tempting to believe that such atrocities as school shootings or terrorist attacks or massacres in a house of worship are commonplace, and not extremely rare in a nation of 330 million people.

Be aware of current events, pray for the victims of tragedies (sadly, even doing that has become a source of contention) and do what you can to try and make things better.

After that, there's nothing wrong with a reminder that this is still a good and noble nation – and a comfortable old TV show is one way to do that.

Escapism was always one of *The Love Boat*'s selling points, even if viewers were escaping something as mundane as winter. From 1977 to 1987, the show embarked on each new season as autumn leaves began to fall, and sailed through the months when days were shorter and weather forecasts promised blizzards and cold, bleak temperatures.

Growing up in the Chicago suburbs I can still recall watching *The Love Boat* on Saturday nights and gazing, longingly, at the bright sunshine and clear blue skies as the Pacific Princess sailed out of port. As each week's swimsuit-clad voyagers lounged on the Lido deck, sipping tropical drinks and discussing day trips into Mazatlán or Puerto Vallarta, it felt like a virtual vacation from the frozen wasteland outside my bedroom window.

Critics hated it, predictably. It didn't have the gravitas of *Hill Street Blues* (as if that was the objective). How dare any series possess no higher aspirations than showcasing nice people in attractive scenery, and simple stories of romance? But in the era that brought us the Iran hostage crisis, the last throes of the Cold War, the Unabomber, the murder of John Lennon and other depressing news, I'm sure millions of viewers appreciated the break. The show came along at a good time.

Timing was also favorable when it came to casting. In the late 1970s and early 1980s, many of Hollywood's golden age stars were still performing, even if opportunities to do so were not as frequent. *The Love Boat*'s prestigious passenger list included June Allyson, Van Johnson, Lana Turner, Joseph Cotten, Olivia de Havilland, Greer Garson, Joan Fontaine, Stewart Granger and Ginger Rogers.

Television stars past and present filled out the remaining roles, along with a few frequent travelers who qualified as celebrities, though at the time we didn't know why, exactly: Fannie Flagg, Dr. Joyce Brothers, and the ubiquitous Charo, who seemed to check in at least once a month.

The *Love Boat* crew was as responsible for the series' success and longevity as its guest stars. I can't prove it (academia is shockingly bereft of scholarly research on *The Love Boat*) but for me it was the friendly and reliable presence of Gavin MacLeod, Fred Grandy, Ted Lange, Bernie Kopell and Lauren Tewes that anchored the series through episodes good and bad.

What a wonderful job that must have been. With the stories carried by the passengers, your captain, yeoman purser, doctor, bartender and cruise director received scripts with one-third of the lines they would have to memorize on a typical hour-long series. Kopell and Grandy had so much free time they also wrote several stories. And once or twice each season a crewmember would get to play a moment that required extra depth and effort, and they were always up to the task.

As with other Aaron Spelling-produced shows from the 1970s, *The Love Boat* was attacked for peddling prime time porn and loosening the morals of America. From our perspective now we clearly didn't know how good we had it back then. Yes, there were stories about single men on the prowl, groups of college friends helping a nerdy buddy hook up, and married people flirting with breaking the Seventh Commandment. But they were always more talk than action. The characters that left the ship having made the right choices were those that found genuine love.

As with any long running series, even one with such a pliable premise, *The Love Boat* eventually began to lose its mojo. I never thought Jill Whelan was the Cousin Oliver of the cruise lines, but most people didn't get why Vicki was necessary. Lauren Tewes' one-season departure disrupted crew chemistry, and the late addition of the Love Boat Mermaids and Ted McGinley (as ship photographer Ace) smacked of desperation.

I remember it most fondly now as a time capsule for an era of film, television and popular culture that we rightly recall as magical. Artist Andy Warhol sailed on the Pacific Princess. So did Donna Reed and Dolly Parton, Hulk Hogan and Lillian Gish, the Hudson Brothers and the Pointer Sisters. Luise Rainer, who won back-to-back Oscars in 1936 and 1937, appeared on *The Love Boat* (playing twins!). Janet Jackson was there at the beginning of her career, and it was where Janet Gaynor, the first Best Actress Oscar winner in 1928, gave her final performance.

But even in its least inspired moments, *The Love Boat* was a refreshing oasis of optimism in a desert of cynicism. It was weekly wish fulfillment that reassured all of us losers that there really was someone out there for everyone.

The Best Episodes

"The Old Man and the Runaway/The Painters/A Fine Romance" (1977)

A good *Love Boat* episode is comprised of equal parts sweetness, spice, silliness and sentiment. Among the highlights here: a grouchy old codger (Will Geer) forms an unlikely friendship with a teenage stowaway (Bayn Johnson).

And Captain Stubing gets his cabin painted by the two most incompetent painters in the business (Arte Johnson and Pat Morita). As soon as the Captain tells them to "paint everything blue," you can guess what happens next.

"Alaska Wedding Cruise, Parts 1 and 2" (1979)

It's not surprising that a series sold largely on dreams of travel to exotic places would feature several episodes shot on location in popular vacation spots around the world. Along for the ride on this cruise to Alaska are Mark Harmon, Lisa Hartman, Lorne Greene, Ray Milland, Eleanor Parker, Audra Lindley and more.

"Alas, Poor Dwyer/After the War/Itsy Bitsy/Ticket to Ride/Disco Baby" (1979)

The Pacific Princess hosts Julie's high-school reunion. This two part episode features another impressive array of guest stars, including Raymond Burr, Kim Darby and Michael Cole, and a surprisingly moving story about one Vietnam draft dodger's trepidation over meeting a former best friend who served in the war.

"This Year's Model/The Model Marriage/Vogue Rogue/Too Clothes for Comfort/Original Sin: Part 1 and 2" (1981)

Better known as the fashion show episode, this is a wonderful encapsulation of the fads and trends in vogue when it was shot. Some of the top fashion designers of the day appear as themselves - Geoffrey Beene, Halston, Bob Mackie and Gloria Vanderbilt.

"Farnsworth's Fling/Three In a Bed/I Remember Helen/Merrill, Melanie & Melanesia/Gopher Farnsworth Smith" (1981)

Probably a stretch to compare this to *King Lear* – but we do have Lloyd Bridges as a wealthy man who brings his daughters (and other relatives) together to decide how he wants to divide up his kingdom, and who is going to hit the jackpot. It was shot on location in Australia.

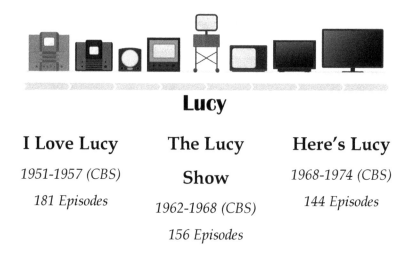

Lucy

I Love Lucy
1951-1957 (CBS)

181 Episodes

The Lucy Show
1962-1968 (CBS)

156 Episodes

Here's Lucy
1968-1974 (CBS)

144 Episodes

Lucille Ball made her last public appearance as a presenter at the Academy Awards in 1989. *Variety* noted that she received a rousing standing ovation that left her "noticeably overwhelmed."

The tribute was richly deserved - in that audience of show business royalty there was likely not one person who did not grow up watching her on television. Another 30 years have passed since her final bow but there is still only one Lucy when you're talking about TV, just as there is only one Elvis in music.

She is a towering figure in the history of the medium. Where many performers achieve pop culture immortality from one successful series, Lucy starred in three hit shows spanning more than 20 years. If you were five years old laughing at her antics on *I Love Lucy*, she was still making you laugh on TV every week in new episodes of *Here's Lucy* after you had graduated college and started your first job.

I Love Lucy wasn't the first television situation comedy, but it was the first to rival any comedy playing in a movie theater as something so special that audiences just had to see it. Along with Milton Berle's *Texaco Star Theater*, it convinced millions of Americans that a TV set, back then a fairly sizable investment, was something they needed to have. By the end of the 1950s there was a television in nine out of every ten American households. We can only surmise that Lucy should have earned a commission on a lot of those purchases. This is when television first brought us together, and what a way to begin.

We look back at *I Love Lucy* as a breakthrough advancement in how great television could be, but such greatness did not materialize out of nowhere like a Marian apparition at Fatima. There was groundwork laid, even if the audience never saw it.

In 1948, Lucille Ball began a four-year run in *My Favorite Husband*, a situation comedy that played on radio, produced by Jess Oppenheimer and written by Bob Carroll, Jr. and Madelyn Pugh. They recognized Lucille's strengths and began to create the "Lucy" character that was fully-formed when they all made the transition to television; Lucy recognized the quality of the material and rehearsed tirelessly to perfect her timing, her physical movement, and her handling of props, to get the most out of every comic set piece.

Richard Denning played her husband on radio but Lucy wanted her real husband, Desi Arnaz, for the TV series. The network whined about his accent, but relented. Their natural chemistry enhanced the on-screen relationship between Lucy and Ricky Ricardo, and Desi's talents as a singer, musician and bandleader added another engaging element to the series. And Lucy mocking Ricky's accent became another of the show's great running gags (though people now lose their jobs for doing that).

In its first handful of episodes *I Love Lucy* created such classic moments as Lucy and Desi's performance of "Cuban Pete" in "The Diet," and Lucy's hilarious turn as 'The Professor' in "The Audition." These and other bits were staples of the nightclub act Lucy and Desi performed dozens of times across the country. By the time they brought them to the show the material had been honed to perfection.

So this was a series that launched with audience-tested material from a radio series and a nightclub act, top writers, the spot-on casting of Vivian Vance and William Frawley as the Mertzes, and a star who at age 40 was eager to finally have a vehicle worthy of her potential. It was an enormous hit within weeks.

When Lucy and Desi had a baby (future *Here's Lucy* costar Desi Arnaz, Jr.). an episode of *I Love Lucy* filmed weeks earlier aired in which Lucy and Ricky Ricardo also had a baby. That episode drew more than 44 million viewers. The baby's picture graced the cover of the first issue of a new magazine devoted to covering a still new medium – *TV Guide*.

After countless classic episodes over six seasons, exhaustion and estrangement between the Arnazes (they divorced in 1960) ended *I Love Lucy* after a series of 13 expanded episodes billed as *The Lucy-Desi Comedy Hour*. Lucy returned to television two years later in *The Lucy Show* as Lucy Carmichael, widowed mom to two children. Thankfully, Vivian Vance also returned, along with the same stable of writers from *I Love Lucy*. Gale Gordon (who was considered for the role of Fred Mertz) appeared as Lucy's vituperative boss, Theodore J. Mooney.

It was a different show, not as consistent or groundbreaking, and one that underwent several major changes during its six-season run: Vance was written out after three seasons, along with Lucy's kids – her character moved from Danfield, New York to Los Angeles, though she would continue to work in a bank for Mr. Mooney. If audiences cared it didn't show in the consistently high ratings – *The Lucy Show* was a top ten hit from first episode to last.

The prevailing opinion among TV intelligentsia goes that *I Love Lucy* is one of television's crown jewels, and that *The Lucy Show* is not as highly regarded, though perhaps its best moments rivaled the quality of its predecessor.

By contrast, *Here's Lucy*, an unofficial continuation of *The Lucy Show*, surpassed the freshness expiration date for its antiquated sitcom formula – and its leading lady.

But as is often the case with television, those who make such pronouncements did not speak for the public at large. *Here's Lucy* also ran for six seasons and ranked among the top ten highest-rated programs in its first four years, rising as high as #3 in 1970-71.

It's likely that Lucy's basic brand of comedy may have seemed outdated to those that preferred more substantive sitcoms like *All in the Family*, *M*A*S*H* and *Good Times*. But clearly there were just as many viewers who enjoyed a weekly visit with a friend they had watched for 20 years. For them, it was comfort TV.

Looking back on *Here's Lucy* now, it's easy to appreciate its old-world craftsmanship: the way standard plots unfold with clockwork predictability; Lucy's comic incompetence at office work and blustery Gale Gordon, back again as her exasperated boss (and in this case, brother-in-law); the lavish musical production numbers, expertly arranged and choreographed within the show's standard shooting schedule, and performed for a live audience.

The series frequently featured big-name guest stars, something *The Lucy Show* did in its later seasons as well. At the time these appearances were not considered all that special, but more than 40 years later it's wonderful to watch so many classic film and television icons sharing the stage with Lucy: Richard Burton and Elizabeth Taylor, Ginger Rogers, Sammy Davis, Jr., Vincent Price, Dinah Shore, Danny Thomas, Phil Harris, Joan Rivers.

Lucille would try once more, joined by Gale Gordon and her same stalwart writers, in *Life With Lucy* (1986), but this time it would not work. The world had changed too much, and Lucy at 75 could not be the spry physical comedienne she was 30 years earlier.

By then her status as the First Lady of Television was secure. There's a story in Geoffrey Mark Fidelman's *The Lucy Book* from a fan who recalled driving on the 405 Freeway in Los Angeles when news came over the radio that Lucy had died. He instinctively slowed down to absorb the news, and then noticed that all the other cars, on both sides of the freeway, had done the same. Within hundreds of separate cars heading for separate destinations, Lucy brought them all together one last time.

The Best Episodes

I Love Lucy

"Lucy Does a TV Commercial" (1952)

If there were a Louvre Museum for television comedy, the Vitameatavegamin bit would be its Mona Lisa. While the brilliance of Lucy's performance in this one seminal scene deserves every accolade it has received, it also overshadows the fact that the rest of the episode is packed with laughs as well.

"Job Switching" (1952)

As with "Lucy Does a TV Commercial," Job Switching" is an episode famous for one unforgettable scene, that also delivers big laughs before and after its most memorable moment. Disastrous attempts by Ricky and Fred at ironing and cooking 'pollo y arroz' are nearly as entertaining as Lucy and Ethel frantically wrapping those accelerating assembly line chocolates.

"L.A. At Last" (1955)

In the show's fourth season the cast temporarily relocated from New York to Los Angeles, after Ricky is invited to screen test for a movie. It was a shrewd decision that inspired several standout episodes in which starstruck Lucy kept running into Hollywood's top stars. "L.A. At Last" features William Holden and Eve Arden, and the famous scene of Lucy lighting her nose on fire.

"Lucy's Italian Movie" (1956)

After Vitameatavegamin and the chocolate factory, the scene of Lucy stomping grapes in Italy is the show's third most famous moment. It's another instance where a script can only tell Lucy what to do – how she does it, and the facial expressions and comedic touches she adds to her confrontation with a surly fellow grape-stomper, are the kind of inspired choices that great comedic actors instinctively know how to create.

"Lucy Does the Tango" (1957)

In its final season, *I Love Lucy* created yet another classic comedy set piece, one that turned a horde of eggs into the longest laugh Ball ever received in any of her shows. Some of the audience response had to be cut for the broadcast to fit the rest of the story in its running time.

The Lucy Show

"Lucy Puts Up a TV Antenna" (1962)

By now fans knew what to expect from an episode with that title – and they knew Lucy and Viv were probably going to surpass those expectations. The scenes on the roof of their house rival the best comic set pieces from *I Love Lucy*.

"Lucy and Viv Build a Shower" (1963)

While Vivian Vance would remain with *The Lucy Show* for another two seasons, this episode features the final classic physical comedy sequence that she and Lucy would share.

They worked so well together by this time, here trapping themselves in a shower as it slowly filled with water, the scene did not have to be rehearsed before it was filmed.

"Lucy Plays Florence Nightingale" (1964)

Lucy is a volunteer nurse at the hospital where Mr. Mooney is recovering from a broken leg. From the moment you see Mooney in his hospital bed, his injured leg suspended above him, you know he's about to be subjected to every form of comedic torture the writers can devise.

"Lucy Meets the Merm" (1964)

Guest star Ethel Merman moves to Danfield under an assumed name – Agnes Schmidlapp. Lucy hopes to pass Agnes off as the real Merman so she can perform at one of her son's Cub Scout events. Fans remember Lucy Ricardo's frustrated show business ambitions from *I Love Lucy*, so when this Lucy tries to teach "Agnes" how to sing, the scene is hilarious because of that familiar association.

"Lucy, the Bean Queen" (1966)

When the owner of Bailey's Baked Beans offers a double-your-money-back guarantee if his beans aren't the best you ever tasted, Lucy buys every can in town to get the refund, so she can use the money to buy new furniture. What could possibly go wrong?

Here's Lucy

"Lucy Visits Jack Benny" (1969)

Jack Benny was among Lucy's closest friends and a frequent guest on her TV shows. What makes this episode special is not its trite premise – Lucy's family rents rooms at Jack's Palm Springs estate, offering Benny several opportunities to display his tightwad persona – but a remarkable cameo at the end when a busload of tourists is dropped at the home for a tour. The bus driver is Jackie Gleason as Ralph Kramden. It's a brief moment, but a special one.

"Lucy the Fixer" (1969)

Lucy meets Harry at his home to finish up some office work. She discovers a lamp isn't working and sets out to fix it. When she's done, Harry's house is in a shambles. "Lucy the Fixer" delivers a master class in the kind of physical comedy that dates back to the silent movie era. The timing, the steady build from minor trouble to major disaster, the reactions of Lucy and Harry every time the destruction escalates – it's flawless.

"Lucy and The Andrews Sisters" (1969)

Watching *Here's Lucy* now is a nostalgic experience, but here's an episode that generated nostalgic emotions when it first aired 50 years ago. Lucy and her daughter join Patty Andrews in recreating a big band era concert featuring the music of The Andrews Sisters. The performance is (mostly) played straight, to give these classic songs their due.

"Lucy Meets the Burtons" (1970)

This is the most famous *Here's Lucy* episode, as well as the highest-rated, thanks to its Hollywood royalty guest stars, Richard Burton and Elizabeth Taylor. The couple is nearly upstaged by Taylor's 60-karat ring, which figures prominently in the story when Lucy tries it on and can't get it off. The show's comic centerpiece was recycled from the *I Love Lucy* episode "The Handcuffs," and works just as well the second time.

"Lucy and Ann-Margret" (1970)

For the children of Lucille Ball and Desi Arnaz, watching all the classic Lucy shows is like watching home movies. This episode like brought back special memories for Desi Arnaz, Jr., who had a crush on guest star Ann-Margret, which inspired the show's funniest scene.

How Times Have Changed: Air Travel

Airplanes were popular settings for sitcom stories, including on the shows featuring Lucille Ball.

In the *I Love Lucy* episode "Return Home From Europe" (1956), Lucy wraps a large package of Italian cheese in blankets to smuggle it onto a plane disguised as a baby.

Passenger: "What's his name?"
Lucy: "Cheddar...uh, Chester!"

In "Lucy and Carol Burnett," a 1967 episode of *The Lucy Show*, Lucy and Carol train to be stewardesses (still the accepted term at the time). The gag is that Carol is afraid of heights, which predictably triggers a panic attack when the plane takes off. Half the show is musical numbers, which are hokey in the best possible way.

It's not surprising that TV shows incorporate air travel into stories. It's a setting familiar to most viewers, which also lends itself to heightened moments of comedy, drama and action. Sometimes you get all three at once, as in the *Laverne & Shirley* episode "Airport '59" (1977), when Laverne has to land a plane after the pilot passes out. As so many of us do when faced with a challenge, she drew inspiration from classic TV, imagining herself in an episode of the 1950s western *Sky King*.

Even with such comic calamities, flying was usually portrayed as a pleasant and even luxurious experience. And that's what it actually was back then. At the start of a vacation, going to the airport and getting on a plane used to be part of the joy of travel, instead of the ordeal that had to be endured before the fun could start.

Today, many more of us share the fear of flying that gripped Emily Hartley in "Fly the Unfriendly Skies" (1972), the first episode of *The Bob Newhart Show*. But not just because we place our safety in the hands of a pilot we've never met. We do the same with train conductors and taxi drivers and the restaurant chef that cooks our dinner. We assume professionals know their trades and won't do their jobs in a way that might kill us.

No, the dread of air travel today emanates from systemic, industry-wide policies that have turned most commercial jets into flying cattle cars.

The suffering begins long before you board the plane: by then you've been nickel-and-dimed for services that used to be free, and forced to participate in a security theater performance by the TSA, where they still make everyone take off their shoes because one idiot tried to stuff his with explosives 20 years ago.

Will your plane be delayed or overbooked? Probably. Some of that can be attributed to the hub-and-spoke system, one of many debacles unleashed by industry deregulation in 1978. Now each carrier routes their fleet through hub cities, which is why your flight from Chicago to Miami can be delayed for six hours because it snowed in Denver.

Could be worse, though: if the delay occurs after you board, you'll be stranded on the tarmac for hours because the gate it left is no longer available, another consequence of the hub system.

Once airborne you'll cope with ever-shrinking seats, nonexistent leg room and restrooms so small that passengers routinely get stuck in them mid-flight. And let's not dwell on the cuisine that has inspired five minutes of material from every standup comic at The Comedy Store.

When did it become acceptable to treat paying customers this way? What happened to the pride airlines used to take in presenting a comfortable travel experience? Some may recall when Eastern Airlines president Frank Borman would appear in his company's commercials, talking about why customer service was paramount, and how his employees strived to "earn our wings every day." As comedian Jay Leno observed, even the slogans would eventually be downgraded, as evidenced by Delta replacing "The airline run by professionals" to "We get you there."

"We get you there?" That's the most we can expect? When deregulation dissolved the Civil Aeronautics Board, it resulted in a free market that should have offered travelers a range of options. Instead, major airlines tried to fend off challenges from discount carriers, like those parodied in the No Frills Airlines sketches on *The Carol Burnett Show*. The result was a race to the lowest common denominator that continues to this day.

Why has flying become such a miserable experience? The answer is simple: if you want to traverse a long distance in a short period of time, there are no other options available. You know it, and they know it. So you endure the misery, or you hop in your car and get where you're going in days instead of hours.

Actually, that sounds rather nice.

Outside of a handful of foreign carriers that still deliver a luxury travel experience, the days of "Something special in the air," "Going beyond expectations," "We'll take more care of you" and "Fly the friendly skies" are long gone...unless you happen to be in Los Angeles. If so, you might want to visit the Pan Am Restaurant, which recreates the experience of flying in the 1960s – retro elegance, great food, great service, comfortable cabins, and no lost luggage. You'll never leave the ground, but sometimes that happens with the real airlines too.

The Mary Tyler Moore Show

1970-1977 (CBS)

168 Episodes

The Dick Van Dyke Show was a tough act to follow, but when Mary Tyler Moore returned to television, this time as a headliner, her new series would equal its predecessor in quality and genre impact.

Moore's Mary Richards was not a variation on Laura Petrie – though memories of Laura influenced how she would be introduced. She was to be a divorcee, but the network didn't want anyone to think Mary left New Rochelle for Minneapolis. Perhaps that seems silly now, but this was a time when audiences cared about the characters from their favorite shows as if they were real people. And television, which strived to create those connections, afforded them the respect they deserved.

So Mary became a 30-ish single woman out on her own, entering the workforce at a time when that was still evolving from an uncommon circumstance into a familiar lifestyle. In doing so she became a feminist icon and that's great – but it wouldn't have mattered if the show weren't funny as well.

To illustrate, consider *Julia* (1968-1971), which starred Diahann Carroll as the first African-American woman to headline a series (in a non-stereotypical role). Her show too often crumbled under the weight of that status. Television was already on its way to being more inclusive: *I Spy* and *Mission Impossible* had debuted, and *Room 222* premiered the following year. These shows were all much better, in part because they just told interesting stories with an integrated cast. *Julia* spent too much time being "about" its own milestone achievement, too often forgetting that once you get that platform, you need to do something with it.

Thankfully, *The Mary Tyler Moore Show* was a landmark in modern feminism, as well as a high-rated, Emmy-winning (33 of them!) success with critics and audiences. Everything about it worked.

It was clear from the first episode that Moore learned two valuable lessons from her previous classic series – create engaging home and workplace settings that could each inspire good stories, and surround yourself with a cast of characters that bring their own métier to the mix.

In fact, though Mary gets top billing most of the laughs are generated by the antics of those around her: Rhoda's sass and Ted's bumbling news broadcasts; Murray's insults and Phyllis's self-centeredness; Lou Grant's bulldog bark and Sue Ann's lascivious come-ons.

Mary Richards was the grounded center around which these eccentric characters circled, reacting with bemusement or disbelief or appreciation at their foibles. But when Mary Tyler Moore was called on to deliver a big comic moment, as in the series of mishaps leading to her Teddy Award in "Put on a Happy Face," or the funeral scene in "Chuckles Bites the Dust," she always delivered.

As with all of the classics celebrated in this book, *The Mary Tyler Moore Show* was beloved and successful because it introduced wonderful characters, gave them attention-grabbing things to say, and provided a place to visit once a week that helped us forget our own troubles and the worries of the world. That it remains a classic, decades later, can also be attributed to its non-partisan approach to humor.

Given that much of the series was set in the WJM-TV newsroom, there may have been a temptation to incorporate current events into the stories, from Richard Nixon and Watergate to the election of Jimmy Carter. But instead the show declined to take strong positions on the issues of the day. Back then, the first rule of situation comedy was to entertain, not proselytize; why alienate half of your audience?

That was an admirable outlook at the time. It wouldn't last much longer.

Murphy Brown, a series that shared DNA with *The Mary Tyler Moore Show*, debuted in 1988. Name-dropping was one of its richest sources of humor. But how many people today would laugh at a Strom Thurmond joke? Combine that dated quality with a stridency of one-sided political opinion, and the result is a series that played well in its day but now offers the same experience as reading an old newspaper.

In 1990, Michael Jordan was chastised at the height of his fame for not taking more stands on political issues – when asked why he responded, "Republicans buy sneakers, too." He took a lot of heat for that. And had he come out in support of a conservative cause or candidate he'd have been criticized even more. Activism is only applauded in our culture if it's the approved kind.

The Mary Tyler Moore Show understood this, as most shows from its era did. Television has since become more hostile and more divisive, and that has inspired many of us to return to the TV from past generations, when great shows respected their audience enough to give them a laugh instead of a lecture.

The Best Episodes

"Rhoda the Beautiful" (1972)

While the series strived to portray Mary as the adorable all-American girl and Rhoda as the frumpy, date-starved mess, audiences couldn't help but notice that Valerie Harper was a fit and beautiful woman as well. So the show gave her a well-deserved moment of self-confidence, fueled from a beauty pageant win at her workplace.

"The Lars Affair" (1973)

A prime example of how Mary Tyler Moore could step back and let her standout supporting cast carry a classic episode. Here it is Betty White's "Happy Homemaker" Sue Ann Nivens (in her series debut), no longer happy after she is discovered having an affair with Phyllis's husband. Cloris Leachman won an Emmy for her performance in this episode.

"The Dinner Party" (1973)

Mary's disastrous parties were one of this show's best running gags. This get-together features a Congresswoman, a guest appearance from Henry Winkler, and the unforgettable main course of Veal Prince Orloff.

"Chuckles Bites the Dust" (1975)

"A little song, a little dance, a little seltzer down your pants"

I've never read the script David Lloyd wrote for this episode, but for the funeral scene I can't imagine it gave Mary Tyler Moore any more to work with than "Mary tries to suppress her laughter." And look at the magic she created from such a simple directive. That scene is justifiably famous but the whole episode is brilliant, from Lou and Murray swapping tasteless jokes about Chuckles' demise to Ted's on-air obituary: "I'd like to think that somewhere, up there tonight, in his honor, a choir of angels is sitting on whoopee cushions."

"Ted Baxter's Famous Broadcasters School" (1975)

The idea of Ted lending his name to a school of broadcasting is already funny; the fact it was a scheme floated by a con artist is even funnier, but the best part is when the WJM news team show up for the first class and find only one student in the room. On the short list of things that always make me laugh, there is Ted singing the school's theme song, and Lou Grant's Ralph Kramden-like reaction.

Sidebar: Why Rhoda Mattered

The precept of casting today decrees that roles should be filled by actors who share the ethnic and cultural experiences of their characters. We are told it is more appropriate and more inclusive.

But had that directive been in place in the 1970s, we might never have met Rhoda Morgenstern – at least, not as exceptionally played by Valerie Harper.

Harper was not Jewish but she created perhaps the most famous and beloved Jewish character on television. And that's not something to just acknowledge in passing, especially at a time when anti-Semitism is sadly on the rise again.

She wasn't the first – *The Goldbergs* (1949) debuted two years before *I Love Lucy*, and the show's writer, producer and star, Gertrude Berg, ranks among television's pioneers. In the 1960s, Buddy Sorrell honored his heritage on *The Dick Van Dyke Show* with a decades-belated bar mitzvah ("Buddy Sorrell Man and Boy").

But even by the 1970s there were shows that depicted Jewish families as something "other"; I recall episodes like "Danny Converts" on *The Partridge Family*, and "Bitter Herbs" on the Saturday morning superhero series *Shazam*.

So it was no small thing that when viewers met Mary

Richards in the first episode of *The Mary Tyler Moore Show*, they also met Rhoda. And near as I can recall, no one had any concerns or complaints. Everyone just liked her.

As much as we must always acknowledge the show's writers for Rhoda's witty dialogue, the credit for the character's acceptance and the affection she engendered in viewers belongs entirely to Valerie Harper.

By the show's second episode one of TV's most enduring opposites-attract friendships had been established. Where Mary was upbeat and optimistic, Rhoda was sarcastic and self-deprecating. Where Mary seemed to get asked out by every eligible male in Minneapolis, Rhoda attracted nothing but losers. Where Mary always seemed stylish and pulled together, Rhoda struggled with her looks and her weight.

> Mary: *"Why don't you eat something?"*
> Rhoda: *"I can't. I've got to lose 10 lbs. by 8:30."*

But these perceived flaws and insecurities never made Rhoda the butt of jokes. Phyllis took her shots but she always ended up on the losing end of the skirmish. Audiences eagerly sided with the plucky Jewish girl over her pompous WASP-y landlord.

The contrast wasn't always religious as much as it was geographic – Mary was a product of the friendly and welcoming Midwest, while Rhoda's roots were planted in the kill-or-be-killed streets of The Bronx. But religious intolerance was front and center in the season two show "Some of My Best Friends are Rhoda," in which Mary's new friend belongs to a tennis club that doesn't welcome certain types of guests. Mary's response spoke for all of us.

Maybe this wasn't the same type of door that opened when Bill Cosby was cast in *I Spy*, but there is a parallel in finding the right actor with enough talent and charisma to bring a non-traditional character into America's living rooms, when safer choices were a less risky option.

Today we think of Mary and Rhoda with the same affection as Lucy and Ethel or Laverne and Shirley. But that was no sure thing in 1970, and for proof one need only look at the fate of *Bridget Loves Bernie*, the CBS sitcom that served as the lead-in for *The Mary Tyler Moore Show* in 1972.

Meredith Baxter played Bridget Teresa Mary Colleen Fitzgerald, an Irish Catholic schoolteacher who falls in love at first sight with Jewish cab driver Bernie Steinberg (David Birney). The couple's inter-religious marriage and the culture clash of their respective in-laws was the launching point for many episodes.

The network canceled the series after 23 episodes, though it ranked fifth among all shows that season. Were there adverse reactions from a few anti-Semitic viewers? Probably. But there was also an objection from The Rabbinical Assembly of America, which described the series as "an insult to the most sacred values of both the Jewish and Catholic religions."

More than 40 years later *Bridget Loves Bernie* remains the highest-rated TV series to be canceled. That same year, Valerie Harper won the Emmy for Best Supporting Actress, and Rhoda left Minneapolis to headline her own CBS series, in which her Jewish character would marry a non-Jewish man. Maybe there were grumblings about that too, but for each one there were 500 viewers looking forward to the wedding.

Was *Rhoda* a good show? Yes, as was *The Mary Tyler Moore Show* after Harper's departure. But there was magic when Mary and Rhoda were together that was not there when they were apart.

Unfortunately, when they reunited in the 2000 TV movie *Mary and Rhoda*, that special something had disappeared. Disappointing, but now it's little more than a footnote, easily ignored for a character that appears in more than 150 episodes of classic television.

Can we say that Rhoda paved the way for Fran Fine and Monica Geller? Perhaps, or perhaps not. But more than one generation of TV fans is still on a first-name basis with her, and for that we must say one last thank you to Valerie Harper – who also turned the world on with her smile.

How Times Have Changed: The Nightly News

Perhaps the greatest irony of broadcast journalism is how there is so much more access now to news on television, yet we are less well-informed (or at least accurately informed) than we were 40-60 years ago.

For most of television's history, viewers got their information from the six o'clock news. The ABC, CBS and NBC networks each presented a 30-minute broadcast, in which an anchorman would read the day's headlines (hopefully with more competence than Ted Baxter), interspersed with on-the-scene accounts from reporters in the field.

I'm sure there were people back then who didn't pay much attention to the news, but it didn't seem that way. When a family watched a network news broadcast, whether it was before, during or after dinner, they knew that most of the nation was doing the same. And headlines that evening would be discussed the next day in schools and offices and other workplaces. Rarely would someone be unaware of what had been reported the day before. Having a vested interest in what was happening in one's country was a trait of good citizenship.

Because of this, the men (and Barbara Walters) entrusted with delivering the news every weeknight became as familiar to viewers as any actor in a top-ten series. It was said at one time that Walter Cronkite, who anchored the *CBS Evening News* for 19 years, was the most trusted man in America. Other anchors such as Chet Huntley and David Brinkley (NBC) and John Charles Daly, Harry Reasoner and Peter Jennings (ABC) held an equally esteemed status with the general public.

When the news was bad, as it was almost every night (planes that land safely don't make the headlines), the anchors were a reassuring presence – most held their jobs for decades, building a relationship with millions of Americans on the other side of the camera.

There was not, as there is now, widespread suspicion that the stories being told were not trustworthy, or were selectively edited to reflect the bias of the broadcast's producer, news director or anchor. And there was not justification for such suspicions, as there certainly is now.

Journalism – real honest-to-God journalism – is dead. I can't pinpoint an exact time of death, but it's been on life support since the escalation of the internet, and about 20 years ago finally gave up the ghost. There are still reputable journalists plying their trade, but they do so in opposition to a tsunami of predetermined agendas, arrogance and flat-out incompetence.

What happened?

It's not that journalists have become more political. Walter Cronkite was liberal in the extreme, but this was not evident from how he delivered the news. However, the accusation of liberal bias dates back to at least 1969, when then-Vice President Spiro Agnew stated as such in a once-famous speech in Iowa. They "read the same newspapers, and draw their political and social views from the same sources," he claimed of the media. The result is "a narrow and distorted picture of America."

Public response tended to support Agnew's statement. The NBC network reported that more than 85 percent of those contacting the network agreed with Agnew's views.

Back then, however, the leftward slant was more of a slight tilt. Picture a carpenter's level that denotes objective reporting when the bubble is in the middle. From the 1950s through the 1970s, that bubble drifted slightly over the left hash mark. Today, that tilt has steepened to the angle of an Olympic downhill ski run. Anchors and reporters are no longer content to tell America what is happening, but what they think about it. And these actions are not just condoned but encouraged by the networks where anchors are employed.

We didn't know how good we had it.

It is ratings, not adherence to the standards of journalism, that now determines whether a news broadcast is a success.

And unlike the network TV era, when the battle for news supremacy was waged between just three main combatants, nightly news shows now face competition from 24-hour cable news channels, hundreds of sports and entertainment channels, streaming services, social media, and millions of websites.

Getting the country's attention amidst such a cacophony of noise is a challenge that won't be overcome by a serious and objective tone. Gone are the days when anchors read their copy in measured, even tones, free of partiality or sensationalism.

Most people wouldn't think of watching news broadcasts from that era now, unless it was part of a research project. But if you do, you'll understand how it was once possible for biased and imperfect people, working within a clear chain of command, to produce something that could accurately be called "the news."

Mission: Impossible

1966-1973 (CBS)

171 Episodes

"Please slow it down – I get stomach cramps!"

That quote was taken from a letter sent to the producers of *Mission: Impossible* from someone who apparently couldn't take the stress.

I'm glad they didn't listen. The show's frenetic pace was one of its greatest assets, comparable to nothing else on TV until Jack Bauer began his first race against the clock on *24*. From the lit match that kicked off the opening credits to the final freeze-frame, *Mission: Impossible* just flat-out *moved*, and demanded that you pay attention.

If you did, and your stomach didn't hurt, your efforts were rewarded. *M:I* rarely insulted the intelligence of its viewers. Don't expect the surplus exposition found in other hour-long dramas – you won't watch scenes in which Jim Phelps turns to Cinnamon and says, "So that means the agent we captured yesterday is planning on contacting his government at midnight, to receive his final instructions on the assassination attempt of General Morales!" No, sorry, you keep up, with no help from the characters.

The title was well chosen because the focus is always on the mission, not the operatives who carried it out. That made casting critical, as an audience used to building familial attachments to TV characters would now have to cheer on a team of emotionless government workers.

Who were they? One-sentence descriptions will suffice: Leader Dan Briggs (Steven Hill, later replaced by Peter Graves as Jim Phelps), a brilliant tactician of stoic demeanor; Barney Collier (Greg Morris), electronics genius; Willie Armitage (Peter Lupus), the team's muscle, Rollin Hand (Martin Landau), master of disguise, Cinnamon Carter (Barbara Bain), fashion model turned Mata Hari. The characters were not further developed, because their personalities or lives before the Impossible Missions Force mattered not at all.

Instead, the drama emerged from the high stakes at play; while detective Joe Mannix was beating up small-time hoods, and Steve McGarrett was chasing Wo Fat on *Hawaii Five-O*, the IM Force was toppling foreign governments and averting nuclear holocaust.

It wasn't just what they did that made them special, it was how they did it. Viewers used to the near misses and lapses of judgment that were written in to pad out episodes could now watch a team that didn't make mistakes. The IM Force got its orders in the first scene and then, step by step, carried them out flawlessly.

Because of this, on those rare occasions when something did go wrong, the sense of danger was far more pronounced. When enemy agents captured Cinnamon in "The Exchange," it wasn't like Dan Tanna having to rescue Binzer on *Vega$*. The threat seemed real.

This was a team that triumphed because they were smarter than their adversaries, not stronger. In fact, muscleman Willie was the least utilized in almost every mission. When he did have a job, it was usually carrying Barney's toolbox.

Theirs was a partnership of professionals, who often went about the task at hand in blessed silence and without commenting on their own cleverness. Every episode featured long scenes with little or no dialogue, which ironically constituted some of the best writing in 1960s television.

Not everyone liked it. In its first season more viewers watched bandleader Lawrence Welk, and one critic in *Saturday Review* wrote a scathing piece that condemned agents who break the laws of other nations and are never brought to justice.

He had a point. At a time when half the nation was incensed about U.S. forces in Vietnam, here was a show that proudly depicted saboteurs getting their marching orders from "the Secretary" (presumably Secretary of State), who then undermined the domestic affairs of other nations by manufacturing evidence, framing and entrapping government officials, and killing without remorse.

Heaven knows how many advocacy groups would demand that *Mission: Impossible* be taken off the air if it were introduced today. But times were different in the 1960s, and I leave it to you to decide if that's a good thing.

The Best Episodes

The Pilot (1966)

The IM Force is dispatched to Santa Costa to recover two stolen nuclear devices. Everything that made the series a classic was already in its first episode – the soon to be iconic self-destructing tape recorder, Lalo Schifrin's brilliant theme, Rollin's rubber masks, Barney's technological wizardry, a cracking pace and a plot that kept viewers on the edge of their seats for a full hour. Also joining the team – Wally Cox, in a memorable one-shot appearance as a safecracker.

"Operation Rogosh" (1966)

This first-season show was the first of many episodes in which the team creates an elaborate charade to convince an enemy agent that he has been transported through time or across a great distance. Here, they have just 36 hours to break an "unbreakable" terrorist planning a series of attacks on Los Angeles.

"The Legacy" (1967)

Four men, all sons of Adolf Hitler's most trusted officers, meet in Switzerland to recover a Nazi fortune, which will be used to start the Fourth Reich. Rollin impersonates one of the heirs, prompting many anxious moments. There's also a great, unexpected twist at the end.

"The Astrologer" (1967)

Mission: retrieve missing microfilm and a kidnapped freedom fighter; the challenge, do it while 40,000 feet in the air on a two-hour airline flight. The tight quarters, limited time frame and lack of escape route all intensify the suspense.

"The Mind of Stefan Miklos" (1969)

"I don't think there has ever been a more difficult show to write in the history of American television than *Mission: Impossible*," said one veteran TV writer. Episodes like this one, which may be the series' best, are the reason. The team has to lead a brilliant intelligence officer to a false conclusion, by leaving clues that can't look like clues.

Sidebar: Elevator Pitch

Most of us don't approach elevators with any sense of wonder anymore. But back when television brought us together, these simple conveyances provided a plethora of plot lines and punch lines.

Their comedic possibilities were explored frequently on *The Bob Newhart Show*, while many other series opted for a one-off story about a stuck elevator that trapped incompatible characters inside. You've seen that plot on *The Dick Van Dyke Show* ("4½"), *That Girl* ("The Elevated Woman"), *WKRP In Cincinnati* ("Fire"), *Gimme a Break* ("Porko's II") and *Night Court* ("Earthquake"), among others.

On *Mission: Impossible*, elevators were taken more seriously. From the staged elevator crash in "The Widow" to Rollin's quick-change from an old man to his regular self during a 30-second elevator ride in "The Bargain", the show found several ways to incorporate this everyday object into its arsenal of espionage tricks.

The best example of this is "Doomsday" (1969), in which a corrupt industrialist tries to auction a hydrogen bomb off to the highest bidder. While Jim, Rollin and Cinnamon pose as auction participants, Barney spends nearly the entire episode climbing through elevator shafts, to get access to the room where the bomb is housed. Once there he must render it harmless before it can be used to start World War III.

Musical Sitcoms: The Monkees/The Partridge Family

The Monkees	The Partridge Family
1966-1968 (NBC)	*1970-1974 (ABC)*
58 Episodes	*96 Episodes*

As with *Bewitched* and *I Dream of Jeannie*, *The Monkees* and *The Partridge Family* are two series inextricably linked in our collective consciousness. Here the common denominator is not magic but music.

Music touches our nostalgic pleasure centers the same way these old TV shows do, so here we have two series that deliver a double-dose of generational joy. For many of us, the songs they introduced were the soundtracks of our formative years. But even if "Daydream Believer" and "I Think I Love You" and so many others were not associated with happy memories, they would not sound out of place alongside the best pop music released by any artist in the 1960s and '70s.

Most of the world has finally come around on The Monkees, who have worn down their critics through persistence and sheer longevity. *Good Times*, a 2016 CD released to celebrate the band's 50th anniversary, earned rave reviews even from detractors like *Rolling Stone*.

A similar reconsideration has not happened with The Partridge Family, which is understandable as the series was created with no regard for musical authenticity. The concept was to cast photogenic actors who would lip-sync to tracks recorded by professional singers and musicians. It was serendipity that David Cassidy, hired for his teen idol looks, asked executive producer Bob Claver if he could try singing as well.

Johnny Ray Miller's excellently researched book *When We're Singin'* provides some long-overdue recognition for the outstanding songwriters, producers and studio musicians that made the Partridge Family records so popular. And despite whatever demons David Cassidy battled during and after his Keith Partridge fame, he was not just a *Tiger Beat* cover story. That man could sing.

Of the two series I think *The Partridge Family* holds up better, though *The Monkees* won the Emmy for Best Comedy Series in 1967. Whether intended or not, Micky Dolenz, Mike Nesmith, Peter Tork and Davy Jones put a family-friendly face on the counterculture. The show spoke to its teen audience in a language they understood, while easing the fears of some parents; those four silly long-haired musicians may have worn fringe jackets and talked all about peace and love, but at least they weren't taking trips on LSD and hanging out with the Hell's Angels, like Ken Kesey and his Merry Pranksters.

Through the course of its first season, this series about a fictional band evolved into a series featuring one of the most successful pop groups of the decade. By April of 1967, the Monkees had released two #1 hits and two multi-million selling albums. Like Pinocchio after a visit from the Blue Fairy, they found themselves unexpectedly transformed from something fake into something real.

That didn't happen with the Partridge Family, and it never could because the family viewers watched on TV couldn't perform live. But this was a witty and genuinely funny sitcom that balanced the challenges of everyday family life – first dates, getting braces, passing a tough high school course – with the responsibilities of making a living as a touring band.

Exactly how successful they were was always a little confusing. In the series' first episode, the Partridge Family is introduced by music icon Johnny Cash, and headline Caesars Palace in Las Vegas. But they spent the next four years playing tiny supper clubs and town picnics where the tickets were probably free. Doesn't say much for Reuben Kincaid (Dave Madden) as their manager.

But through great episodes and those less memorable, *The Monkees* and *The Partridge Family* always gave us a song to send us smiling into the closing credits. And I don't think a month has gone by in the decades since that I haven't listened to at least one of those songs, and smiled again.

The Best Episodes

The Monkees

"The Spy Who Came In From the Cool" (1966)

The band gets mixed up with the CIA, Russian spies and stolen microfilm. The episode is packed with silly throwaway gags, moments of breaking character and talking to the audience at home, and no less than four great songs, including "(I'm Not Your) Steppin' Stone".

"Monkees Get Out More Dirt" (1967)

All four Monkees fall in love with April, the girl at the neighborhood Laundromat (played by Julie Newmar). Who will win her hand?

"The Monkees on Tour" (1967)

The evolution of the Monkees from fake band to real band culminated in "The Monkees on Tour," the final episode of the show's first season. It was an unscripted documentary that follows the group as they land in Phoenix for a concert before more than 10,000 fans. This was the moment in Monkee history when the quartet went from being along for the ride to deciding they'd rather drive the car.

"Everywhere a Sheik, Sheik" (1967)

The story is typical Monkee silliness (Davy has to marry a beautiful princess or be executed by her father). But this episode is elevated by guest appearances from 1960s icon Donna Loren, and dancer-choreographer Anita Mann, who joins Davy in a delightful song and dance routine to "Cuddly Toy," composed by Harry Nilsson.

"The Devil and Peter Tork" (1968)

The band actually gets serious (almost) in this retelling of the Faust legend. Peter falls in love with an ornate harp in a music store window. The store's owner offers it to him and gives him the ability to play – in exchange for his soul.

The Best Songs

"I'm a Believer"

This is not only one of the band's most popular and successful songs (seven weeks at #1), I think it belongs in the select company of the most perfect pop records ever made, alongside The Ronettes' "Be My Baby" and "California Girls" by The Beach Boys.

"Mary, Mary"

Given the master plan behind The Monkees machine it's doubtful that Mike Nesmith's songwriting played any role in his casting, but it became an essential element in the band's evolution. That's Glen Campbell playing the distinctive lead guitar riff on "Mary, Mary," a song also covered by the Paul Butterfield Blues Band and Run DMC.

"Daydream Believer"

Another obvious pick, another #1 hit, and featuring Davy's best vocal on a Monkees track (though if you prefer "She Hangs Out" I won't argue the point). How many other bands could boast three lead singers as distinctive and as good as Davy, Micky and Mike?

"The Girl I Knew Somewhere"

History tells us this is the first fully self-contained Monkees song. Mike wrote it, and the group played the instruments and performed all the vocals. Peter Tork plays a mean harpsichord on this top-40 classic.

"Last Train to Clarksville"

It was about a soldier leaving for Vietnam, as most fans know by now. It's fascinating to me that the first single from this manufactured band of TV goofballs not only tackled such a serious subject, but was also climbing the charts before the series even debuted. Personally I think "Clarksville" is slightly (just slightly!) overrated, but it was their first #1 hit and deserves to be here.

The Partridge Family

The Best Episodes

"But the Memory Lingers On" (1970)

Better known as the skunk episode. A stowaway skunk sprays the family in their bus, putting their charity performance at a children's hospital in doubt. Fans remember it for the costumes the group borrows for the show, and another great song in "Brand New Me."

"Soul Club" (1971)

A booking mix-up sends the Partridges to a Detroit nightclub, where owners A.E. (Richard Pryor) and Sam (Louis Gossett, Jr.) were expecting The Temptations. The club is on the verge of being lost to a loan shark, so the family agrees to perform, unaware of whether anyone will actually show up. The episode is one of many great showcases for Danny Bonaduce as the family's resourceful middle child.

"The Undergraduate" (1971)

Family matriarch Shirley (Shirley Jones) goes back to college, where a classmate half her age develops a crush on her. This is one of the funniest shows in the series.

"Don't Bring Your Guns to Town, Santa" (1971)

Returning from a holiday concert, the family bus breaks down in a ghost town, where they are greeted by its only resident, an old prospector named Charlie (played by Dean Jagger). When the kids worry about missing Christmas, Charlie tells them a story about the town back in its heyday, which triggers a delightful western fantasy sequence with everyone in the cast playing different roles. When the Partridges return to serenade Charlie with "Have Yourself a Merry Little Christmas," his wordless, tear-filled reaction packs an emotional wallop, especially after such a whimsical story.

"Bedknobs and Drumsticks" (1973)

The family agrees to film a commercial for Uncle Erwin's Country Fried Chicken. Erwin (William Windom) rejects the classy first attempt and insists on a second version – with the family wearing chicken suits. The cast hated this episode because of those suits but it's one of the better third-season shows. From a one-note role, Windom manages to create a complete character that you can easily imagine having a real life beyond his few minutes of screen time.

The Best Songs

"I Think I Love You"

This was the biggest Partridge Family hit, and the one song that is probably familiar even to someone who never watched the show. "I Think I Love You" went to #1 in 1970 and stayed there for three weeks. It has everything fans love – memorable words and music from songwriter Tony Romeo, that ever-present harpsichord, and a great David Cassidy vocal, double-tracked for added impact.

"Only a Moment Ago"

From our current perspective of decades after the series debuted, "Only a Moment Ago" takes on added resonance. It's a song about longing for happier, simpler times, which is something that many of us do every time we hear Partridge Family music. "Why has the music stopped," indeed.

"Together We're Better"

The best song on the group's *Notebook* album was immortalized in the episode where the family visits the King's Island amusement park and hangs out with Mary Ann Mobley. The playful opening notes of the organ sound like a circus calliope, setting the perfect mood for one of the most ambitious Partridge records. From a foundation laid by writer Tony Romeo, a lot of gifted people crafted an intricate musical arrangement and vocal backing tracks that complement Cassidy's lead. There's a lot going on here in just 2 minutes and 30 seconds, and it's all pretty wonderful.

"I'll Meet You Halfway"

"I'll Meet You Halfway" doesn't sound like a typical Partridge Family record. There's a sophistication to it, and an almost classical quality to the strings and piano arpeggio that set the mood before the singing starts. Partridge record producer Wes Farrell wrote it with Carole King's songwriting partner Gerry Goffin.

"Summer Days"

Yet another Tony Romeo song, and this one is irresistible from the explosive opening riff to Cassidy's exuberant vocal to a buoyant chorus that bounds and rolls out of your speakers with unbridled joy. Why "Summer Days" was never released as a single remains a mystery. It's not just my favorite PF song – it's one of my favorite records from any group and any musical era. The 1970s may not always have been as carefree and innocent as the song suggests, but for those three minutes you can close your eyes and pretend they really were that wonderful.

How Times Have Changed: Christmas

Both *The Monkees* and *The Partridge Family* aired memorable Christmas shows that are watched every holiday season by fans old and new.

While I believe there is ample justification for looking back on the lives, values and worldview of previous TV generations and regretting what has been lost, it is also true that every generation has felt a similar longing. Evidence of this can be found in many of the stories told by Christmas-themed episodes of classic television shows.

We may be convinced that the Christmas celebrations of 40 or 60 years ago were more reverent and more congenial, and less crass and commercial, but don't tell that to Jim Anderson on *Father Knows Best.* In an episode entitled "The Christmas Story" (1952) Jim is disillusioned by his family's cynicism. "Why can't we have Christmas the way it used to be? Quiet...simple..." Later, he chastises his children for their materialism. "Have you forgotten the meaning of Christmas? Have you forgotten everything you learned at Sunday school?"

Determined to celebrate the holiday right, Jim drags the whole family up to the mountains so they can cut down their own Christmas tree. His plan goes awry when the car gets stuck in a snowdrift, and they are forced to seek shelter in an abandoned fishing lodge.

By episode's end they've all rediscovered the true meaning of Christmas, thanks to a kindly stranger in a white beard – but it's Jim's nostalgic reflections that are most interesting. He'd be in his early 40s in 1952, so his memories of when Christmas was celebrated right would date back almost to the turn of the 20th century. And if there were TV shows back then, I'm sure someone would regret how the holiday has changed since the glory days of the 1870s.

"A Very Merry Christmas," from the first season of *The Donna Reed Show*, aired on Christmas Eve of 1958. The story focuses on Donna's concern that nothing is apparently being planned for the children's ward of the hospital where her husband Alex works. She later discovers that the hospital's janitor, Charlie (played by legendary silent film comedian Buster Keaton) is in charge of the annual Christmas party, which takes place right on schedule.

But earlier in the episode, Donna watches her daughter Mary fret over whether she should buy a gift for one of her friends, since that friend hasn't given her anything yet, and hears her son Jeff complain that he's probably going to lose money on Christmas because he spent more on presents than he's received. She also barely survives a trip to a frenzied department store to buy a last minute gift for one of Alex's co-workers.

"Was Christmas always like this?" she asks Alex. "Christmas should be warm, and friendly, and peaceful." "Christmas hasn't changed," he tells her. "Maybe wrapped up in too many ribbons, but it's still Christmas."

These moments do not negate our nostalgia for Christmas past – but perhaps they reflect how many of us associate our best Christmases with those we experienced in childhood, when we celebrated both the joy of Jesus's birth and the excitement of a visit from Santa Claus, and those colorful boxes that appeared under the tree on Christmas morning as if by magic. Sometimes maturity has its drawbacks.

Shows like these and many others also remind us of holiday traditions that have either been lost, or are endangered of becoming so. Are there still neighborhoods where groups of friends get together and go caroling from door to door? There's a scene featuring this activity on countless shows from *The Adventures of Ozzie & Harriet* to *Wings*.

Television homes decorated for the holiday always show dozens of Christmas cards arrived through the mail and displayed on strings over fireplaces and doorways. Now most people don't bother sending them, or they send e-cards. I appreciate when one arrives because it's the thought that counts, but you can't gather them on the mantle.

And where will children like Cindy Brady go to visit Santa with department stores going under and malls sitting empty? Hopefully the North Pole has Zoom.

Classic shows preserve these traditions, which now seem even more heartwarming at a time when television has mostly lost interest in Christmas-themed episodes. The fear of offending a small but very loud core of professional whiners has made the prospect less palatable. That's not just disappointing because Christmas shows will never again be a treasured memory in collective holiday celebrations – it's regrettable because ignoring the holiday also devalues it. Maybe that was the idea.

What should we take away from this? That how television celebrates Christmas has changed, and there have been actions taken in the name of political correctness that many of us find unsettling. But none of this can or will impact the way we choose to celebrate the holiday. If Christmas today doesn't seem as special as the ones you enjoyed as a child, that's probably as it should be. Just ask Donna Reed.

The Patty Duke Show

1963-1966 (ABC)

105 Episodes

The longer a TV show runs, the greater the temptation to indulge in one of the medium's most time-honored clichés – having one of its stars take on a dual role.

Most of these moments are little more than one-shot gimmicks, but occasionally a series will elevate this dubious set-up into something memorable. Lindsay Wagner did it so well on *The Bionic Woman* as Jaime Sommers and Lisa Galloway that she won the Emmy. And on *Bewitched*, the episodes featuring Elizabeth Montgomery as Samantha and Serena encapsulate the social and generational conflicts of the 1960s. Note the contrast between Sam, the sophisticated New England suburbanite who dresses formal for country club dinners, and her free-spirited, flower child cousin who wouldn't be caught dead with all those stiffs.

But on *The Patty Duke Show*, the dual role was no gimmick. The entire series was built around the concept of identical cousins, both played by a teenage actress who had already earned an Academy Award. Hardly surprising then that Patty Duke was able to create two fully realized characters and keep them both distinct and appealing through 104 episodes.

Patty Lane was the typical teenage girl of her time – boy crazy, rock and roll crazy, hanging out at the local malt shop and talking in slang that mystified her parents.

Cathy, her cousin from Scotland, had traveled the world with her father, a foreign correspondent. Quiet, sophisticated, confused but charmed by the Brooklyn Heights youth culture she found herself in, she admired Patty's free-spirit exuberance even when it landed her in trouble at home or in school.

The show's theme song contains the lyrics "they laugh alike, they walk alike,"- but it won't take long before you find out that's not true. Patty's laugh was large, loud, and open-mouthed, while Cathy would just curl up the corners of her mouth in a demure grin, and bow her head slightly, as if reluctant to show her emotions. And while Patty would burst into a room, Cathy would make a more ladylike entrance, with the poise one might expect from someone who attended European boarding schools.

Through the use of a split screen and a body double, viewers watched Patty and Cathy regularly appear in the same scene and even the same frame. It would not surprise me at all if younger viewers watched an episode having no clue they were seeing one person play two roles. Notice the breakfast table scenes, where Duke makes Cathy left-handed and Patty right-handed, or how natural the conversational rhythm seems when the two characters are talking to each other – after a while you completely forget the novelty of what's happening.

Several stories called for Patty to imitate her cousin Cathy, or vice versa, and the modulation that Duke employs here is astonishing. Just by the way she holds her eyes, or the suggestion of a mannerism that doesn't quite fit, she depicts the character she is playing, and the character her character is trying to play. Even with the sound off, you can always tell what's going on.

Had Duke's virtuosity taken place in a sub-par show it would still be worth our attention. Thankfully, *The Patty Duke Show* also featured William Schallert, the hardest-working man in television's first three decades.

Schallert seemingly turned up in guest spots on dozens of popular series in the 1960s and '70s, playing everything from priests to farmers to folk singers. *The Patty Duke Show* gave him the chance to finally settle into a role for more than one episode; as Patty's father, *New York Chronicle* editor Martin Lane, he finds himself both exasperated by the chaos his exuberant daughter foists on his family, and eager to see what crazy scheme she'll come up with next.

Jean Byron, another familiar face from sitcoms of that era, complements Schallert in a more conventional role as Patty's mother. The Lanes also have a younger son, Ross, played by

Paul O'Keefe. It's hard to figure out what purpose he served on this series, or even if he had one. Just six of the show's 105 episodes focus on Ross. That's a sign that the writers realized the character wasn't working. He seems like an afterthought even among members of his own family.

We can call that a misstep, but it's a minor one in an otherwise marvelous show featuring one (or two) of the very best performances in the classic TV era.

The Best Episodes

"The French Teacher" (1963)

One of the most popular family sitcom stories is the student who develops a crush on a teacher. *The Patty Duke Show* wasted no time getting there – "The French Teacher" was the show's first episode. Patty is failing French ("a moth-eaten drag") until her teacher leaves to get married and is replaced by dashing substitute Andre Malon (Jean-Pierre Aumont). Starry-eyed looks turn to genuine hope after Andre offers to show her Paris if she ever visits. But when Patty starts to make plans for their future, Andre turns to her father for help:

Andre: "I think she wants to marry me!"

Martin: "It would serve you right."

"Patty Pits Wits, Two Brits Hit" (1965)

This episode features a guest appearance from Chad & Jeremy, the British singing duo that rode the Beatlemania wave into several American TV appearances and a handful of hit singles. Here they play Nigel & Patrick, an undiscovered act that Patty helps propel to stardom. It's a show that illustrates how the musical generation gap that started in the 1950s only widened after the British Invasion. "Mindless, monotonous drivel" is how Patty's father describes the then-current music scene. Chad & Jeremy perform two of their best songs, "Yesterday's Gone" and "A Summer Song," plus the equally catchy "The Truth Often Hurts the Heart."

"The Perfect Hostess" (1965)

Two characters? By now that was easy for Patty Duke – so why not add a third one? Here, Duke also plays cousin Betsy, a manipulative Southern Belle who makes a play for Cathy's boyfriend.

"Operation: Tonsils" (1965)

Classic family sitcom plot – Patty has to have her tonsils taken out – meets classic sitcom misunderstanding – she overhears her handsome doctor praising the trim lines and beauty of his new boat, and thinks the compliments are all for her. The doctor is played by one-time matinee idol Troy Donahue.

"Do You Trust Your Daughter?" (1966)

Next to Duke's virtuosity in a dual role, one of this show's greatest joys is the loving relationship between Patty and her "Poppo." "Do You Trust Your Daughter?" opens a rift between them that reminds us how great sitcoms could also produce potent dramatic moments. When Martin realizes he had mistakenly accused Patty of lying, he expresses his *mea culpa* through an oddly beautiful 19th century song called "Keemo-Kimo." Schallert's tender performance and Duke's emotional reaction makes for one of those scenes that justify the love we share for television classics.

How Times Have Changed: Teenage Hangouts

From the Malt Shop to the Mall

The 1950s was a pivotal decade for both television and teenagers. It's when the new electronic medium came of age, as well as when America first saw the emergence of a distinctive youth culture with its own music, clothes and language.

As a result, one cultural trend that can be traced through television is where teenagers liked to hang out with their friends. Our first stop is the malt shop. If you see one in the show you're watching, you know you're safely ensconced in a more benevolent time.

Which one would you visit first? Maybe Marty's Malt Shop, across the street from Madison High School in *Our Miss Brooks*. Hopefully it wasn't something in the concoctions on the menu that made Walter Dennon (Richard Crenna) speak in that ear-splitting falsetto.

New York was home to Charlie Wong's on *The Many Loves of Dobie Gillis*, where Thalia Menninger tried to mold the hapless Dobie into the wealthy man of her dreams. Over in Brooklyn Heights, Patty Lane was hatching another ambitious scheme at the Shake Shop on *The Patty Duke Show*.

When Mary Stone set out to change her wholesome image on *The Donna Reed Show*, she headed to the local malt shop ("The New Look"). And on *The Mickey Mouse Club* serial "Annette," the malt shop was where the kids gathered to rehearse their next school show. Annette Funicello and David Stollery performed a duet that salutes the place they first met:

"We'll drink a double malted, sittin' on a stool
Meetin' at the malt shop, after school"

The malt shop on *The Adventures of Ozzie & Harriet* was located near the college campus, where it was popular both with the students and some of the parents – several episodes had Ozzie stopping by to bring home ice cream.

The first malt shops opened in the 1930s and '40s, so by the 1950s and '60s they already had a retro quality to them. The circular, wrought iron ice cream tables, the jukebox in the corner, the burgers and fries on the menu, and the uniforms worn by the waitresses and soda jerks were introduced before World War II, and were still there when Elvis was drafted.

The most significant change to the malt shop was the one portrayed at Arnold's on early-season episodes of *Happy Days*: the addition of carhops and drive-up access, so teens could stay in their roadsters and listen to Jerry Lee Lewis on the radio while enjoying their burgers and shakes.

This was also the heyday of the drive-in movie, another favorite teen hangout that, unlike malt shops, was still doing business by the 1970s. Gradually, however, most of the drive-ins were shut down, and malt shops were supplanted by national fast food chains with similar menus.

In a 1971 episode of *The Partridge Family* ("Why Did the Music Stop?"), Shirley tries to encourage her performing family to have a "normal" life, and tells Keith and Laurie to "go down to the malt shop, and meet some of your friends."

Keith: "The malt shop?"

Shirley: "Well, wherever young people hang out these days."

Keith: (laughs) "Maybe Andy Hardy will be there, and we can all go over to Polly Benedict's house!"

That's how quickly malt shops became an artifact of times gone by.

For the Partridge kids, the hangout was the local taco stand. For the kids on *The Brady Bunch*, it was the pizza parlor. And if you were lucky enough to live in California or some other coastal state, you also had the beach. *Gidget* (1965-1966) offered an ebullient salute to that thriving surf culture, but sadly this delightful series didn't find an audience until after it was canceled. No one suffered more from this than its top-billed star, Sally Field, who then got stuck on *The Flying Nun* for three seasons.

Disco peaked in the '70s but that was more of an adult scene. Video game arcades? You'll see them pop up in some *ABC Afterschool Specials*, and occasionally in other shows like *Square Pegs*, which aired a 1982 episode called "Pac Man Fever." "Skateboard Wiz" (1978) was a great time-capsule episode of *Wonder Woman* that featured a skateboard competition (and possibly the first look at a half-pipe in scripted TV), and an arcade filled with early video games (Sea Wolf!).

But if the malt shop had a successor as a preferred teen hangout, it had to be the indoor shopping mall. There teens could gather at the food court after school, share a drink at Orange Julius, check out the latest LPs at the record store, and play with the Magnus chord organs until a salesperson came by to shoo them away.

You'll hear malls mentioned a lot in TV shows through the 1980s, but you won't often see them on screen, because to do so would require shooting on location, or building a pretty enormous set.

These days all the malls are starting to close as well, victims of the convenience of online retail and the shuttering of the specialty shops that filled the spaces between the anchor tenants (many of whom are also disappearing).

Where do teenagers hang out now? Coffeehouses, maybe – though back when I was in high school only the more sophisticated or bohemian kids were already drinking coffee.

Perhaps the need for a hangout is also something we can relegate to history. With texting and video chats and social media, a physical place to meet is no longer necessary. Now you can spend time with your friends while scattered throughout your community. Easier, yes. Better?

Perry Mason

1957-1966 (CBS)

271 Episodes

Perry Mason exemplifies how television could once define and idealize a profession to such a profound extent that it transformed the lives of thousands of viewers.

The show inspired many young fans to consider the law as a profession. We'll never know how many cases were tried successfully by men and women who defended the innocent in court because they once saw a gallant man do it on TV. Series star Raymond Burr may have known, as he heard the stories. Burr was frequently in demand to speak before bar associations and other gatherings of attorneys, and experienced the strange phenomenon of someone pretending to do something being idolized by those who actually do it.

It was not the only show to have real-world career impact; *Star Trek* instilled dreams of space flight in hundreds of scientists, astronauts and technicians, many of whom joined NASA. Medical dramas from *Dr. Kildare* to *Marcus Welby, M.D.* to *St. Elsewhere* increased medical school admissions.

But *Perry Mason* may be the most effective testimonial for a single vocation. On this series the attorney isn't a stuffed shirt who spends hours in a law library researching precedent court cases, or a seedy charlatan exploiting a loophole to get a dangerous felon off the hook. He (or she) is a tireless crusader for justice, with a single-minded devotion to the law and the welfare of a client. The stakes: literally life and death. Who wouldn't find such valor appealing?

This wasn't TV's first courtroom drama, though today no one remembers early examples like *Famous Jury Trials* (1949-1952), or *The Amazing Mr. Malone* (1951-1952). But *Perry Mason* was the series that lasted the longest and set the standard for dozens of subsequent legal shows.

Erle Stanley Gardner created the character in a series of novels that sold tens of millions of copies. There were four Perry Mason feature films and a radio series, neither of which the author found appealing. So when the TV series was proposed Gardner was consulted on casting, and chose Raymond Burr over such contenders as Fred MacMurray and Efrem Zimbalist, Jr. Burr, big and burly with a commanding voice, was often cast in villain roles before he began using his imposing figure to break down reluctant witnesses and guilty parties on the witness stand.

Where Joe Friday lived to put bad guys away, Mason lived to save the innocent from the gas chamber. Any trace of a social life is an afterthought. When Mason faced off against Los Angeles District Attorney Hamilton Burger (William Talman), it was like the Harlem Globetrotters playing the

Washington Generals. No TV lawyer had a higher winning percentage – in more than 270 episodes he lost only three cases, albeit with technicalities that later impacted the outcome. According to the book *Cult TV*, the first time Mason apparently lost, CBS received 30,000 letters warning against any more verdicts like that.

You'd think viewers might tire of the formula that pervaded through nine seasons – an innocent client, though one that may still have something to hide; Perry and his investigator Paul Drake (William Hopper) digging into the case, ably assisted by Perry's loyal secretary Della Street (Barbara Hale). When court is in session Perry starts badgering nervous witnesses with "Isn't it true…" questions, as D.A. Burger accuses him of "going on a fishing expedition," or "making another grandstand play for which counsel is so noted."

The result – a startling confession (to everyone but Perry), sometimes from the witness stand, sometimes from the gallery, and amidst the histrionics Mason calmly chalks up another victory.

It just worked. Every time. Viewers not only kept watching, they came back when Raymond Burr returned as Mason in a series of popular TV movies, the last of which aired in 1993, the year Burr passed away.

Perry Mason is another example of a television series from an era when the medium was perceived as not just a source of entertainment, but one capable of contributing to the betterment of society. Aristotle once said the best way to know how to live a moral life is to find the good man, watch him, and imitate him. Once television gave us many such examples to follow. It probably still happens here and there – but with the proliferation of programs and networks and the fracturing of a viewing audience that was already dwindling, it is highly unlikely a series will ever have the same impact on a generation's career aspirations.

The Best Episodes

"The Case of the Moth-Eaten Mink" (1957)

Usually clients come to Perry with their troubles; here, a case begins when Perry and Della are out to dinner and hear gunshots, followed by a waitress fleeing the restaurant and getting hit by a car. One of the more dark and violent cases (there's even gunfire at Mason's office) shot in a film noir style that is even more impressive given the budget limitations on a weekly series. A great case, presented with great craftsmanship.

"The Case of the Fugitive Nurse" (1958)

A woman is accused of murdering her philandering husband – who later turns up alive in Mexico. So who was the murder victim – and did she actually kill him? This episode offers a fine showcase for Ray Collins as Lt. Tragg, who frequently found himself in opposition to Mason's defense of his clients. No cop likes to be told repeatedly that he arrested the wrong person.

"The Case of Constant Doyle" (1963)

In 1962, during season six, Burr was recuperating from surgery, though he still appeared in episodes from a hospital bed (where Mason was recovering from his own medical procedure). Since he couldn't appear in court, cases were litigated by guest actors, in this case Bette Davis as attorney Constant Doyle. With Peggy Ann Garner in the cast as well, this episode features two Academy Award winners. While there is no substitute for Mason's courtroom theatrics, watching Davis grill a witness is almost as satisfying.

"The Case of the Deadly Verdict" (1963)

Janice Barton (Julie Adams) figured she had to be in the clear when Perry agreed to defend her against a charge of murdering her aunt. But the jury disagreed, and Janice is sentenced to die. Perry remains convinced of her innocence, but how can he prove it?

"The Case of the Final Fade-Out" (1966)

This was not a series acclaimed for its comedy, but while there is still some serious business in this, its final episode, there are also inside jokes and meta references presented as a wink to loyal viewers. Perry's client is a television producer accused of murder, and that opens the door to plenty of cracks about the cutthroat entertainment industry. As you look at the background players in each scene keep in mind that you're seeing all of the grips, gaffers, prop men, and electricians who had worked behind the scenes on the series. And the judge in the case is played by Perry Mason creator Erle Stanley Gardner.

Rocky & Bullwinkle

1959-1964 (ABC/NBC)

163 Episodes

If you're under 50, you probably believe *The Simpsons* is the most sophisticated, subversive and hilarious animated series ever created. If you are over 50, that distinction still belongs to *The Bullwinkle Show*, aka *Rocky and His Friends*, aka *Rocky & Bullwinkle*.

Its attention to show titles may have been as haphazard as the quality of its animation, but satire and silliness have rarely coexisted so brilliantly as they did in the adventures of one plucky squirrel and one dimwitted moose.

The series didn't get much attention when it debuted in 1959, the same year as *Bonanza, The Many Loves of Dobie Gillis* and *The Twilight Zone*. But like *Star Trek* it found its audience after being canceled, and remained a television staple for the next four decades.

Created by Jay Ward and Bill Scott (Scott also provided Bullwinkle's voice), *Rocky and His Friends* would raise bad puns to an art form and would turn obscure historical and political references into punch lines long before Dennis Miller anchored *Saturday Night Live*'s Weekend Update.

Ward assembled an all-star team of guys used to being the smartest person in every room they entered – Chris Hayward, Chris Jenkins, George Atkins, Al Burns, Lloyd Turner – and they wrote jokes more for themselves than the kids in the audience. How many 7-year-olds would laugh when Boris Badenov's boss, Fearless Leader, was described as "Pottsylvania's answer to Bernard Baruch?" But the parents were laughing.

Today, maybe the grandparents laugh. The parents probably don't get it either.

I once had the pleasure of interviewing Jay Ward's daughter Ramona, who told me that her father thought that, "children need to come forward, and the show should not talk down to them." That was a belief shared by every titan of children's entertainment, from Dr. Seuss to Fred Rogers.

The Genius of Wossamotta U

You can watch any of the serial-style adventures of Rocky and Bullwinkle and understand what made the show a classic. But the story of Wossamotta U best exemplifies the series' perfect blend of sophistication, silliness and social commentary.

The tale begins when the regents of financially strapped Wossamotta University vote to increase revenues by "recruiting the best football team money can buy."

"How will we pay for it?" asks one administrator.

"How else?" replies his colleague, "We'll fire a few English teachers."

Bullwinkle is recruited and given the standard course load for a football player on scholarship, which includes a class in crochet and reading *Dick and Jane at the Seashore*. When the coach tells quarterback Bullwinkle, "Let's see you throw one," Bullwinkle replies, "Throw a game already? I haven't even practiced yet!"

Boris and Natasha turn up with plans to clean up by gambling on Wossamotta games. When the money starts rolling in from the football program, the professors make plans to buy new books and lab equipment, but instead the funds are spent on an indoor baseball diamond and a new home for the football coach.

For the final game of the season, between Wossamotta and Boris's team, the Mud City Manglers, Boris borrows his game plan from the Civil War. He is then accosted by a representative from the "League of Confederate Corrections," who insists the Civil War be referred to as "The War Between the States." Rocky and Bullwinkle take on the absurdities of political correctness, decades before the term was even coined.

While paying homage to the writers, I should also mention the enormous contributions made to these shorts by William Conrad's intense narration ("When our last episode was switched off in utter disgust by 37 million viewers...") and June Foray, who voiced both Rocky and Natasha.

A best episodes list doesn't quite fit for this series, so instead here are five other classic moments from the Jay Ward canon.

A Promo Generates Public Outrage

At the end of one program, Bullwinkle tells the kids of America to pull the knobs off their TV sets, so they couldn't change channels "and that way we'll be sure to be with you next week." The following week, Bullwinkle had to tell the 20,000 kids who did so to glue the knobs back on.

Fractured Fairy Tales: Sleeping Beauty-land

This series added satiric twists to famous bedtime stories. When they tackled Sleeping Beauty, the handsome prince, who happens to look a lot like Walt Disney, has second thoughts about waking his true love with a kiss. Instead, he turns her into the main attraction at the Sleeping Beauty-land theme park. "Disney loved it," said Mrs. Ward.

Moosylvania

In this clever and insightful send-up of government bureaucracy, Bullwinkle campaigns for Moosylvania statehood. When the government declares the region a disaster area, it offers to provide assistance. The first airlift consists of helium, maple syrup and bubblegum.

Peabody and Sherman: William Shakespeare

The puns and wordplay in the time-traveling Peabody shorts were hard to top. When the WABAC machine brings Sherman and Peabody to Stratford-on-Avon, they find Sir Francis Bacon accusing Shakespeare of stealing his plays. When he clobbers Will with a flower pot, Shakespeare angrily yells, "Bacon! You'll fry for this!"

The Lawsuit That Wasn't

Durward Kirby, a popular 1950s television personality, threatened to sue Jay Ward over a story in which Rocky and Bullwinkle search for a hat known as the "Kerward Derby." Ward responded in the press by saying, "Oh, that would be wonderful. Sue us fast because we need the publicity." That was the end of the lawsuit.

I started this piece by splitting the generations between those who love Bullwinkle and those who love *The Simpsons*. Obviously it's possible to love them both; *Simpsons* creator Matt Groening does. Homer Simpson's middle initial, J, is a tribute to Jay Ward.

How Times Have Changed: Commercials

You probably still remember a lot of TV commercials from back in the day, even if you haven't watched them in decades.

"From the valley of the Jolly (ho, ho, ho) Green Giant"

"Here's to good friends, tonight is kind of special…"

"There's a fragrance that's here today and they call it…Charlie"

"Sometimes you feel like a nut…sometimes you don't"

Why is that?

We know why the shows were memorable – we looked forward to watching them and they made us happy. Many of us now own our favorites on DVD and they remain as close as our bookshelves.

But those old commercials stopped airing decades ago and you can't see them anywhere now except YouTube. With few exceptions we didn't enjoy them – they were annoying interruptions, or bathroom break opportunities.

Sure, a few were genuinely entertaining – for me the series of Lite Beer ads with Rodney Dangerfield, Bob Uecker and a host of celebrities and athletes were always fun to watch. And the Polaroid camera ads that teamed James Garner with Mariette Hartley were sometimes more enjoyable than the shows they sponsored.

But I still remember countless individual commercials that had nothing remarkable about them: Ads for Pepsi showcasing the active and fun-loving lifestyle of the Pepsi Generation; A commercial for the game Connect Four where a sister wins with a diagonal lineup of pieces, and the brother responds, "Pretty sneaky, sis" before spilling all the pieces across the table. A mother in Boston yelling "Anthony!" out her kitchen window, and little Anthony running home because Wednesday is Prince Spaghetti day.

Repetition had something to do why they stuck with us. No one was keeping count but I'd estimate that those like me who watched a lot of television were exposed to the same commercials dozens, if not hundreds of times. They were bound to sink into our psyches sooner or later.

Commercials also used music to break through our barriers, a phenomenon that the geniuses behind *Schoolhouse Rock* harnessed for the noble aim of education, instead of the mercenary quest to sell snow tires. If you are really bored one day, take out a piece of paper and try to list all of the jingles from the 1960s onward that have taken permanent residence in your head.

"Hold the pickle, hold the lettuce, special orders don't upset us..."

"I'm a Pepper, he's a Pepper, she's a Pepper..."

"When it says Libby's Libby's Libby's on the label, label, label..."

I have one more theory about why older commercials have such staying power. They were better than commercials are now.

By "better" I don't mean they were works of art – some were dull and many tried to be funny and failed miserably. But for the most part they behaved themselves as guests in your home. They didn't scream to get your attention. They wouldn't upset the appetite of anyone eating in front of the television. They didn't contain content that had to be muted if there were children in the room.

They also, by and large, shared the values of the television shows during which they appeared. You could laugh at the "Time to make the donuts" guy as he trudged out of his home before sunrise to beat the morning crowds at Dunkin Donuts – but you also had to admire his work ethic. Same with the truck drivers and loggers and oil men who put in a tough eight hours before they could say "Now, it's Miller time."

Women took pride in keeping a clean house and cooking good dinners for their families. And they were not looked down upon for doing so, any more than a woman who chose to pursue a career outside the home deserved criticism for her decision.

A phone call from an old friend or distant family member was something special. Families could take their kids to McDonald's or another fast food eatery without being rebuked for choosing a burger over a tofu kale salad. Gas stations had attendants who would fill your tank, clean your windshield and check your oil.

Sometimes watching these ads now is a bittersweet experience, as we view once prominent businesses proudly promoting themselves in their glory days: Sears, Montgomery Ward, Toys 'R' Us, Kinney Shoes, B. Dalton Booksellers, and too many more to mention.

Commercials now have changed in two significant ways. First, there's now more text on the screen. As advertisers know most viewers now mute or fast-forward these spots, it's an attempt to get their message through these obstacles.

The other difference is that sometimes selling something isn't the point.

The primary purpose of every commercial used to be to promote the benefits of one brand over another. Now, the objective is to be funny, or titillating, or outrageous enough to get people talking or achieve the ultimate dream of going viral. If that happens, the hope is brand messaging will take care of itself.

This is especially noticeable during the Super Bowl, the Olympics of television advertising. You can sense the desperation from the modern day Mad Men, aware that their client has paid $4 million for 30 seconds of TV time that most viewers will likely ignore. They offer us supermodels and pop stars, chimpanzees in business suits and slapstick comedy. Whatever product is being sold, the real message is exactly the same; Please, for the love of all that's holy, *notice me*.

Let's see how well this strategy worked by how many people can recall those high-priced ads 20 years from now. If I had to guess, I think there will still be more people who remember the Pillsbury Doughboy.

Sci-Fi Cautionary Tales: The Outer Limits/The Twilight Zone

The Outer Limits	The Twilight Zone
1963-1965 (ABC)	1959-1964 (CBS)
49 Episodes	156 Episodes

Science fiction offers a vision of what our future may hold. Horror brings our worst nightmares to life. When the two genres merge, the result is particularly unsettling. Think you've got problems now? Wait until the alien invaders and evil robots get here.

The Twilight Zone told all kinds of stories in its five-year run, and told them well enough to be lauded as one of the medium's crown jewels. But when you think back on its greatest moments, the stories that still haunt the recesses of your memory years after you last watched them, many will likely fit into that sci-fi/horror hybrid. Think "To Serve Man," or "The Hitch-Hiker."

The Outer Limits had a more narrow focus. With the exception of one episode created as a failed pilot for a different series ("Controlled Experiment"), this show wasn't interested in whimsical fantasy tales. Serious writers and serious actors told serious stories that struggled not to be undercut by silly alien costumes and primitive special effects.

If there's a reason why these sci-fi tales so often contained elements of horror as well, it's because this was the one genre where the first generation of TV writers and producers explored the real-world issues that kept viewers up at night.

Sitcoms and variety shows, whether by chance or network edict, provided an escape from life's troubles. Westerns looked back on a historic era with a different array of dangers. Police and detective shows dramatized threats that were serious, but had already been factored into the acceptable risk of life in a big city. So it was left to science fiction to confront calamities that ranged from the perilous to the unthinkable.

Nuclear war topped that grim list: *The Twilight Zone* debuted just 14 years after the atomic bomb exploded on Hiroshima, and the Cold War of the 1950s deepened fears that Russia might one day drop the big one. That scenario found its way into *TZ* episodes such as "The Shelter," "Third from the Sun," and "Time Enough at Last."

And if the Soviet Union wasn't going to obliterate us, they might settle for conquest and subjugation under merciless totalitarian rule. The sci-fi version cast aliens in the role of the Red Army in such *Outer Limits* episodes as "O.B.I.T."

Or maybe we'd destroy ourselves, through disease or radiation that decimates our food supply and renders the planet uninhabitable, as shown in "The Man Who Was Never

Born" (*The Outer Limits*) and "I Shot an Arrow Into the Air" (*Twilight Zone*).

As more electronic conveniences made their way into the marketplace, some speculated about the risk in creating machines to replace humans, dramatized in the *Twilight Zone* by "The Lateness of the Hour."

And there was always concern over what monstrosities might be created by unfettered or careless science, as Mary Shelley described in *Frankenstein*. It's dramatized in *Outer Limits* episodes like "The Architects of Fear" and "The Sixth Finger."

Many of these concerns are still with us. That, plus the high quality of the writing on these shows, has kept these cautionary tales as cogent as any type of series from this era.

Will they prove accurate in their predictions? Who knows – but we can take some consolation in the knowledge that many of the calamities predicated in 1950s and '60s sci-fi were supposed to have occurred by now. If we're lucky they'll be like the experimental cars on display every year at the Auto Show – always promising to be here soon, but never actually becoming a reality.

The Best Episodes

The Outer Limits

"The Man Who Was Never Born" (1963)

What William Shatner was to *The Twilight Zone*, Martin Landau was to *The Outer Limits*: when you see his name in the credits, you know the episode is going to be a good one. Here, he plays a being from the future that travels back to earth's past to change history before a biological disaster is unleashed. It's a variation on the old "kill Hitler before he grows up" proposition, and you know those never actually work – but the climax will likely still surprise you.

"The Zanti Misfits" (1963)

A bug-like alien species forces the U.S. to turn over part of Arizona for use as a penal colony. That's where we're at when this one opens, as a bank robber with some serious issues (played by Bruce Dern) accidentally breaks into the facility, causing a jailbreak that pits the Zanti criminals against the American military. It sounds like any grade-B monster flick, but the show ends with one of the series' best ironic twist endings.

"The Bellero Shield" (1964)

Arguably the series' best show, "The Bellero Shield" has been described as a science-fiction twist on Shakespeare's *Macbeth*. Martin Landau plays a scientist conducting laser experiments, who unexpectedly contacts an alien being that can project an impenetrable shield. Landau's wife, played by Sally

Kellerman, covets the power of that shield and will do whatever it takes to acquire it.

"Demon with a Glass Hand" (1964)

Harlan Ellison wrote this dark tale that defies easy description. Robert Culp plays a man with no memory and a talking glass hand that is missing a few fingers. He hopes to clear up the mystery of who he is by acquiring those missing fingers, but the people who have them are trying to kill him. This is sci-fi with a film noir style, where shadows and light set an inescapable mood of foreboding.

"I, Robot" (1964)

A robot is put on trial for murder, making for the kind of courtroom drama you'd never see on *Perry Mason*. Since this episode aired more than 50 years ago, we've turned even more of our lives over to technology, and are just beginning to realize what may be lost in the process.

The Twilight Zone

"Time Enough at Last" (1959)

Many *TZ* episodes end their stories with a twist that you (hopefully) didn't see coming. Of these episodes "Time Enough at Last" is the most famous – Burgess Meredith plays a meek bank teller who always wishes he had more time to read. He finally gets his wish, but then…

"22" (1961)

This Rod Serling-scripted episode can still scare the heck out of first-time viewers. Barbara Nichols plays a dancer hospitalized for fatigue. During her stay she is traumatized by a recurring nightmare, in which she follows a shadowy figure down to the hospital basement, where the morgue is located. Just as she approaches the entrance a severe looking nurse appears and says, "Room for one more, honey." But is it just a dream?

"Five Characters in Search of an Exit" (1961)

"Clown, hobo, ballet dancer, bagpiper, and an army major. Five improbable entities stuck together into a pit of darkness." Thus begins one of the series' most brilliant and surreal episodes. William Windom plays the soldier, whose emotional "We're in hell" speech offers one possible explanation for their plight – but not the correct one.

"Living Doll" (1963)

Telly Savales plays the abusive stepfather to a little girl who has a doll named Talky Tina. And Tina did not like Telly. If you haven't seen it but are familiar with the *Child's*

Play movies, you probably have some idea where the story went. Savales's heightened desperation, an ominous Bernard Herrmann score and the voice of June Foray as Tina create an escalating mood of tension that plays with the viewer's loyalties. We enjoy watching the mean old stepdad get his, but the zinger at the end of the episode suggests that Tina may have already chosen her next victim.

"Nightmare at 20,000 Feet (1963)

A nervous airline passenger (William Shatner), recently released from a sanitarium, thinks he's spotted a "gremlin" on the wing of the plane. No one else sees it or believes him. He takes drastic action to save the plane, and for his troubles is carried off in a straitjacket. Rod Serling's closing narration reassures viewers that his allegations won't be doubted much longer.

Sidebar: Wisdom from Willoughby

Classic television shows can serve a higher purpose beyond the entertainment derived from them. Like any work of art worthy of our respect, they have something to teach us as well.

During its five seasons, *The Twilight Zone* presented dozens of issue-oriented stories, including some effective but occasionally heavy-handed allegories about war, racism and intolerance. For me it was the subtler stories that struck a deeper chord, none more so than "A Stop at Willoughby."

Fade up on Gart Williams, a media buyer in New York, sitting amongst other executives in a boardroom, anxiously tapping a pencil. He has just lost a major account, much to the chagrin of his oppressive boss: "This is a push-push-push business, Williams, all the way, all the time."

Gart leaves the office on the verge of a nervous breakdown that's been building for years. Headed home he falls asleep on the train, but when he wakes he finds himself on a 19th century rail coach. The snowy November evening has been replaced by bright summer sunshine, as the train stops at an idyllic small town called Willoughby, circa 1888. Gart wakes up, and dismisses the episode as a dream.

At home his pressures do not subside. "I'm tired, Janie. Tired and sick," he says to his unsympathetic wife, who coldly ponders how she could have married such an over-sensitive loser.

Back at work, the stress resumes unabated – angry clients, constantly ringing phones. The next night, he once again hears the conductor call "Next stop, Willoughby." This time, he gets off the train.

This being *The Twilight Zone*, there's that usually crushing twist at the end. I'll avoid spoilers for anyone who somehow missed this episode during the last 60 years.

In 25 minutes, "A Stop at Willoughby" paints a complete and perfectly rendered portrait of a man who spent the better part of his life doing something for which he had neither affinity nor desire. He sublimated his true self to pursue a lifestyle that was never important to him, to achieve prosperity that brought no satisfaction. Now he's at the end of his tether and willing to grasp at any lifeline, no matter how fantastic.

I can't prove it but I am certain that when this show first aired, someone living Gart Williams' life for real decided to hop off the self-destructive carousel, and to start spending more time doing what he or she loved. Hopefully, after a half-century of syndication and videocassette and DVD releases, many others have been similarly inspired to recalibrate their priorities.

The demands on Gart Williams' time were stifling to him – and this was in 1960! How much faster is life moving now?

How many more electronic devices are commanding our attention, not only in the office but at home and in the car and even when we're supposed to be with our friends and families?

If anything, the lesson of "A Stop at Willoughby" is needed now more than ever: We are more than our jobs, or at least we are supposed to be. And if the world insists on moving at a certain speed, we don't always have to keep up with it. It's a lesson we are never too young or too old to learn.

Star Trek

1966-1969 (NBC)

79 Episodes

The previous chapter looked at shows that warned of a potentially bleak future. *Star Trek* offered a more optimistic forecast.

We are told the 23rd century is a post-scarcity environment. Everyone has enough food to eat, energy to heat their homes, and whatever else is needed for a comfortable life. And the earth finally eliminated poverty and intolerance and lots of other sins.

How? The series skipped over that part.

Creator Gene Roddenberry just assumed that in another few hundred years we would have decided that these things are wrong and will transform our society accordingly. In that sentiment he is not unlike politicians who promise to bring about the same modern day Eden, with plans that are short on specifics, except for how they will raise your taxes.

More gratifying, and thankfully much closer to our present reality, is the casual nature with which Roddenberry presented men and women of different races and cultures working alongside each other in professional positions. It was a bold move at the time – and one rendered more effective by not calling attention to it. Contrast that with too many current shows that constantly pat themselves on the back for achieving an enlightenment that most of us figured out decades ago.

Star Trek's place in television history is a unique one. It is TV's first cult show, and the first to become more popular after it was canceled. Constant reruns and fan gatherings that evolved into conventions further elevated its pop culture profile. It has added expressions to our language, created futuristic technology that has since become reality, and inspired the name of a U.S. space shuttle.

The conventions have come in for some mocking among non-converts, as well as from series star William Shatner in a now famous *Saturday Night Live* sketch, when he told fans to "get a life." But if you ever attended one you'd meet a diverse assortment of kind and imaginative people, with a higher combined IQ level than at most public gatherings. This was taking the concept of television bringing us together to the next level. Not content to discuss the latest episode at school or work the next day, *Star Trek* fans wanted to meet more people who shared their enthusiasm, and convey their appreciation to the show's cast and creative team, who eagerly obliged.

Star Trek could have disappeared after three seasons and less than 80 episodes. Instead, it inspired six movie adaptations featuring the original crew, plus six spinoff series, totaling more than 650 episodes of mostly fine television. No other series can match that legacy - or likely ever will.

The Best Episodes

Balance of Terror (1966)

This episode introduced the Romulans, who played a prominent role in the 2020 revival *Star Trek: Picard*. Inspired by World War II-era submarine films, the story pits the battle strategy of Captain James Kirk (William Shatner) against a Romulan commander played by Mark Lenard, who returned to the Trek universe in a recurring role as Spock's father.

Space Seed (1967)

Kirk and company beam aboard a derelict spaceship, the Botany Bay, and discover a crew of genetically enhanced humans led by Khan Noonian Singh, (Ricardo Montalban) who use their superior strength and intellect to take over the Enterprise. Montalban played Khan again in *Star Trek II*, and it's easy to see why the film looked back to this memorable show for inspiration.

The City on the Edge of Forever (1967)

It's not quite unanimous but most Trekkers consider this to be the series' finest hour. Kirk and Spock (Leonard Nimoy) travel back in time to America in the 1930s, where Kirk falls in love with social worker Edith Keeler (Joan Collins). You probably know the rest, but if you don't it's worth discovering without spoilers. Harlan Ellison wrote the episode, though in typical Ellison fashion he later disavowed the script.

Amok Time (1967)

The Enterprise brings Spock home to Vulcan, in an episode that establishes much of what we know about his culture, and what happens when logic is upended by the ritual of Pon Farr. The battle "to the death" of Kirk and Spock presents a no-win situation, and the smile on Spock's face at the climax is as fondly remembered a moment as the series ever produced.

The Trouble with Tribbles (1967)

Not profound, not philosophical, just a lot of fun. The Enterprise is invaded by a species of furballs that multiply rapidly. A few humorless Trekkers are not amused, but most fans love this show.

How Times Have Changed: Religion

One of the ways the future as depicted in *Star Trek* is better than our present, at least according to Gene Roddenberry, is that mankind had finally gotten over its need for religion.

Since the officers in Starfleet value tolerance, they always show respect for alien cultures that maintain some belief system. But that deference masks a barely concealed smugness, sort of like how we go to the zoo and think it's cute how the bears still eat with their paws.

What kicked God to the curb in the 23rd century? It's suggested here and there that dispatching with religion was beneficial because it separated people into different tribes with opposing views, and disputes over belief instigated violent conflict and war.

While history is indeed rife with religious conflict, it's also true that most of these skirmishes occurred between the 13th and 16th centuries. And we now have data on what happens as we head in the opposite direction, as the move toward secularization is well underway, at least in the United States and Europe. The previous century has been the most secular since mankind stood upright. Was it less violent? Sure, if you don't count World War I, World War II, the Korean conflict,

Vietnam, Germany under Hitler, Russia under Stalin, the Killing Fields of Cambodia, China under Mao – total casualties close to 200 million, at least half of which occurred in places where religion was outlawed. That's not a number you'll spot on any Humanist Association billboard.

Star Trek also suggested that science has supplanted superstition, and answered all the big questions so there's no longer any need for God. That view is referred to as scientism, and it's astounding how commonplace it remains. Especially when one considers how many of the most revered scientists in history were Christians, from Isaac Newton, who formulated the laws of motion and universal gravitation, to Francis Collins, who mapped the human genome.

This is not the place for a full exploration of this, but those interested can find plenty of additional resources online. I would recommend the YouTube videos of Bishop Robert Barron as a great place to start.

Let's leave the 23rd century and return to the 20th, when the shows from the 1950s through the 1970s viewed religion as a prominent aspect of American life. That didn't mean the characters in family sitcoms and dramas were always shown in church or in prayer, but it happened enough for viewers to recognize that they practiced their faith, and that it helped to shape their personal character and their worldview.

It shouldn't take anyone long to recall examples of this:

"Thanksgiving Day" (*Father Knows Best*, 1954)

"The Good Guys and the Bad Guys" (*The Donna Reed Show*, 1961)

"Man in a Hurry" (*The Andy Griffith Show*, 1963)

"Buddy Sorrell Man and Boy" (*The Dick Van Dyke Show*, 1966)

"The Voice of Christmas" (*The Brady Bunch*, 1969)

"The Red Woodloe Story" (*The Partridge Family*, 1971)

"A Funny Thing Happened on the Way to the Vatican" (*Bridget Loves Bernie*, 1972)

"Fonzie's Baptism" (*Happy Days*, 1977)

…and many more. Now? At least have *The Simpsons*.

I don't think religious references or participation have been dropped from most contemporary TV shows because everyone in television production is a godless heathen (okay, maybe at Netflix). The motivation here is more to avoid offending those of a different faith or no faith, and insulate the series from accusations of proselytizing.

Was that the motivation of the older shows? It would be silly to even suggest it. I've never met anyone who converted or switched from agnostic to believer because Carol Brady sang "O Come, All Ye Faithful."

At a time in television when diversity is paramount and lack of inclusion has become the unforgiveable sin, it's sad but perhaps not surprising that for believers, there is still no room at the inn.

The Superheroes: Superman/Batman/Wonder Woman

The Adventures of Superman	Batman	Wonder Woman
1952-1958	*1966-1968 (ABC)*	*1975-1979*
(Syndicated)	*120 Episodes*	*(ABC/CBS)*
104 Episodes		*59 Episodes*

For comic book fans, this is a golden age – not related to the comics themselves, which face the same awkward transition to digital media that have cost newspapers and magazines countless subscribers – but in the ascension of their most iconic characters into motion pictures that have dominated the global box office for 20 years.

Two factors triggered the renaissance in the comic book movie genre; the source material was taken more seriously, and CGI finally caught up to the types of superhero exploits fans expect to see from larger-than-life characters.

The appeal of these champions inspired several earlier attempts to bring them to life, with mixed results. The three most memorable were *The Adventures of Superman*, *Batman*, and *Wonder Woman*.

Superman came first, as he did in the comics. After a popular radio series in 1940s, the Man of Steel debuted on television with George Reeves as Clark Kent/Superman, Jack Larson as Jimmy Olsen, and Phyllis Coates (and later Noel Neill) as Lois Lane.

The first season was played fairly straight, with some surprisingly violent and vicious criminal activity foiled by Superman. Subsequent seasons were tailored more to the show's youngest fans, with more comedy, less genuine suspense, and silly supporting characters like Professor Pepperwinkle. Superman became part boy scout, part Santa Claus, part surrogate parent to the city of Metropolis.

The change was beneficial for George Reeves, who could project innate kindness and warmth with an effortless charm. For the first generation of TV fans he *was* Superman, just as Christopher Reeve will always be for me.

Batman was the dark, grim contrast to Superman's all-American hero, and that quality was best captured in the three Christopher Nolan 'Dark Knight' films starring Christian Bale. They're impressive, no doubt, and they have bestowed a gravitas on the superhero film genre that had not taken hold even after the successes of the X-Men and Spider-Man franchises. But as the end credits rolled on *The Dark Knight Rises*, I was more exhausted than entertained.

Shouldn't watching Batman make you happy? If not, what's the point?

Watching the *Batman* series (1966-1968) always makes me happy. It's like someone put The Lone Ranger, Rocky &

Bullwinkle and *Rowan & Martin's Laugh-In* into a blender and hit the puree button. That "someone" was executive producer William Dozier, who masterminded this eccentric superhero serial and also provided the breathless narration for each episode ("Same Bat-time, same Bat-channel!")

Adam West rarely receives sufficient acclaim for his ability to don blue tights and deliver lines like "Riddler, you can't buy friends with money," in a monotone that rivaled Joe Friday's. His underplaying was perfectly balanced by Burt Ward's high-spirited enthusiasm and the flamboyant antics of Gotham City's assorted evildoers.

It's a series with enduring appeal to all ages, though not for the same reasons. Kids love the action-packed fight scenes punctuated by comic book panel POWs and BAMs, the brass-driven theme song and the rogues' gallery. Older fans will appreciate Adam West's aforementioned deadpan line readings ("Let's go, Robin. We've set another youth on the road to a brighter tomorrow") and the satiric references to everything from politics to pop culture.

When I recall the show now, my first memory is of bright, bright colors. The animated opening credits sequence, the silky midnight blues of Batman's cape, the reds and yellows in Robin's costume, The Riddler's bright green tights and The Joker's hot pink suit, Batgirl's red hair and the rich hues of the library at stately Wayne Manor – they all seemed to pop off the screen so much more vividly than other color TV shows of that era.

Like many overnight sensations it fizzled out as fast as it became a phenomenon, but sixty-some years into the TV medium and it's still hard to find another show as unique as this unapologetically camp take on one of the comics' most dour superheroes.

When you consider how many false starts plagued DC's Wonder Woman revival until Patty Jenkins and Gal Gadot nailed it, you have to marvel at Lynda Carter's ability to personify that character and make it seem effortless.

She appeared to have stepped right out of the pages of the comic – and that is just how she's introduced in the series' opening credits. But the success of her portrayal goes far beyond her obvious statuesque beauty and physical assets.

Wonder Woman is an outsider from paradise forced to not only cope with a more hostile modern world, but to serve as its protector. Carter tapped into the character's compassion, her puzzlement at the dishonesty and casual cruelty that surrounds her, and her sometimes-childlike optimism in a better future for a deeply flawed world.

Sadly, the show itself rarely reached the heights of Carter's portrayal. Wonder Woman rarely faced any of her comic book adversaries, and her super heroics were largely limited to running fast, jumping over fences and bending the barrels of guns.

The series' supporting cast provided no actual support. As co-worker/love interest/perennial kidnap victim Steve Trevor, Lyle Waggoner looked dashing in his military uniform, but that was about it. No one else stuck around long enough to make an impression.

The series' first season, set during World War II, is slightly better than the final two years, but whether Wonder Woman was battling killer gorillas, mad scientists, kid psychics or evil geniuses that hypnotize government agents with disco music (yes, that's an actual episode), Lynda Carter always maintained her grace and dignity. As super heroic achievements go, that's the real wonder.

The Best Episodes

The Adventures of Superman

"Superman on Earth" (1952)

The first series episode recounts the well-known story of Superman's origin – the dying planet Krypton, Jor-El and Lara launching baby Kal-El to earth, where the child is adopted by the Kents of Smallville. Clark grows up, moves to Metropolis, and uses his powers for truth, justice and the American way. Richard Fielding's script remains refreshingly faithful to the comic book, and is all the better for it.

"Crime Wave" (1953)

In this gritty, action-packed episode, Superman pledges to cleanse Metropolis of organized crime. His crusade is threatened when a top mob boss discovers his secret identity. George Reeves plays the angry scourge of the underworld with conviction.

"Panic In the Sky" (1953)

Superman tries to stop a meteor from crashing into Metropolis, but the meteor is filled with Kryptonite. Superman crash-lands on earth, suffering from amnesia. As the meteor drifts closer, the world wonders where Superman has gone. Anyone who wonders why series fans treasure the episodes written by Jackson Gillis, look no further than this superb sci-fi adventure.

"Around the World with Superman" (1954)

A little girl is blinded in a car accident, and her father, guilt-ridden over the crash, deserts his family. Superman uses his x-ray vision to locate fragments of glass in the girl's optic nerve, and helps surgeons restore her sight. He then sweeps her in his arms and flies her around the world. The rear-projected shots of the Eiffel Tower and the Himalayas may not be state-of-the-art, but the emotional impact of these moments is undiminished.

"Jimmy the Kid" (1956)

This episode was a great showcase for Jack Larson, who plays both Jimmy Olsen and a lookalike thug known as Kid Collins. Collins is hired to retrieve incriminating evidence against a Metropolis crime lord hidden in Clark Kent's safe. He breaks into Kent's apartment, opens the safe, and finds Clark's Superman costume. Larson was so good in the dual role that fans often asked him where they found another actor to play his evil twin.

Batman

"Hi Diddle Diddle/Smack in the Middle" (1966)

The pilot introduced the series' most popular villain, The Riddler. Frank Gorshin earned an Emmy nomination for his inspired portrayal, which was influenced by Richard Widmark in *Kiss of Death* and the staccato tough-guy moves of James Cagney. This episode also featured the famous "Bat-dance" sequence at the What a Way to Go-Go discotheque.

"True or False Face/Holy Rat Race" (1966)

Probably the series' best episode, and the only one to give an indication of whether this cast could have played the material straight and still make it work. The camp content is dialed back in favor of action and a particularly slippery villain (played by veteran TV heavy Malachi Throne).

"Hot Off the Griddle/The Cat and the Fiddle" (1966)

This is my favorite of the many outstanding Catwoman stories written by Stanley Ralph Ross and featuring the wonderfully droll Julie Newmar. The cliffhanger finds the Dynamic Duo covered in margarine and tied to griddles under giant magnifying glasses, where they are to be cooked by the sun. "Holy oleo!" exclaims Robin, to whom Catwoman replies, "I didn't know you could yodel."

"A Piece of the Action/Batman's Satisfaction" (1967)

Not a great story, but it's a must-see for the showdown between Batman and Robin and visiting heroes the Green Hornet (Van Williams) and Kato (Bruce Lee). The story goes that Lee refused to lose the fight, script or no script, and there's no question the intensity of the dueling masked heroes is amplified during their standoff.

"The Sport of Penguins/A Horse of Another Color" (1967)

The Batgirl shows of season three were a mixed blessing. Usually they meant a dumber-than-usual story or a lame villain like Milton Berle's Louie the Lilac. But there was also the unforgettable vision of former Ballet Russe dancer Yvonne Craig high-kicking her way through a fight until she is inevitably captured by the evildoer of the week. This was the best of her adventures, as The Penguin (Burgess

Meredith) concocts a horseracing hoax assisted by heiress Lola Lasagna (Ethel Merman).

Wonder Woman

"The New, Original Wonder Woman" (1975)

As in *The Adventures of Superman*, Wonder Woman launched with a refreshingly faithful origin story, marred only by limitations in how a hero's super abilities could be expressed. Where Gal Gadot could convincingly take down squadrons of German troops on a muddy battlefield, Lynda Carter struggled to subdue German spy Stella Stevens.

"The Feminum Mystique, Pts. 1 & 2" (1976)

Wonder Woman returns to Paradise Island to repel a Nazi invasion, with the help of her sister Drusilla, aka Wonder Girl, played by future Oscar-winner Debra Winger.

"The Bushwhackers" (1977)

Wonder Woman takes down a gang of cattle rustlers with the help of legendary cowboy Roy Rogers. That's good enough for me.

"Screaming Javelins" (1978)

Classic? No. Fascinating in its strangeness? Absolutely. Diminutive, mild-mannered Henry Gibson, garbed in a shiny purple jumpsuit, plays the ruler of a tiny island nation, who kidnaps the world's top athletes and blackmails them into competing under his flag at the Olympics. The episode also featured Melanie Chartoff as a Russian gymnast and Rick Springfield as her boyfriend. Gibson's take on Marion Mariposa must be seen to be believed – he's like some twisted offspring of Liberace and Julian Assange.

"Amazon Hot Wax" (1979)

Diana Prince goes undercover to expose a music-extortion ring. This show is well remembered for Lynda Carter's performance of "Toto (Don't It Feel Like Paradise"). Unlike many TV stars that try to parlay that fame into a singing career (and probably shouldn't), Carter really could sing.

How Times Have Changed: Saturday Mornings

In the classic TV era there were patterns of life shared by millions of Americans. Some of them were created by television. The nightly news was on at 6pm; football owned Monday nights come September; and Saturday mornings were for kids.

From the late 1960s through the early 1990s, the national networks devoted their Saturday morning blocs to a mix of cartoons and live-action children's programming. If this is when you grew up, you have a happy shared memory of plopping down on the floor in front of the television, devouring a bowl of sugar-coated cereal, and staying in your pajamas until 11am or later, until it was time to go outside and play.

Were the shows good? Some of them were. But most were derivative and few lasted beyond one season.

Among the staples were series about anthropomorphic animals (*Yogi Bear, Magilla Gorilla, The Pink Panther*), cartoon versions of prime time hits (*Happy Days, Laverne & Shirley, The Dukes of Hazzard*), some with a sci-fi spin (*Gilligan's Planet, Partridge Family: 2200 A.D.*); there were shows featuring comic book superheroes (*The Super Friends, Spider-Man and His*

Amazing Friends), and there were compilations of Warner Bros. cartoons featuring Bugs Bunny, Daffy Duck and the Road Runner, some of which were already 30 years old.

The few original ideas to emerge from Saturday morning kidvid are, not surprisingly, those that are still most fondly remembered.

Scooby-Doo, Where are You? debuted in 1969 and lasted just two seasons, but they are still making new Scooby shows 50 years later. Familiarity accounts for some of why my generation remains loyal – if you grew up with the Scooby gang it's somehow reassuring to know they are still chasing phony ghosts. But in this current age of edgier children's entertainment I have no answer to why today's kids enjoy Scooby-Doo mysteries as much as I did back when the Beatles were still together.

Beyond its own durability, Scooby-Doo also inspired countless variations on its "teenagers solve mysteries" theme, including *Josie and the Pussycats*, *Clue Club*, *The Amazing Chan and the Chan Clan*, and *Butch Cassidy and the Sundance Kids*. All of these series were produced at the studio headed by William Hanna and Joseph Barbera, two men who still own the Saturday morning memories of the first TV generations. Ask someone in their 50s about the cartoons they used to watch, and you'll hear about Fred Flintstone and Jonny Quest, the Jetsons and the Smurfs, Captain Caveman and

Hong Kong Phooey and Penelope Pitstop – all Hanna-Barbera creations or adaptations.

One of the few production companies to rival Hanna-Barbera was Filmation, which produced fewer series but several classics, included an Emmy-winning animated adaptation of the original *Star Trek* series. Their cartoon versions of *Archie* comics added a musical component to that franchise. "Sugar, Sugar," released by "The Archies" and introduced on a Saturday morning show, became the number one song of 1969 on the *Billboard* charts.

Filmation also gave us *Fat Albert and the Cosby Kids*, based on characters created by Bill Cosby. Along with the brilliant *Schoolhouse Rock*, it was the best attempt to bring an educational component to Saturday morning television. Other Filmation hits included the first animated adaptation of Batman, *Tarzan, Lord of the Jungle*, and several popular live-action shows such as *The Shazam/Isis Hour*, *Space Academy* and *Jason of Star Command*.

With Warner Bros., Hanna-Barbera and Filmation occupying three places on the Mount Rushmore of Saturday morning TV, the fourth spot belongs to Sid and Marty Krofft, whose outlandish creations – *H.R. Pufnstuf, Lidsville, and The Bugaloos* – featured remarkable puppetry and a subversive sense of humor.

As with most series from this time, the Krofft shows were short-lived but continued to resonate beyond their initial runs. *Land of the Lost* debuted in 1974, and was adapted into a (terrible) Will Ferrell comedy in 2009. *Electra-Woman and Dyna-Girl* was a female superhero show starring soap opera legend Deidre Hall; there were just eight half-hour episodes, but there have already been two revivals and a third may be on the way.

For the first 20 years of Saturday morning kids programs, the shows tried to entertain us, and the commercials tried to sell us something. But beginning in the 1980s, the shows themselves became advertisements for products – *Care Bears, G.I. Joe, Transformers, He-Man and the Masters of the Universe*. If you grew up with these shows you may remember them fondly, and some were better than they had to be to move the merchandise. But it was a derisive trend that, along with the ascent of cable television, hastened the end of this era.

Saturday mornings aren't special anymore. As of this writing television's original three networks now devote that time to sports and news programming. Thanks to streaming services, DVDs and the DVR, kids' shows old and new can be watched any day, any time. That makes TV viewing more convenient, but it also makes it less significant. If you can do something any time you want, there's nothing special about doing it.

I still remember when a Saturday morning filled with cartoons was enough to make a whole day better. Kids today will never understand how wonderful that was.

The Best Shows

Scooby-Doo, Where Are You? (1969-1971)

What was it about the characters in this series that has proven so resilient? The original episodes are still fun, though hardly any better written or animated than anything else at that time. Some of the later versions tried to add layers of depth to the stories or more mature personality aspects to the characters (such as 2010's *Mystery Incorporated*), but fans seem divided on whether that's necessary. Most prefer the basics: Fred driving the Mystery Machine (and usually getting lost or running out of gas), Daphne tripping over something that triggers a trap door, Velma losing her glasses, Shaggy in desperate search of food, and Scooby mixing occasional moments of bravery with consistent cowardice.

Jonny Quest (1964-1965)

Jonny Quest was the only Hanna-Barbera cartoon with a body count. In the first episode, "Mystery of the Lizard Men," more than twenty bad guys are wiped out by 11 year-old Jonny and his teacher, Race Bannon. That may not be the best way to frame a tribute but it's the genuine sense of danger in Jonny's animated adventures, and his bravery and resourcefulness in fighting back, that cannot be overlooked when probing why the show still holds up. Every aspect of the series was first class, particularly the richly detailed animation by Doug

Wildey that had far more depth and sophistication than the typical H-B output of that era. Put a 6-12 year old boy in front of this 50 year-old show today, and he will be just as captivated as the show's original fans.

The Bugaloos (1970-1972)

It's impossible to explain *The Bugaloos* to someone who has never watched it. But yes, this really was a series about four photogenic British teenagers that portray singing insects (and the ladybug was played by a guy). They live in Tranquility Forest with their pal Sparky the firefly, and their bucolic way of life is constantly under attack from Benita Bizarre, who lives with a Nazi rat named Funky in a skyscraper-sized jukebox. Only Sid and Marty Krofft could have envisioned such a premise. Martha Raye plays frustrated singer Benita, and it's a performance that must be seen to be believed.

Fat Albert and the Cosby Kids (1972-1982)

Between his Emmy-winning stints on *I Spy* and *The Cosby Show*, Bill Cosby created, produced, and hosted this series about the adventures of a group of friends, inspired by his youth in the streets of Philadelphia. This series combined entertainment with education, while representing a significant breakthrough in multiculturalism in children's television.

Wacky Races (1968-1970)

Some of Hanna-Barbera's cleverest visual gags found their way into *Wacky Races*, with narrator Dave Willock adding to the fun with his clever calls of every race. The premise of these ten-minute shorts was simple – 11 tricked-out cars competed in a series of races around the world. While kids in the '70s laughed at the antics of the Ant Hill Mob, the Gruesome Twosome and the Slag Brothers, their older brothers were probably wagering on the results of each race, which were always a surprise every week. I confess that I was among those viewers secretly hoping Dick Dastardly and his snickering canine, Muttley, would actually drive his Double-Zero racer to a checkered flag. He probably had the best car in the field, but was always undone by seeking an extra edge through some dirty scheme. Cheating never pays, kids.

Sidebar: A Sunday Morning Classic:
Make a Wish

Make a Wish (1971-1976) is the kind of show they don't make anymore. Not only that, it's the kind of show they wouldn't even try to make anymore. With 500 channels you'd think any good idea would be revived, recycled or ripped off. But *Make a Wish*, with its canny blend of music, free expression, etymology, animation, live action and documentary filmmaking, was truly of a product of its freewheeling time.

It took me a while to come around on the show back then. At first when it popped up on Sunday mornings, that just meant cartoons were over, so right away there was intrinsic hostility. But it was easier to leave the TV on when there were only three networks and no cable, especially when you're a kid for whom a quiet room was anathema. So one morning I let it play.

As host Tom Chapin (brother of Harry Chapin) strummed his guitar and crooned the theme song, I thought this was going to be another of those overly earnest series that strived to teach me something by "speaking my language." Those rarely ended well.

But then Chapin introduced a word and invited us to "think of all the possibilities," and suddenly *Make a Wish* became a show for poets and dreamers.

All of the chosen word's derivations and diverse meanings were explored through whimsical non-sequiturs and silly puns, illustrated by animation that was similar to what Terry Gilliam concocted for Monty Python. Ancient history mixed with modern slang. A literary reference would segue into a sports cliché. Chapin riffed on the word the way a jazz musician explored a melody, finding hidden beauties and unexpected tangents, before bringing it back to a familiar setting.

And then each inventive journey into the wonder of words (all written by the series' creator, Lester Cooper), would abruptly give way to a short documentary related to one of the themes. This segment was as straightforward and serious as the educational films they'd make us watch in elementary school. I always imagined this bit was the trade-off demanded by the network, to balance out the stuff they probably saw as a bunch of hippie crap.

Following the film, Chapin would return to perform an original song inspired by the word. His soothing voice was a comfortable guide for such flights of fancy, and kept us grounded even as Chapin himself ascended toward the sky at the beginning of each episode. He once described *Make a Wish* as a show for six year-old speed freaks. But there was genuine imagination on display here, and for a young writer already in training it was a building block toward a lifelong relationship with the joys and quirks of the English language.

That Girl

1966-1971 (ABC)

136 Episodes

Does how a television series ends have any impact on its legacy?

I think the answer has to be affirmative. Shows like *M*A*S*H* and *The Fugitive* delivered satisfying conclusions for millions of fans emotionally invested in their characters. But World War II never ended for the prisoners at Stalag 13 on *Hogan's Heroes*. And I can only imagine how *St. Elsewhere* viewers felt about all of its stories unfolding only in the imaginings of an autistic teenager.

That Girl is another series that failed to stick the landing. And here, the culprit in that unfortunate misstep is the same person who made the series such a delight to watch for five seasons – Marlo Thomas.

Let's start with the positive – Thomas is wonderful as aspiring actress Ann Marie, who leaves her hometown of Brewster in upstate New York to launch her career in Manhattan. She receives loving support from two men in her life – her curmudgeon of a father (Lew Parker) and boyfriend Donald Hollinger (Ted Bessell, a master of silent comedic reactions, which is sometimes all he got to play opposite his chatterbox girlfriend).

Every time I revisit this show I like it more, and I think some of the credit Mary Richards receives for breaking ground as a single female making her way in the world should really go to Ann Marie.

Then and now, what brings viewers to *That Girl* is the same comedic tone and breezy stories that fueled most sitcoms of the era. That, and the amazing array of 1960s fashions Ann Marie was somehow able to afford despite being frequently out of work.

In the first episode of the series' fifth and final season, Don proposes to Ann, and she accepts. As the season progresses they announce the engagement to their respective in-laws, Don has a bachelor party, and the couple attend pre-marriage counseling sessions.

So what better way to end the series than with the wedding?

But that didn't happen. Instead, the series' final episode ("The Elevated Woman") is a lazy clip show built around Ann's attempts to get Donald to accompany her to a women's liberation meeting.

Why? The answer is revealed on one of the excellent DVD commentary tracks for *That Girl*, recorded by Marlo Thomas and series co-creator Bill Persky. They discuss how the network also wanted the series to end with a wedding, but

Thomas was having none of it.

"I said 'No way,'" she recalled, with the same pride Susan B. Anthony felt when women got the vote. "I didn't want all the girls to watch it and think the only happy ending would be to get married. It was really important that we didn't do it."

Yeah, take that, you silly, Neanderthal viewers. Why should you expect a series about a young couple in love for five years to end with a marriage?

What Ms. Thomas failed to consider is that Ann Marie wanted to get married, and that should trump her feelings on the subject.

All actors exert some influence on the characters they play, but when personal beliefs contradict the established values and personality of that character, the result is a story that doesn't ring true, exacerbated in this instance by it being the last time we would ever see Ann Marie. As a result, a very sweet series was left with a slightly bitter aftertaste.

If it's any consolation to her, the point that Ms. Thomas was trying to make has eagerly been embraced by the society at large. Cohabitation, parenting without marriage, and single parenting are far more commonplace now than they were when Ann Marie didn't say 'I do.'

How ironic that today, when television reflects our current culture, a traditional wedding finale would be the most untraditional climax anyone could imagine. I'll leave it to you whether that constitutes progress.

The Best Episodes

"What's In a Name?" (1966)

Ann's agent suggests that she change her name, because 'Ann Marie' sounds incomplete. But when her father finds out, he's not having it. A looming guest spot on a TV series requires Ann to make a decision – will her credit read 'Ann Marie' or 'Marie Brewster'? This typically well-written episode showcases Lew Parker's wonderful embodiment of Ann's frequently perturbed but always proud father.

"Pass the Potatoes, Ethel Merman" (1967)

This is the show's best episode. Ann is cast in a musical starring Ethel Merman. When she and Don see Ms. Merman eating alone in her dressing room, they invite the star to dinner at Ann's apartment. The joy expressed by Marlo Thomas as they stand side-by-side, singing and cooking in her kitchen, transcends performance.

"Dark On Top of Everything Else" (1969)

Ann heads back to Brewster for a weekend with her parents, and is surprised to find them not home. She spends the evening in her old bedroom, reminiscing about her childhood. The episode is nearly a solo outing for Thomas and she is always delightful to watch here, especially after a comedic sequence after Ann locks herself in the basement that is worthy of Lucille Ball.

"My Sister's Keeper" (1969)

Ann meets a talented singer and tries to help advance her career, unaware that she is also a nun. The singer is played by Marlo Thomas's sister Terre, and the episode also features appearances from her brother Tony, and a cameo appearance from her famous father, Danny Thomas.

"There Was a Time Ann Met a Pie Man" (1969)

Ann's excitement over landing a role on a national TV series is diminished when she learns she'll be taking a pie in the face. Is the money and exposure worth the potential embarrassment?

How Times Have Changed: Environmentalism

If it seems like there has never been as much emphasis on protecting the environment as there is right now, you were not watching TV in the 1970s.

Today, it's climate change. In the '70s, it was the ecology movement.

"Ecology" is not a word you hear much anymore but it was everywhere back then, defining a movement with its roots in books like *The Population Bomb* and Rachel Carson's *Silent Spring*. The Environmental Protection Agency was founded in 1970, the same year that the first Earth Day was celebrated.

1970 was also the year that television picked up on the crusade, beginning in January with an episode of *Room 222* called "Once Upon a Time There Was Air You Couldn't See."

The setting is Pete Dixon's class at Walt Whitman High School in Los Angeles, a city already infamous for its air quality thanks to all the smog jokes in Johnny Carson's *Tonight Show* monologues. Two of Pete's students raise more than $600 to film a local 60-second TV commercial, urging viewers to support upcoming legislation to study the smog problem.

What I like most about the result is how the ad sounds exactly like what two inner city kids would create, without the help of the episode's writers to make them sound more polished. It's more effective because it is simple and sincere.

Two months later, *That Girl* aired "Soot Yourself," in which Ann joins an anti-pollution group that pickets the magazine where her fiancé works.

There's not much comedy here, just lots of self-righteous speeches. This kind of hammer-over-the-head approach, when people are just hoping for a pleasant 30 minutes of entertainment, tends to alienate more than it rallies the troops.

That same month another take on the same topic aired that was even more impassioned, but also more embarrassing.

A Clear and Present Danger was a 90-minute pilot for the Hal Holbrook series *The Senator*. That show was an outstanding look at Washington politics, but it stumbled badly out of the gate with a story that plays like the *Reefer Madness* of air pollution.

It opens with prospective senatorial candidate Hayes Stowe (Holbrook) arriving in Los Angeles to visit his beloved law professor. He arrives just after the man has died in the hospital. His doctor intones somberly, "I think he would have made it…if it weren't for the smog."

That sets Hayes on a mission to make pollution the central issue of his Senate campaign, which results in his being dubbed "the Paul Revere of smog."

The nadir of the drama comes when Hayes allies himself with a wild-eyed college professor who insists that breathable air on planet earth will not be around much longer. It reminded me of a 1962 *Donna Reed Show* episode in which an astronomer predicts that man will have visited Mars and Venus by the 1980s. If they were both right, at least we'd have other planets to colonize.

A key component of the ecology movement was getting the message out to the next generation, so they would grow up to be responsible stewards of the planet. It was a prominent classroom topic when I was in elementary school, and was incorporated into many of the children's shows back then, once again beginning in 1970. Remember the Willie Wimple shorts on *Sesame Street*?

The Bugaloos (1970) was Sid and Marty Krofft's contribution to the movement. The entire series is a paean to the superiority of natural landscapes over man-made urban jungles. The Bugaloos live a carefree life in Tranquility Forest, singing and celebrating the simple joys of nature. They are constantly under threat from Benita Bizarre (Martha Raye), loud, crass, and garish, like the city where she lives.

Filmation's *Ark II* presented a more dire future. The opening narration describes its cataclysmic premise: "For millions of years earth was fertile and rich. Then, pollution and waste began to take their toll. Civilization fell into ruin. This is the world of the 25th century." But if you've seen the show you know there's a plus side – talking monkeys!

By 1971 it wasn't just the shows but the commercials that delivered a planet-saving message. That was the year Woodsy Owl first exclaimed: "Give a hoot, don't pollute!" And if that didn't get your attention, a close-up of a crying Indian on a trash-filled riverbank certainly did. That spot remains one of the most famous public service announcements of all time.

Did any of these efforts have lasting impact? The United States did pass many pieces of environmental legislation in the early 1970s, such as the Clean Water Act, the Clean Air Act, the Endangered Species Act, and the National Environmental Policy Act. Perhaps television served to educate the public as to why such measures were necessary.

The climate change debate hopes for a similar result, but with more severe legislative edicts. And we must act now, they warn, because so many prominent "experts" are putting timelines on the end of the world.

If you're worried, take some comfort in the fact that both *The Population Bomb* and *Silent Spring* made dire predictions about the future that never came to pass.

No one should have any issue with respecting nature, and doing what we can to make the world a better and healthier place. What has changed from the ecology movement to the current climate change crusade is the tone of the rhetoric, and the lengths to which some are eager to fundamentally change how we live, work and play.

Even with TV's spotty track record in prognostication, if I were betting on when civilization was going to fall into ruin I'd put my money on *Ark II* over Alexandra Ocasio-Cortez.

The Waltons

1972-1981 (CBS)

221 Episodes

The 1970s brought its share of challenges, as every decade does: the Iran hostage crisis, gas shortages, and the Watergate scandal that ended Richard Nixon's presidency. Into this era of economic and political unrest came *The Waltons*, a series that said, "You think times are tough now?"

The source material was Earl Hamner, Jr.'s recollections of growing up with a large family in rural Virginia during the Great Depression. He first told the story in the 1961 novel *Spencer's Mountain*, which was adapted into a film two years later starring Henry Fonda. It failed to capture the qualities that made the book successful, in part because it changed the setting from Virginia to Wyoming.

Hamner's second biographical novel, *The Homecoming: A Novel About Spencer's Mountain* (1970), received much better treatment in a 1971 TV movie that became a holiday tradition for many families through annual Christmas broadcasts.

Its success convinced CBS to take a chance on what seemed like an unlikely prospect for a hit series – would viewers then embracing Sonny and Cher and the Bunkers on *All in the*

Family be that interested in a dirt-poor farm family struggling to get by in 1933? Yes they were, as it turned out: *The Waltons* was a top 20 hit for its first six seasons.

Credit CBS also for some canny cast changes from the family as played in *The Homecoming* that contributed to the series' popularity and longevity.

Replacing the flinty Patricia Neal as family matriarch Olivia Walton was Michael Learned, who exuded home-and-hearth benevolence. Ralph Waite stepped in for the more rough-around-the-edges Andrew Duggan as her husband John. Richard Thomas was wisely retained as John-Boy, the eldest son who represents Hamner in his youth. Ellen Corby returned as Grandma Esther, and replacing Edgar Bergen as Grandpa would be the affable Will Geer.

As in *The Homecoming*, each story is told as a remembrance of John-Boy's, now a writer living in New York City. Hamner provided the voiceover narration that introduced every one of the series' 221 episodes.

Why did the series resonate with millions of viewers? Perhaps Americans weary of Vietnam headlines were eager to embrace this portrait of a loving family. Perhaps they wanted to escape from the contentious political debates on shows like *Maude* and *All in the Family*. Maybe it was just nice to see dirt roads and general stores and quiet country nights on TV again, now that westerns had largely disappeared from prime time.

There was frequent struggle and real hardship in these stories, but *The Waltons* also taught lessons on how to endure tough times with grace. It reminded us that it was okay to miss the things you can't afford right now, but that's also a reminder about acknowledging a greater appreciation for the things you have. And even when your life seems especially low, there is always someone even worse off, so try to help them if you can.

Faith was an integral part of that perspective, and was sometimes personified on Walton's Mountain in the unlikely form of John Ritter as the young Reverend Matthew Fordwick. Ritter made his final appearance on the series in 1976, the same year he debuted as Jack Tripper in *Three's Company*.

The Waltons is also a show that writers like because it's about John-Boy's aspirations to that profession. In a time and place where a less volatile career pursuit would have been prudent – his father had aspirations only of earning enough money to feed a large family and scrape together another mortgage payment – John-Boy was encouraged to pursue his dream, even when a luxury like a typewriter was out of the question. Richard Thomas became the series' breakout star for his sensitive portrayal of John Walton, Jr., as audiences followed his journey from college to starting a local newspaper, to having his first novel published, and leaving the Blue Ridge Mountains for New York and Europe, where he covered World War II for the military newspaper *Stars and Stripes.*

Finally, the series served up a perfect grace note at the end of every episode with those wonderful, memorable "good nights." These scenes were widely parodied at the time but fans always looked forward to those final lingering conversations between rooms before the last light went out in an upstairs window.

Like many shows *The Waltons* overstayed its welcome, losing beloved cast members along the way to real world health issues and the desire to pursue other opportunities. The grandparents were the first departures and perhaps the most detrimental, as they were such a wonderful mismatch: Esther, the stern, Scripture-reading disciplinarian, and jovial Zeb, who also loved the Lord but figured he wouldn't object to a little drinking and carousing every once in a while.

Then Richard Thomas left, followed by Michael Learned and Ralph Waite.

When episodes focused more on new characters played by Patty Duke's dad (William Schallert) and Lulu Hogg (Peggy Rea), viewers knew they weren't watching the same show anymore.

But even after nine seasons, some viewers still were not ready to come down from the mountain. *A Wedding on Walton's Mountain* aired just eight months after the series aired its final episode, and was succeeded by two more revivals the following year: *Mother's Day on Walton's Mountain* and *A Day of Thanks on Walton's Mountain*. The last of six reunion movies, *A Walton Easter*, aired in 1997, 25 years after the show's first episode. John-Boy, who had covered the Hindenburg airship disaster in the series' fifth season, was now anchoring a television network's coverage of the Apollo 11 mission to the moon. Hopefully by then he could afford a typewriter.

The Best Episodes

"The Literary Man" (1972)

John-Boy never had much chance to interact with other writers in an isolated rural community – until the day his truck breaks down and a stranger stops to help him fix it. That stranger is A.J. Covington (David Huddleston), a published writer who travels the world telling stories about the places he visits. John-Boy is enthralled. But is A.J. really who he says he is, or is he just looking for a free meal?

"The Deed" (1973)

You would think there would be no debate about land ownership if your name is Walton and you live on Walton's Mountain. But when a lumber company claims to have purchased timber rights, threatening the future of the family's sawmill, John needs to fight the claim in court. There's no question that he'd win – the problem is raising $200 for court costs. John-Boy gets a job in the city to help raise the money, which proves more adventurous than he expected.

"The Prophecy" (1975)

John's high school class returns for a reunion. He is the only one among the graduates who stayed on the mountain, and feels like the class disappointment. But he discovers instead that his classmates hold him in the highest esteem, and that few achievements in this life are as great as raising a happy, loving family. That's a message that used to be more prevalent, and one we need to hear more often now.

"The Burn Out" (1976)

Just when viewers wondered how many more hardships this series was going to inflict on one family, we get an episode where their house nearly burns down. John-Boy finally has a piece of his novel that he's ready to send to publishers – until that is lost in the fire as well. But it's not all gloom – the kids move in with various neighbors while the house is rebuilt, and all return with greater appreciation for their own family when they are finally back together.

"The Fire Storm" (1976)

John-Boy publishes excerpts from Hitler's *Mein Kampf* in his newspaper to raise awareness of the danger he poses to the world. The reaction is swift and severe – threats, ostracism, and a book burning. It's enlightening to watch this episode in a time when the efforts by some to silence speech they don't like has resulted in politically motivated censorship in the press and on social media. It's a reminder of how a fire started to quench hate speech can quickly spread to consume legitimate and even sacred speech as well.

How Times Have Changed: The Emmy Awards

More than 25 years before *The Waltons* received an Emmy Award as Best Drama Series, the first Emmy Awards were bestowed. The year was 1949, a time before most American homes had a television. Just six statues were presented in Hollywood before a live audience of 600 people.

For the first generations to grow up with TV, the annual Emmy broadcast was something to get excited about. As with other awards shows from this era, the Academy paid due homage to the icons of generations past while honoring the best shows and performances from the previous year. Hosts, presenters and recipients were gracious and engaging, even while reading scripted jokes that usually fell flat. No one decided this was the proper time to mention how much they hate the president, or air a list of grievances against the nation that gave them the opportunity to become wealthy and famous.

There will always be controversy among fans over winners and losers. While the Emmys deserve generally high marks for recognizing excellence, they have also had some colossal misses over the decades: Jackie Gleason (*The Honeymooners*),

Andy Griffith (*The Andy Griffith Show*), Patty Duke (*The Patty Duke Show*), and David Janssen (*The Fugitive*).

Still, as long as the competition field was limited to three (later four) broadcast networks and PBS, most quality series ran long enough to be acknowledged. Name just about any successful show from the 1950s through the 1980s, and it will have been recognized with nominations, if not always with a gold statue.

That changed with the ascent of cable television. At first, a separate award was created to honor excellence in cable broadcasts – the Ace. And that made sense because network television broadcasts were (and still are) regulated by the Federal Communications Commission, and are limited by standards and restrictions implemented by that government agency. They have to play by different rules.

But no one thought the Ace Award had much status, so cable shows became eligible for Emmys. And then they started to win everything.

Over time, those who chose not to invest in cable, or preferred more family-friendly network fare, became disenchanted with the Emmys as shows they never watched swept every category, while brilliant, critically acclaimed shows like *The Gilmore Girls* and *Buffy the Vampire Slayer* were ignored.

In 2000, when the first season of HBO's *The Sopranos* lost the Emmy to ABC"s *The Practice*, it was deemed such a travesty of justice that the Television Academy actually changed its voting procedures. How dare this show that doesn't curse every ten seconds and wallow in graphic violence be considered the greater artistic achievement?

After that, for the next ten years, just about everything on HBO won Emmys as if the mere existence of these series entitled them to adoration. In 2001, four of the five nominations for Best Writing went to *The Sopranos*. *Sex and the City* and *Six Feet Under* dominated other categories during their broadcast histories. Today, the cool cache once traded upon by HBO has moved to the streaming services. This is now where television's top stars and creators have opted for short-run shows where anything goes, that do not require seven-season contracts or worry about restrictions on language, sex or violence.

Why should we care? Because one of the ways we recognize that the television of decades past is worth celebrating and preserving is the number of Emmys these series received. For more than 20 years now, network TV shows have largely been denied that measuring stick of achievement, because Emmy nominations and statues are going to shows on cable by at least a 5:1 margin.

And because of the perception that all the good stuff is found elsewhere, many outstanding performances on network shows have been ignored: Charles Esten in *Nashville*; Jonny Lee Miller in *Elementary*; Megan Hilty in *Smash*;

Madeleine Stowe in *Revenge,* and Dana Delaney in *Body of Proof.*

Would an Emmy nomination for Dennis Quaid have saved *Vegas* (2012) from early cancellation? It was Emmy nominations that once convinced viewers to try a sitcom called *Cheers* that finished dead last in the ratings after its first season. Had that series debuted after 2000, it would now be long forgotten.

There have been many brilliant cable shows, as well as series that originated on streaming services like Netflix and Hulu. They deserve to be recognized as well. But two decades of non-cable series being beneath the notice of those that reward excellence in the medium is worrisome, and may hasten the extinction of network television.

The Westerns

The Great Train Robbery, an 11-minute film released in 1903, is often credited as the first narrative motion picture shot in the United States. It was a western.

For most of the 20th century, there were more westerns made than any other type of movie. Once television came of age that trend continued, beginning in 1949 with *The Lone Ranger* and the debut of *The Gene Autry Show* one year later.

The peak of the TV western craze was 1958-1959, when 30 westerns aired simultaneously in prime time. Television fans wanted to see cowboys – more than cops or doctors or lawyers or detectives. Despite the fact that most of these shows had a similar look and setting, viewers could not get enough of fast-draw marshals, gunslingers for hire, barroom brawls, territory disputes between ranchers and homesteaders, and heroes who lived by the code of the west.

But those days, like the days of saloon showdowns and stagecoach travel, are now long gone.

Why has the popularity of the western diminished? Changing times and tastes may be partly to blame. The superhero genre is where audiences now cheer the battles between good guys and bad guys; Wyatt Earp can't compete with Batman and Captain America.

But I suspect the main culprit for westerns falling out of popular favor is a generational condemnation of the old west era. As *Smithsonian Magazine* observed in 2016, "Dismantling cherished fables about the Old West and stripping the romance from the history of "Westward Ho," newer studies have exhumed the human casualties and environmental costs of American expansion. Offering little glory, these interpretations of how the West was lost have accented the savagery of American civilization."

That era is just one of many recipients of harsh reassessment. According to the revisionists, if you lived in America during its first 200 years you were probably part of the problem. It's another component in the ongoing effort to portray the U.S. not as the beacon of hope and freedom that it still remains, but as a nation built on violence, racism and subjugation.

Such jaundiced evaluation is now often accompanied by the *Avatar*-advanced myth of peaceful Indians living in harmony with the land and not bothering anyone until evil white men wiped them out so they could build interstate highways and fast food restaurants. Those history books tend to omit the enslavement of blacks by prominent members of all five so-called "Civilized Tribes" (Cherokee, Chickasaw, Choctaw, Creek and Seminole). They don't divulge that the

Anasazi practiced cannibalism, or describe in graphic detail the tortures and atrocities committed by Comanche tribes.

To be clear, none of that justifies broken treaties or the Trail or Tears or the Sand Creek Massacre. No one would deny that Native Americans were here first, and that they got a raw deal. But we should be capable of comprehending history with accuracy and authenticity, and not reduce all of its aspects to a one-dimensional conflict of oppressors and oppressed.

When we take a more clear-eyed look at the 19th century without applying our preconceptions and prejudices to its way of life, we can still find much to admire from our ancestors.

While the exploits of chiefs and sheriffs and outlaws captured the popular imagination, the overwhelming majority of Americans who headed west in the 1800s were just regular people looking for a better life for themselves and their families. They were motivated by the same desires shared by Europeans who sailed to America in the previous two centuries: to have the freedom to make their own choices; to live on land they could call their own; to trade the disquiet of urban squalor for wide open spaces.

Westerns may romanticize that colorful period, but they also depict the challenges and dangers of taming a frontier, as shown on shows like *Wagon Train*, *Rawhide* and *Tales of Wells Fargo*.

Perhaps the traits of these pioneers that we once admired (thankfully, some still do) have fallen out of favor as well: Individualism, hard work, courage, respect for law and order, doing more and talking less, earning your own way in this world without expecting a handout, but giving one to those in need.

These are the messages instilled in the first generation of television westerns, personified in the old-school chivalry of Hopalong Cassidy, Marshal Matt Dillon (James Arness) on *Gunsmoke*, and Clint Walker as Cheyenne Bodie (*Cheyenne*).

What also shouldn't be lost in this discussion is that these were good shows. Some of the best and most popular are listed at the end of this chapter, but there's not much drop in quality from those cited to many others watched by millions every week.

And if the stories sometimes played like something we just saw on another series, a charismatic lead could make sitting through the same adventure more enjoyable: Chuck Connors in *The Rifleman*; Ty Hardin in *Bronco*; James Drury in *The Virginian*; Steve McQueen in *Wanted: Dead of Alive*; Robert Culp in *Trackdown*; John Smith and Robert Fuller in *Laramie*.

We should be able to acknowledge the harsh reality of a less enlightened time, but that does not negate the bravery of those who set out west in search of a brighter future, the hardships they endured or the accomplishments they achieved despite those challenges.

And cowboys are just cool. Always have been, always will be.

The Best Shows

Bonanza (1959-1973)

Bonanza mixed comedies with tragedies, action-packed outings with social commentary. Viewers never knew what type of story they'd find from week to week, which helped the series avoid the formulaic stories of some TV westerns and contributed to its remarkable longevity.

Our guide through these varying stories was an appealing cast of characters, portrayed by an outstanding ensemble cast. Eric Cartwright, better known as Hoss (Dan Blocker) was the series' heart and soul, and despite his imposing presence he was particularly beloved by younger viewers. Ben (Lorne Greene) was a rock of stability, faith and optimism, despite being three-times widowed. Adam (Pernell Roberts) was the intelligent but brooding eldest son. Handsome Joe (Michael Landon) was the youngest, the most hotheaded, and the Cartwright most often left heartbroken by a girlfriend's death or betrayal.

Gunsmoke (1955-1975)

Television's longest-running and most respected western (more than 600 episodes) was the only dramatic series to span two defining decades in American pop culture. There were better TV westerns but this is definitely a good one, anchored as it was by the steadfast presence of James Arness as Marshal Matt Dillon. Arness received three Emmy nominations for that portrayal, but the greater achievement was keeping the character consistent, relevant and appealing through two decades of turbulent American history. From the optimistic era of President Dwight Eisenhower through Vietnam, the JFK assassination, the moon landing, Woodstock and Watergate, and long after the rest of the TV cowboys were gone, Dillon protected the streets of Dodge City, and gave millions of Americans a reassuring place to visit when the rest of the world wasn't as safe.

Have Gun Will Travel (1957-1963)

Know someone who doesn't like westerns? Show them this one. As Paladin, Richard Boone played a more sophisticated and complex hero than most of the buckaroos of his day. A hero dressed in black, with a West Point education and a quick draw, Paladin preferred fine music and literature to carousing in the saloon. His sense of chivalry was reflected in the knight on his famed calling card.

Lawman (1958-1962)

In the midst of a primetime era dominated by western series, *Lawman* lasted four years without a gimmick. Good scripts and an appealing cast were enough. As Marshal Dan Troop, John Russell had one of those faces that looked like it was carved from marble, and indeed sometimes it seemed like he was part statue. But he could move quickly when he had to, which was about once every three episodes.

The Life and Legend of Wyatt Earp (1955-1961)

What separated this series, starring Hugh O'Brian as the legendary marshal, was its attention to historic detail, and the decision to chronologically dramatize this real lawman's life as it happened, from Ellsworth to Dodge City to Tombstone.

The Lone Ranger (1949-1957)

He's not as instantly recognizable as he was about 50 years ago, but for most of the 20th century The Lone Ranger ranked alongside Superman, Tarzan and Sherlock Holmes as a fictional character that was known by everyone around the world. Despite two big-budget movie revivals (that flopped), no one has yet been able to compete with original series stars Clayton Moore as The Lone Ranger, and Jay Silverheels as his faithful Indian companion, Tonto.

Maverick (1957-1962)

This irreverent, non-traditional western was an audience favorite thanks to James Garner as the affable Bret Maverick, a gambler who, when trouble beckons, is ever ready to climb out the window and run away.

The Wild Wild West (1965-1969)

The parallels between unflappable Secret Service agent James West (Robert Conrad) and British Secret Service agent James Bond were not coincidence. Michael Garrison, who created *The Wild, Wild West*, had previously purchased the movie rights to Ian Fleming's 007 novels. That was in 1955, when Hollywood wasn't interested. By the time they came around, he had already sold them. Undaunted, Garrison finally did his version of Bond, transferring the character to the American west in the 1870s. It was a risky move, since the boom in TV westerns had largely subsided by 1965. But the series' mix of western elements with espionage and science fiction was something new and fresh.

The Best Episodes

Bonanza

"The Crucible" (1962)

Pernell Roberts is featured in what is arguably the series' best episode. Robbed and left for dead in the desert, Adam is apparently rescued by prospector Peter Kane, played by Lee

Marvin. Adam's relief turns to terror when Kane is revealed as a madman, who seeks to prove through torture that a morally upright man can be driven to murder. Their twisted battle of wills is riveting.

Gunsmoke

"The Jailer" (1966)

A distraught widow, played by Bette Davis, imprisons Matt Dillon and Miss Kitty (Amanda Blake) to avenge her husband's hanging. The legendary Davis is mesmerizing as she elevates a western adventure into something akin to a Greek tragedy.

Have Gun Will Travel

"Hey Boy's Revenge" (1958)

The exploitation of the Chinese immigrants who built the first railroads was rarely explored in TV's golden-age westerns. Perhaps that's why this episode found its way onto *TV Guide*'s 1997 list of the 100 Greatest TV Episodes.

Maverick

"Shady Deal at Sunny Acres" (1958)

Mr. Bates (John Dehner) is a crooked banker, as Bret Maverick discovers after his $15,000 deposit disappears. To retaliate, the ultimate man of inaction pulls up a rocking chair across from the bank and spends the next several days whittling. Or does he? By episode's end the money is back in Maverick's wallet, and Bates is in jail for embezzlement.

The Life and Legend of Wyatt Earp

"Gunfight at the O.K. Corral" (1961)

After more than 200 episodes, the West's most famous lawman finally takes that legendary walk down a dusty street with Doc Holliday, to confront the Clantons in the series penultimate episode.

Why We Still Miss Johnny Carson

Memory is a curious thing. I can recall few specific moments from 40 years ago, but I still hold on to an assortment of seemingly random recollections that are as vivid now as if they just happened yesterday.

In 1980, I watched the annual anniversary episode of *The Tonight Show*. These, you may recall, were always special shows featuring clips from the series' long and illustrious history. After it was over I distinctly recall lying in bed that night and thinking, "What are we all going to do when Johnny Carson retires?"

That such a question would even occur to anyone is suggestive of the central place Carson long occupied in our popular culture. There had been plenty of shows I liked that were canceled or that ended their runs, and it was sad but hardly traumatic. Losing Johnny Carson was something else entirely.

For more than 30 years his *Tonight Show* was America's night-light. There may have been fights over the remote during prime time but anyone still awake at 11:30, 10:30 central, was almost certainly watching NBC, as Carson emerged from behind that rainbow-colored curtain for a monologue that was funny when the jokes worked and even funnier when they didn't.

If there is an overriding theme that has run through this book, it's the celebration of an era in television that was shared more intimately than it is now, and a reminder of how those shared experiences seemed to bring us closer together as a generation and as a nation. No one personified that unity more than Johnny Carson.

We've had no shortage of late-night talk show hosts over the last three decades, some brilliant in their own right, but none have approached Carson's eminence. There wasn't any part of the job that he had not mastered – effortless class and charisma, quick wit, perfect comic timing, the sketches and his staple of recurring characters (Tea Time Movie host Art Fern was genius every time), and how he adapted his interviewing style to present each guest in the best possible light.

But it's the nightly monologue that most defined Carson's preeminent position as a commentator on current events, and a national barometer on the issues of the day. There was no agenda behind the jokes except for the crafting of a solid punch line. When Democrats where in charge, they got skewered. When Republicans took over, they got it too.

In a *60 Minutes* interview, Mike Wallace asked Carson why he never took a more serious stand on a political issue. "Tell me the last time that Jack Benny, Red Skelton, any comedian, used his show to do serious issues," he replied. "That's not what I'm there for...once you start that, you start to get that self-important feeling that what you say has great import."

Back then, the perception was that all of us, the regular folks, were on one side, and the dopes we elected into office were on the other side. Now, it's more about my dopes vs. your dopes. David Letterman was still making nightly Sarah Palin jokes two years after she and John McCain lost the election. It doesn't matter if you liked her or not, that was lazy. And it was something that Carson, Letterman's idol, would never do.

Most of the successful hosts that have come along since – John Stewart, Steven Colbert, Jimmy Kimmel, Seth Meyers, and Trevor Noah – were Letterman fans and are following his divisive blueprint. Result: one less opportunity for television to bring us together.

Johnny Carson, like Will Rogers in an earlier era, united people by pointing out the absurdity inherent even in the best type of government, and by deflating the pomposity of our most prominent public servants. I know many of today's hosts now fulfill that role for many, but there's more anger in their attitudes than bemusement. Perhaps that is fitting for our times.

And so I return to the original question I asked in 1980: "What are we all going to do when Johnny Carson retires?" Now I know the answer. I wish I didn't.

Epilogue: Can We Go Back?

"We all want progress, but if you're on the wrong road, progress means doing an about-turn and walking back to the right road; in that case, the man who turns back soonest is the most progressive."
– C. S. Lewis

Why do millions of people love classic television shows? Why do they still watch them every day and collect them on DVD? Why does the MeTV network, with its 24/7 schedule of television series from the 1950s-1980s, attract more viewers than CNN and 80 other cable outlets?

One reason is that many Americans have become disenchanted with the current TV landscape, which by and large is a reflection of the current culture.

Television won't change unless the culture does, but prevailing wisdom tells us that the past belongs to the past, and trying to recapture it in the present is a fool's endeavor.

But I'm not so sure.

Can we go back? How often has any country reversed course to return to an earlier status quo? When it happens, it is only after circumstances reach a desperate state. France eventually restored responsible leadership after a Reign of Terror that grew out of an idealistic revolution. But that occurred only after tens of thousands of people were executed, religious monuments were destroyed, Christian graves were desecrated, public and private worship were outlawed, and the possession of property was considered robbery.

We're not there yet. But we're getting closer.

Searching for signs of optimism? Let's turn once again to television, where the renewed appreciation for Fred Rogers gives me hope.

He was a daily presence on TV for 33 years; most of them in a pre-cable era when few children's shows aired on weekdays other than those on PBS. He communicated with millions of kids, and we'll never know how many were comforted by his benevolent words and gentle support. Not just those who may have needed it most – the children of a bitter divorce, or abused kids with nowhere else to turn. I think also about all the kids who were lonely, or ostracized because of their race or religion or how they looked. Perhaps they were too short or tall, too thin or overweight, a little slower to learn, or they just didn't fare as well in the DNA lottery as their more popular and attractive classmates. For these children, every day at school was a reminder of what they were not.

How do we begin to measure the solace provided to so many by a soft-spoken neighbor who reminded them that they are special, and they can be liked just for who they are?

How many kids grew up to be better parents by remembering the lessons he taught?

Fred Rogers made television a better place to visit, and no one before or since has established a more enduring bond with his audience. But his approach, which stressed quiet words, understanding, tolerance and love of all people, now seems out of step in a loud, confrontational, my-way-or-the-highway world. And yet, over the past decade there has been a resurgence of interest in the man and his work, with the 2018 documentary *Won't You Be My Neighbor?* and the film *A Beautiful Day in the Neighborhood*, starring Tom Hanks as Mr. Rogers.

A heartfelt reaction from nostalgic adults could be expected, but those who didn't grow up with *Mr. Rogers' Neighborhood* reacted as if they could not believe someone that kind and sincere actually existed – or didn't have some dark side or secret vice that could be used to undermine all of the good work he did. When Mr. Rogers invited his friend Francois Clemmons, an African-American police officer, to cool off on a hot day by spraying his feet in a wading pool, no one mocked that moment or dismissed it as "ambivalent prejudice" – because such assessments were given little credence by intelligent people.

Isn't the way Mr. Rogers regarded others the way we're supposed to be treating people now? Fifty years ago many shows sent that message. Perhaps the seeds that he planted may still take root.

But before we can determine if it's possible to recover what has been lost, we have to identify exactly what must be restored, and to what extent most people believe it is worth saving.

Obviously there are some aspects of the classic TV era that are best left in the past. But can we resign those to history, and focus instead on bringing back a degree of professionalism that has been lost in the workplace, along with an honest, objective media? Can we stop building walls that separate religious faith from the public square? Can we recognize that none of us will ever ace the purity tests now being applied to everyone in public life, and bestow a more appropriately measured response to decades-old transgressions? Can forgiveness be tendered when it is warranted?

If such reversal is not possible, we face a decision about where the culture is headed – go along for the ride, or get off the train. Neither choice promises that life will get easier. Continue to assert beliefs that are no longer prevalent, and you risk exile from relatives, un-friendings on Facebook, and perhaps even the loss of your job and community standing. Or, follow the crowd and pretend that a box of Land O' Lakes Butter supports sex trafficking.

On those days when it seems everything that was once right is now wrong, and what used to be regarded as unacceptable has become the noblest of objectives, there are still places where hope can be found. The classic shows of the past and the lessons they taught us are a valuable reminder of the days before America went stupid in the head.

"Classic television is a medium, one of many but perhaps the most visible and most personal one, that tells us about ourselves - who we were, who we are, who we aspired to be. Forget that, banish it from our collective memories, fail to learn from it, and we have forgotten an integral part of ourselves and our American culture." – Mitchell Hadley, *The Electronic Mirror*

Television may never bring us together again, but for many of us it can make the separation more bearable.

Afterword: 25 More Shows

Love the shows featured in this book? Here are 25 more classics you'll also enjoy.

Alfred Hitchcock Presents (1955-1962)

The story quality in this anthology series may not be as consistent in quality as *The Twilight Zone*. But when the material was there, as it was in the show's many adaptations of classic short stories, Hitchcock presented some very memorable tales indeed. "An Unlocked Window" (1965) may be the scariest prime time program ever broadcast, at least until *The X-Files* served up "Home."

Charlie's Angels (1976-1981)

Popular enough in its day to earn ratings comparable to Super Bowls and to grace the cover of *Time* magazine, *Charlie's Angels* was also derided for introducing a genre that became known as "jiggle TV." But what some once criticized as sleazy looks pretty chaste now, and its first three seasons offered pleasures besides the beauty of its stars – Kate Jackson earned two Emmy nominations and helped make the Angels credible as investigators. Several film and television remakes have attempted to capture the appeal of the original – none came close.

Columbo (1971-2003)

Peter Falk's trenchcoat-clad police lieutenant, who annoyed suspects into confessions, was one of several characters featured in NBC's *Sunday Mystery Movie* series. But while *McCloud*, *McMillan and Wife* and *Hec Ramsey* all had their moments, *Columbo* was the only one that earns a place alongside the creations of Edgar Allen Poe and Sir Arthur Conan Doyle in the annals of classic detective fiction.

The Courtship of Eddie's Father (1969-1972)

It lasted just three seasons and 73 episodes, and should have stuck around longer. Tom Corbett, as played by the marvelous Bill Bixby, belongs on every TV fan's short list of the best television dads. Great theme song, too.

The Defenders (1961-1965)

It is rarely syndicated, and only the first season is currently available on DVD, but it's a show worth pursuing anytime and anywhere it may appear. A courtroom drama starred E.G. Marshall and Robert Reed as father-and-son lawyers, *The Defenders* is must-see viewing for anyone who appreciates great writing, great acting, ambitious stories, and entertainment that actually expects viewers to have an IQ above double-digits.

Doctor Who (1963-present)

There are two distinct eras of *Doctor Who*; the first was launched with the character's debut adventure in 1963 and ended in 1989; the second began when the series was revived in 2005. Both are mostly wonderful, though in recent years the series has become another proponent of woke storytelling. As with the original *Star Trek* series, one had to overlook the rudimentary special effects and Styrofoam monsters in its earlier run, and appreciate the quality of the writing and performances. But there are great rewards here for those able to do so, not the least of which is more than 600 episodes of delightful sci-fi stories to enjoy. That should keep you busy for a while.

Eight is Enough (1977-1981)

This may be television's most authentic portrayal of the advantages and drawbacks to growing up in a crowded household. There is a genuine family "feel" that pervades, even if some of the situations are heightened for dramatic effect beyond what most of us will experience in our non-scripted lives. I also cannot recall any other series that moved as easily from sitcom style humor, complete with laugh track, to serious moments, and then back again. That tonal switch is fraught with peril, and only the best television shows can pull it off without undermining the drama or overplaying the comedy. *Eight is Enough* gets it just right.

The Ernie Kovacs Show (1952-1956)

Where other comedians were content to play on television, Ernie Kovacs was the only personality who would play *with* television, creating surreal audio and visual tricks that were decades ahead of their time. Possibly an acquired taste, but give it a chance.

Family (1976-1980)

After 20 years of sensationalized reality TV, the idea of dramatizing the normal low-key reality of life with one Pasadena family now seems like an incomplete pitch; what's the hook? Is the father psychic or is the mother leading a double life? Does the son have super powers? But when the writing and the acting are as perfect as they are here, no other incentive should be necessary. To watch *Family* is to be wholly drawn into the joys and sorrows and relationships of fictional characters, and to believe that every word they say is extemporaneous, and could not possibly have been typed by someone else months earlier.

The George Burns and Gracie Allen Show (1950-1958)

Viewers probably expected a traditional husband and wife sitcom from this married comedy team who honed their skills in vaudeville and on radio. Instead, Burns and Allen essentially played themselves in stories that mixed reality and fiction. Burns would regularly step out of character (and off the set) to offer comments on the episode's plot – or he'd turn on the TV in his den that was playing the same episode that viewers at home were watching, so he could view the scenes he wasn't in. This remarkable series offers more proof that TV's earliest sitcoms were capable of innovative storytelling.

Gidget (1965-1966)

Gidget had the misfortune of becoming a hit after it was canceled. Scheduled against *The Virginian* and *The Beverly Hillbillies*, the series was a flop the first time around, but the ratings soared in summer reruns. By then it was too late to bring it back, so ABC did the next best thing by casting Sally Field in a new series - *The Flying Nun*. *Gidget* was and remains the better show, and Sally Field could not have been more adorable as the sassy, surf-loving beach bunny.

The Golden Girls (1985-1992)

Building a show around four senior citizens was distinctive, but in every other way *The Golden Girls* was as traditional as comedies get. It holds up thanks to the steadfast expertise of three TV sitcom vets, and an unknown stage actress (Estelle Getty) who consistently trumped their punch lines.

The Honeymooners (1955-1956)

Episodes from "the classic 39" have been on television almost non-stop for more than half a century. Jackie Gleason and Art Carney were the medium's first great comedy team, and Carney's Ed Norton is the forefather of every wacky TV neighbor from Gladys Kravitz to Cosmo Kramer.

Leave it to Beaver (1957-1963)

A family situation comedy that defined both its era and its genre, and that introduced a character in Eddie Haskell that became synonymous with sycophantic weasels.

Little House on the Prairie (1974-1983)

Michael Landon was one of TV's most beloved stars. While he also enjoyed long-running success in *Bonanza* and *Highway to Heaven*, *Little House* is his best TV work. Based on the classic books by the once beloved and now canceled Laura Ingalls Wilder, the series also introduced adorable half-pint Melissa Gilbert, and the delightfully wicked Nellie Oleson.

Lou Grant (1977-1982)

During its original run, watching *Lou Grant* helped the masses understand what goes into putting together that morning paper that arrived on all of our doorsteps. Today, it plays like a eulogy for a once-proud vocation. If the sounds of a typewriter make you more nostalgic than the songs played at your prom, this is the show for you. After a few episodes you'll long for the days when news came from a newspaper, and not from a million websites and politically charged blogs of dubious intent.

The Man From U.N.C.L.E. (1964-1968)

The 1960s box-office success of James Bond inspired a wave of secret agent facsimiles, including this popular series starring the suave Robert Vaughn as Napoleon Solo. The twist was having Solo partner with a Russian (David McCallum) at the height of the Cold War, inspiring millions of teenage girls to ponder how Communism could be bad when Illya Kuryakin was so dreamy.

The Many Loves of Dobie Gillis (1959-1963)

A head-in-the-clouds slacker, the girl genius that loved him (and who he couldn't stand), television's first beatnik, and a gorgeous blond teenage gold-digger were among the draws of this atypical sitcom from TV's golden age. The stories were often more pessimistic than those on other series back then, but the dialogue was razor sharp, and no other show offered a better satiric take on the idle rich, represented first by

Warren Beatty as Milton Armitage, and later by Stephen Franken as Chatsworth Osborne Jr.

Mr. Ed (1958-1966)

Yes, it's about a man and his talking horse. It probably shouldn't have worked but it does. And what other series can boast guest appearances from Clint Eastwood, Mae West and Hall of Fame Dodger great Sandy Koufax?

My Three Sons (1960-1972)

Next to *The Adventures of Ozzie & Harriet*, this was the longest-running family situation comedy of the classic TV era. It was a very different show at the end of its run than it was at the beginning, but with Fred MacMurray anchoring the series as unflappable widowed dad Steven Douglas, it coasted through multiple cast changes and additions while always giving viewers the gentle, heartwarming stories they loved.

The Odd Couple (1970-1975)

The classic Neil Simon play became an equally successful film, before television got hold of the material and made it work once more. Tony Randall and Jack Klugman were ideally cast as the mismatched roommates, one neat, one sloppy, whose friendship survived honking sinuses, smoke-filled poker games, and a hilariously disastrous appearance ("Aristophanes!") on the game show *Password*.

The Phil Silvers Show (1955-1959)

As inveterate gambler and con man Sgt. Ernie Bilko, Phil Silvers created one of television's most lovable rats. Concerns over portraying a military man as a flim-flam artist dissipated after voluntary army enlistments actually rose during the years the series aired.

Room 222 (1969-1974)

Room 222 tackled real-world issues, and also introduced in Pete Dixon an American history teacher as admirable as those educators from a more innocent era. Dixon challenged his students to question conventional wisdom. He guided them through a chaotic time by leading from an example of compassionate common sense that, had it been shared by more folks in 1969, might have eased some of the tensions that nearly broke the country in two. "I better ask you straight out – do you prefer 'colored,' or 'negro,' or 'black'?" inquires naïve young student-teacher Alice Johnson (Karen Valentine). Responds Dixon, "I always preferred 'Pete.'"

WKRP in Cincinnati (1978-1982)

I'm not sure why this show seems to bubble just under confirmed "classic" status. Maybe it wasn't on long enough. But I still can't get through Thanksgiving without one reference to flying turkeys.

The Wonder Years (1988-1993)

The music and the fashions and the Vietnam references set this coming-of-age series in a very specific time and place, but there was also something universal about the struggles of Kevin Arnold. One hundred years from now, adolescent boys will still identify with his sibling issues, school issues, and the agony and ecstasy of falling in love with the exquisite Winnie Cooper.

Acknowledgements

After a ten-year hiatus from writing books I wondered if anyone would still be interested in my thoughts on television, so I must first thank my publishers for telling me I would always have a home at Black Pawn Press. We signed our contracts the day before most of the country shut down for the COVID-19 pandemic – let's try not to take that as a portent.

A sincere thank you to Kathy Garver, Mitchell Hadley, Kathryn Leigh Scott, and Ed Robertson for the kind words about this book, and the era in television it celebrates.

Jack Condon, my friend and co-author on a previous book, generously shared some of his insights on two of his favorite shows, *The Waltons* and *Laverne & Shirley*, which I know made those chapters better.

Thank you to my parents, for believing that growing up in front of the television was not the worst thing that could happen to a kid.

This book has its roots in my blog, Comfort TV, which would not have launched without the design and IT talents of Ron Zayas and Greg Dorchak, which are very much appreciated. One day I'll get the hang of these computer things.

Thank you to everyone who ever stopped by the blog, and to those who joined in on our classic TV discussions.

Finally, this book is dedicated to all my fellow TV fans – especially anyone who was invited out to dinner or a concert or a ball game, and politely passed because they'd rather curl up in a quilt, prepare a few snacks on a TV tray, and spend the evening with Ozzie and Harriet, Patty and Cathy, Friday and Gannon, Lucy and Ethel, or any of the other characters that brought us so much joy for so long. You are not alone.

Bibliography

Note: Some of the chapters in this book are expanded, revised and/or updated versions of material that first appeared on the blog Comfort TV (comforttv.blogspot.com).

Articles

Stephen Aron, "The History of the American West Gets a Much-Needed Rewrite," *Smithsonian Magazine*, August 16, 2016

https://www.smithsonianmag.com/history/history-american-west-gets-much-needed-rewrite-180960149/

Patricia Ward Biederman, "Here's the Story, of a Man Named Davy," *Los Angeles Times*

https://verybradyblog.blogspot.com/2018/05/davy-jones-reprised-his-role-on-stage.html

Justin Harp, "John Schneider isn't happy about Dukes of Hazzard being pulled from TV Land: 'It's overly PC,'" *Digital Spy*, June 7, 2015 https://www.digitalspy.com/tv/ustv/a656774/john-schneider-isnt-happy-about-dukes-of-hazzard-being-pulled-from-tv-land-its-overly-pc/

Cynthia Littleton, "Remembering Lucille Ball, Pioneering 'I Love Lucy' Star and TV Mogul, on Her Birthday," *Variety*, August 6, 2020
https://variety.com/2020/tv/news/lucille-ball-birthday-i-love-lucy-1234726557/

Madeline Kaplan, "'Dukes Of Hazzard' Pulled From TV Land Schedule Amid Confederate Flag Controversy," Huffpost TV
https://www.huffpost.com/entry/dukes-of-hazzard-tv-land-pulled_n_7706752

Thomas H. Maugh II, "Conclusive evidence of American Indian cannibalism found," *Los Angeles Times*, September 7, 2000
https://archive.seattletimes.com/archive/?date=20000907&slug=4041058

Dennis McLellan, Paul Henning obituary, *Los Angeles Times*, March 26, 2005
https://www.latimes.com/archives/la-xpm-2005-mar-26-me-henning26-story.html

David Moya, "Land O'Lakes Removing Native American Woman From Packaging After 92 Years," *Yahoo News*, April 15, 2020
https://news.yahoo.com/land-o-lakes-dumps-native-america-mascot-235156343.html

Shruti Mukherjee, "Why Did Michael Learned Leave 'The Waltons' After 6 Successful Years?," *Republic World*, March 9, 2020
https://www.republicworld.com/entertainment-news/rest-of-the-world/why-did-michael-learned-leave-the-waltons-after-6-successful-years.html

Naomi Schaefer Riley, "'The 1619 Project' Enters American Classrooms," *Education Next*, Summer 2020
https://www.educationnext.org/1619-project-enters-american-classrooms-adding-new-sizzle-slavery-significant-cost/

Nathan J. Robinson, "I Can't Believe They Still Make Students Recite The Pledge Of Allegiance," *Current Affairs*, June 25, 2018
https://www.currentaffairs.org/2018/06/i-cant-believe-they-still-make-students-recite-the-pledge-of-allegiance

Jody Rosen, "Commentary: It's time to cancel 'The Star-Spangled Banner.' Here's what should replace it," Los Angeles Times, July 14, 2020

https://www.latimes.com/entertainment-arts/music/story/2020-07-14/national-anthem-star-spangled-banner-lean-on-me

Ryan P. Smith, "How Native American Slaveholders Complicate the Trail of Tears Narrative," *Smithsonian Magazine*, March 6, 2018

https://www.smithsonianmag.com/smithsonian-institution/how-native-american-slaveholders-complicate-trail-tears-narrative-180968339/

Books

Tim Brooks and Earle Marsh, *The Complete Directory to Prime Time Network and Cable TV Shows, 1946-Present, Ninth Edition* (New York, Ballantine Books, 2007)

Steve Cox, Dreaming of Jeannie (New York, St. Martin's Griffin, 2000)

Geoffrey Mark Fidelman, *The Lucy Book* (Los Angeles, Renaissance Books, 1999)

Mitchell Hadley, *The Electronic Mirror*, Minneapolis, Throckmorton Press, 2018)

John Javna, *Cult TV* (New York, St. Martin's Griffin, 1985)

Websites

The American Civil War Museum
https://acwm.org/blog/myths-misunderstandings-confederate-flag/
American Minute with Bill Federer
https://myemail.constantcontact.com/French-Revolution---Bastille-Day---Reign-of-Terror--libert----galit---fraternit--.html?soid=1108762609255&aid=1rW4pOVTIp0

The Center for Cowboy Ethics and Leadership
http://cowboyethics.org/cowboy-ethics/

It's About TV
https://www.itsabouttv.com/

Robert Feder
https://www.robertfeder.com/2020/07/08/metv-flags-objectionable-content-shows-another-era/

Superman Homepage

https://www.supermanhomepage.com/other/other.php?topic=phonebooth

Television Academy Foundation: Paul Henning interview
http://www.emmytvlegends.org/interviews/people/paul-henning

Wikipedia: Criticism of the Pledge of Allegiance
https://en.wikipedia.org/wiki/Criticism_of_the_Pledge_of_Allegiance

About the Author

I was born in Skokie, IL, where I lived for the first 18 years of my life, with the exception of two years that need not be elaborated on here. I was an only child and an introvert, plugged into pop culture from a very early age. The shows that I grew up with are the ones still closest to my heart today – *The Brady Bunch*, *The Mary Tyler Moore Show*, *The Partridge Family* – and the shows slightly before my time that aired daily in syndication – *The Dick Van Dyke Show*, *I Love Lucy*, *Bewitched* – plus the Saturday morning cartoons and live action kids series of the 1970s.

In 1982, after graduating high school, I moved with my family to Las Vegas. I attended UNLV and began a freelance writing career that encompassed articles on everything from silver mining to the quality of convenience store cuisine. Whenever I could, I wrote about television.

Over the past two decades I've had several books on television published, including *What Were They Thinking?*, *The 100 Dumbest Events in Television History*, *Obsessed With TV*, and companion guides to *Charlie's Angels* (written with Jack Condon) and *The Dukes of Hazzard*. My blog, Comfort TV, has received more than 750,000 visits since launching in 2012.

I'd tell you more, but *I Love Lucy* is about to come on

Keep up with all of my favorite shows and observations by
subscribing to the Comfort TV blog at
http://comforttv.blogspot.com

CPSIA information can be obtained
at www.ICGtesting.com
Printed in the USA
BVHW050849090223
658199BV00012B/183